P9-CDK-357

Please remember that this is a library book,
and that it belongs only temporarily to each
person who uses it. Be considerate. Do
not write in this, or any, library book.

AAW 4574

JC GEN

AN INTRODUCTION TO THE SOCIOLOGY OF JUVENILE DELINQUENCY

AN INTRODUCTION TO THE SOCIOLOGY OF JUVENILE DELINQUENCY

David Musick

Department of Sociology
University of Northern Colorado

State University
of New York
Press

Published by
State University of New York Press, Albany

©1995 State University of New York

All rights reserved

Production by Susan Geraghty
Marketing by Dana Yanulavich

Printed in the United States of America

No part of this book may be used or reproduced
in any manner whatsoever without written permission.
No part of this book may be stored in a retrieval
system or transmitted in any form or by any means
including electronic, electrostatic, magnetic tape,
mechanical, photocopying, recording, or otherwise
without the prior permission in writing of the publisher.

For information, address State University of New York
Press, State University Plaza, Albany, N.Y., 12246

10 9 8 7 6 5 4 3 2

Library of Congress Cataloging-in-Publication Data

Musick, David.
    An introduction to the sociology of juvenile delinquency / by
David Musick.
        p.   cm. — (SUNY series in oral and public history)
    Includes bibliographical references (p. 279) and index.
    ISBN 0-7914-2351-4 (hardcover : acid-free paper). — ISBN
0-7914-2352-2 (pbk. : acid-free paper)
    1. Juvenile delinquency—United States. I. Title. II. Series.
HV9104.A5M87 1995
364.3'6'0973—dc20   94-14576
                                                                    CIP

This book is dedicated to Kristine

CONTENTS

PREFACE

This book is intended for use as an introductory text in under-graduate juvenile delinquency courses. It is also addressed to the general reader who is looking for a basic overview of juvenile delinquency in the United States. This book resulted from my teaching courses entitled "Introduction to Juvenile Delinquency" at five different universities and colleges over a period of nineteen years.

I have worked as a teacher and counselor with inmates in state and federal prisons. As a child, mostly in California, I weathered five stepfathers. Before the age of fifteen, I acquired expertise in criminal violence, theft, grand larceny, burglary, drug and alcohol use, income tax evasion, and embezzlement. Thus, in addition to my academic credentials, I bring a large base of practical experience about crime and delinquency to this book.

Juvenile delinquency is a complex and confusing topic. Each time I teach Introduction to Juvenile Delinquency I have trouble finding a suitable textbook. Most delinquency texts include material I consider irrelevant. For example, most delinquency texts report in detail on poorly conducted, unsubstantiated research. In this book I minimize the use of research findings that seem likely to be proven incorrect as social science concepts, theories, and methodologies are strengthened in the future. Many delinquency texts also leave out information I believe is important. For example, usually too little attention is paid by authors to the connection between juvenile delinquency and other problems that "at risk" children face in industrial societies. In order to overcome this deficiency, I include information not only about delinquents but also about other types of problem children. Thus the broader social environment of delinquency can be better understood, and delinquency can be put into a more general conceptual context.

Another problem with many available texts is that they pay too little attention to history. Ignoring the past leaves an impression that delinquency and related childrens' problems have only recently appeared upon the scene. Historical data, on the other hand, reveal that problem children, and youthful law violation, are recurring dilemmas confronted by all large urban civilizations. Histories of problem children, and of childrens' law, show that many young persons have been exploited, and pushed toward criminality, in all large societies. Consequently, the early focus of this book is on what Robert Nisbet calls "the history of ideas," on identifying and defining basic concepts, and on exploring their connections to the past.

My approach throughout this book is conceptual and historical. While I have tried to make information throughout the book current, in keeping with my historical approach, the citations you will find are, in my opinion, the most useful and appropriate.

The book is relatively brief. My objective was not to write a compendium of everything that social scientists have written about juvenile delinquency but to record the fundamental concepts, interpretive perspectives, and methodologies that are used to describe and analyze juvenile delinquency. I take, wherever possible, a comparative-historical approach. In most cases, this involves a comparison of things in time, rather than in space.

This is a challenging book that, while brief and straightforward, makes no attempt to simplify the highly complex subject of juvenile delinquency. This book is written in the tradition of works like *The Social Bond* (Nisbet, 1970), *Social Processes* (Shibutani, 1986), and *American Dilemmas* (Turner and Musick, 1985), which resist the temptation to assume that college and university students require oversimplified, condescending course materials.

An Introduction to the Sociology of Juvenile Delinquency is divided into five parts. Part 1 presents the basic concepts that must be understood in order to study juvenile delinquency. Part 1 also traces the history of problem children, parenting, and children's law. Chapter 1 examines basic types of problem children, including delinquents, status offenders, and dependent and neglected youth. In chapter 1 information about basic parenting styles, such as infanticide, abandonment, ambivalence, intrusion, socialization, and helping is presented. Chapter 1 also examines childhood in preindustrial Italy, France, and England.

Chapter 2 traces the history of problem children in colonial and industrial America. It describes five phases of juvenile legal development, including the early juvenile court movement, early juvenile law, recent developments in juvenile law, changes by the U.S. Supreme Court in juvenile law and American juvenile law today. Chapters 1 and 2, taken together, show that America has, since colonial days, spawned a large population of problem children and that many adults in this country find ways to profit from youth in trouble. We also learn that U.S. childrens' law has expanded considerably. Today, government agencies and private child-saving organizations claim jurisdiction over millions of at risk children.

Part 2 of *An Introduction to the Sociology of Juvenile Delinquency* examines popular ways to measure the extent of juvenile delinquency. Chapter 3 shows how police arrest statistics and surveys are used to measure the extent of delinquency. Police arrest statistics are by far the most popular measure of delinquency. However, surveys uncover far more delinquency than arrest data reveal. In general, both arrest statistics and surveys indicate that delinquency is widespread in American society.

Part 3 presents theories that attempt to answer two questions about juvenile lawlessness: What causes delinquency? And what kinds of children become delinquent? Chapter 4 presents clinical and observational ideas about delinquency. Clinicians and field observers generally agree that American delinquency is a sizable problem. Clinicians and field observers learned that American delinquency had many causes, as they developed a multitude of important ideas about the etiology of children's problems. Chapter 5 examines micro delinquency theories like demonism, the "free will" perspective, physical type theories, varieties of modern positivism, behaviorism and labeling ideas. Chapter 6 outlines macro and midrange delinquency theories, including structural functionalism, early Marxist ideas, modern Marxism, the "natural areas" perspective, anomie, differential association, and group conflict. Taken together, chapters 5 and 6 demonstrate that there are many causes of delinquency and that no current theory adequately explains its genesis for all children.

Part 4 looks at social units most closely involved in preventing, controlling and, ironically, causing juvenile delinquency. Chapter 7 reports on three important aspects of family organization and process: cultural influences, intrafamily factors, and the effects of rapid social change on family life. Chapter 8 focuses on mass industrial education and on school-related causes of delinquency. Chapter 8 also presents recent data showing the extent of violence and property crime in American schools. Chapter 9 explores the connection among policing, gangs, and delinquency. We examine the history and structure of community-level police organizations, police officer roles, tools, and police options with juveniles. Interaction between the police and gangs is considered. Chapter 10 describes American courts and shows how juvenile cases compete for judicial attention with many other types of litigation. Chapter 10 also describes the basic stages of juvenile court process.

Part 5 of *An Introduction to the Sociology of Juvenile Delinquency* focuses on programs designed to prevent and correct juvenile delinquency. Chapter 11 considers the relative merits of punishment versus rehabilitation, public versus private operation of programs, and community-based treatment versus incarceration of problem children. It describes several types of community-based prevention and corrections programs, including those run by schools, probation offices, public corrections agencies, and private organizations. Chapter 12 looks at the practice of incarcerating problem children in places like juvenile halls, detention centers, industrial schools, training schools, camps, ranches, adult jails, and prisons. Finally, parole is examined. Chapter 13 summarizes basic themes and lessons of the book.

ACKNOWLEDGMENTS

No book is written and published without the help of many persons. I appreciate the input and encouragement of students in my juvenile delinquency classes at the University of Northern Colorado. Inmates taking my classes at the Federal Correctional Institute in Englewood, Colorado, helped in numerous ways. Special thanks are due to Jonathan H. Turner for his encouragement throughout the project. Daniel O'Connor helped with early chapters of the book. Ron Warncke provided direction and support. Priscilla Ross and Susan Geraghty at SUNY Press gave kind, enthusuastic, and efficient assistance.

Many thanks are due to persons at the University of Northern Colorado who typed text, prepared graphics or helped with editing. In particular, Margaret Lambeth deserves acknowledgment. The UNC Graduate School provided much-needed aid. Lindy and Greg at Wordsmith's in Greeley, Colorado, gave valuable assistance with preparation of graphics.

I am deeply indebted to the many scholars whose prior work enabled me to compile *An Introduction to the Sociology of Juvenile Delinquency*. A list of references at the end of the book serves as a more complete acknowledgement of their contributions.

PART 1

Concepts, Definitions, and Links to the Past

CHAPTER 1

A Conceptual and Historical Basis for Studying Juvenile Delinquency

Sociological interest in juvenile delinquency dates back to the turn of the century. Sociologists are drawn toward juvenile delinquency for a variety of reasons. Many sociologists would like to better understand what causes delinquency. Other sociologists look for ways to prevent or correct delinquency. A good number of sociologists get involved with delinquency through work on a related subject like the family, drug abuse, or education. Regardless of why, delinquency has become a focus of hundreds of professional sociologists. We must remember, however, that delinquency is a multidisciplinary subject, attracting the interest of historians, psychologists, journalists and novelists, lawyers and judges, political scientists, and social workers, as well as sociologists. For this reason, our approach to the study of delinquency must also be multidisciplinary.

The discipline of sociology can be broken down into three parts. First, sociology is conceptual. It focuses on the histories and definitions of important concepts. Second, sociology is structural. It describes and explains how and why people organize in order to interact with each other. Finally, sociology examines process. It provides information about human behavior as it actually occurs. Throughout the book we will see how again and again all three parts of sociology shed light on delinquency. In chapter 1 we begin our analysis by first considering the conceptual history of children's problems. It is important to understand that delinquency and other children's problems are cross-cultural, historically rooted, and common to the history of humanity. In order to illustrate these facts in this chapter, we first identify and define core concepts related to delinquency. We consider basic types of problem children, basic parenting styles, and the history of child care in civilizations that influenced American society.

BASIC TYPES OF PROBLEM CHILDREN

In legal terms, there are four basic types of problem children in any large civilization at almost any time throughout its history. First, there are young persons known today as *delinquents,* children who are caught, found guilty, and punished for violating local, state, or federal criminal laws (Barnes and Teeters, 1959: 69; Empey and Stafford, 1991: 5). Delinquents are divided by legal officials into minor offenders (vagrants, prostitutes, petty thieves, etc.) and major offenders (murderers, rapists, arsonists, etc.).

Second, *status offenders* are children who violate no criminal law but engage in offensive behavior (Thornton and Voigt, 1992: 15). Status Offenses involve a breach of morality or of a strong social norm (frequenting gaming houses, promiscuity, truancy, possession of alcohol or tobacco, etc.). Status offenders are often considered predelinquent by law enforcement personnel, prime candidates to graduate into full-fledged delinquency.

Dependent and *neglected children* form the third and fourth basic categories of problem youth. Dependent children have lost at least one parent, or their parents are unable to provide them with sustenance and care. Studies have shown that dependent children come from families living in poverty (Thurston, 1930: 398; Empey and Stafford, 1991: 5). Neglected children have parents who intentionally treat them violently or cruelly and who withhold sufficient care (Carstens, 1930: 403; Empey and Stafford, 1991: 5). While neither dependent nor neglected children necessarily violate criminal law, they are often considered predelinquent. When dependent or neglected children do get into trouble, they are commonly incarcerated with, or close to, delinquents and status offenders. It is sometimes difficult to tell whether a child is neglected or dependent. Dependent and neglected children are often treated interchangeably by members of the law enforcement community.

OTHER IMPORTANT TYPES OF PROBLEM CHILDREN

Children with physical, mental, or learning *disabilities* do not fit easily into a legal model of basic types of problem children. Yet, disabled children are more likely to be caught violating the law, and more likely to be processed as delinquents, than are children without disabilities.

It is possible that disabled children often fail to respond to social cues and tend toward impulsive behavior. Some parents, teachers, legal officials, and other control agents probably misunderstand such behavior, thus feeling frustration and anger toward disabled children. Disabled children who are misunderstood can easily grow alienated from family, school, and legal authority. Alienated disabled children are likely to associate with other alienated children, who encourage each other to commit acts of hostility and delinquency (Murray, 1976; *Rocky Mountain News*, Aug. 13, 1988: 66; Shibutani, 1986: 326).

Disabled children are also often ridiculed by classmates and potential playmates. For example, Amy, a nine-year-old disabled third-grader who lives in Indiana, wrote "[I] have a problem at school. Kids laugh at me because of the way I walk and run and talk. I just want one day where no one laughs at me or makes fun of me" (*Daily Camera*, Dec. 22, 1993: 9A). Exposure to continuous ridicule can turn disabled children away from the very groups other children depend upon for support and guidance.

Suicidal children also do not fit well into a legal model of basic types of problem children. Yet, suicide is surpassed only by accidents as a leading cause of death among teenagers in the United States. About 400,000 teenagers attempt suicide each year. Approximately 5,000 are successful (Gaines, 1991: 7). In 1991, 29 percent of a national sample of high school students reported having suicidal thoughts during the twelve months preceding the survey, and 7 percent reported attempting suicide.

Before 1960, suicide among teenagers was hardly noticeable in the United States. The teenage suicide rate in 1960 was 3.6 per 100,000 American adolescents. By 1970, the rate was up to 5.9. In 1980, the suicide rate climbed to 8.5 children. Currently, 11.3 out of each 100,000 adolescents in the United States commits suicide. Today, roughly 5 percent of all teenagers try to take their lives each year, compared to 1 percent in 1960 (Bennett, 1993: 12). The number of American youth taking their lives continues to climb (Gaines, 1991: 7).

Teen suicide touches all social classes, although poor children are most at risk. Suicide engulfs honor students as well as underachievers (*Daily Times-Call*, Dec. 4, 1993: 10A). Teen suicide eliminates alienated youth, those left without hope, children who have given up on their families, schools, communities, friends, and neighbors. Suicidal teenagers are often labeled burnouts, dropouts, dirtbags, druggies, grinders, mall rats, or punks. They rebel against the favoritism shown other teens called preps, jocks, or brains (Gaines, 1991: 9). Girls report thinking about suicide more than do boys. There is some disagreement over whether boys or girls more often attempt suicide (see U.S. Dept. of Justice. Bureau of Justice Statistics, 1993: 319; Gaines, 1991: 7). Some suicidal teens are known to school and legal authorities as "fuck-ups," long before they "do it." Other suicidal adolescents gain public attention only with their last act (Gaines, 1991: 3).

Data about teen suicide, for many reasons, probably underestimate the dimensions of the problem. For example, because of the stigma attached to suicide in the United States, many young persons who take their lives are recorded as having experienced accidents involving automobiles or drugs. If we accept the assertion that suicidal people are also often murderous, when an object of aggression is available, then many teenagers engaging in extreme violence—youth out "wilding," skinheads, gang bangers, as well as robbers, murderers, arsonists and rapists—might be trying to get someone else to take their lives, possibly a victim, a rival gang member, or a police officer. If, as Gaines suggests, the United States is one of the most dehumanizing and alienating of all countries, if growing numbers of children feel exploited, dominated, and hopeless, then teen suicide can no longer be considered inconsequential (12).

BASIC TYPES OF PARENT-CHILD RELATIONSHIPS

Juvenile delinquency begins, like socially desirable behavior, in the home. Parent-child relationships are the cornerstones upon which good citizenship and misbehavior are built. According to De-Mause, six basic types of parent-child relationships exist (1974a: 553–56). In some cultural and historical settings one or two types prevail. In other societies, especially in mass, postindustrial civilizations like the United States, several basic types of parent-child relationships operate side by side. Demause observes that all six types exist today and combine to form a fairly good scheme for classifying contemporary parental behavior. Below, the history of each type of relationship is described.

Infanticide

Infanticide is the willful murder of newborn children, usually by exposing, starving, strangling, smothering, or poisoning them or by employing a deadly weapon (Langer, 1974: 353). Infanticide is a common solution to the problems presented by handicapped or weak babies. Murder is an option pursued by parents who lack the material, emotional, and physical resources necessary to raise children. Mortality data suggest that children risk infanticide until the age of five, although most murders occur early in the first year of life. Fathers usually decide which children will be kept, if any, and girls are at greater risk than boys (Langer, 1974: 354). Infanticide minimizes the number of problem children in a society by eliminating many who would presumably be dependent, neglected, and delinquent. Infanticide has been employed by parents throughout history, and it remains in use today.

Abandonment

Another option is dumping unwanted children in places where they are likely to die, or where they will be found and kept alive by others. In ancient China urns were put in public places for this purpose. Before the twentieth century, dung heaps and irrigation ditches were favored by the parents of problem children in other countries. Wet nurses and their intermediaries were used in early France, England, and America. In the United States, churches, public parks, spots adjacent to freeways, and even dumpsters have been favored places to abandon children.

In England, France and the United States, numerous organizations emerged to take care of unwanted children. The earliest were almshouses, which sequestered and exploited children for their labor alongside destitute, handicapped, diseased, and deranged adults. Before 1875, placement in the almshouse, for the young, or indenture, for older youth, was the most likely fate for children abandoned in the United States (Thurston, 1930: 399–400).

In France, hospitals for poor, abandoned children were opened by the church and government. This development lessened the rate of infanticide and precipitated a torrent of abandonment. Most abandoned children in French hospitals died shortly after arrival.

Few thrived. Abandonment places children where they can be exploited by uncaring adults.

It is possible that some more affluent parents favor short-range abandonment, a practice where children are kept within the household and are cared for by surrogates but at a distance from parents. For rich children, this means care by nurses, nannies, teachers, and tutors. Today, short-range abandonment may mean care outside the home by entrepreneurs, care at the hands of an older sibling, or care provided by some other relative.

Ambivalence

In the fourteenth century some well-educated parents began to read that children must be shaped through violent training if they are to become moral, disciplined, and productive adults. Parents fused this new information with the age-old beliefs that children are impediments to adult happiness and should be avoided whenever possible. Out of this amalgam of thoughts came the practice of ambivalent parenting, which emphasized beating children into accepting the dictates of adult society. Ambivalent parents might have loved their offspring, but training manuals asserted that sparing the rod would surely spoil the child (DeMause, 1974a: 553–54). Children raised by ambivalent parents enjoy some of the economic and physical protections life inside the family can offer, but they also acquire feelings of fear, hostility, and anger, along with a tendency to try solving problems through violence.

Intrusive Approach

As civilizations expanded and became more complex, material wealth also expanded greatly, and many European families were set free from the immediate drudgery of working long hours in order to survive. Some parents used their leisure and resources to get more involved with their children. Jean-Jacques Rousseau, a philosopher, helped them by writing *Emile* (1762), a book dedicated to an aristocratic female friend about how to raise her son, Emile. Rousseau prescribed an approach that would have the parents, especially the mother, interact more with their children. Although the children would remain in the hands of nurses and male tutors who lived in the family home, the parents would "intrude" more into the child's development. Emile was set free from the bondage of swaddling wraps and was allowed into his mother's chambers at regular intervals to be coddled and fed at her breast.

Rousseau expanded these ideas in *The Social Contract* (1762). He portrayed the mother and child as central figures in a movement to reform and strengthen French society. Rousseau believed that, while nursing, mother and child form a love bond that becomes the cement of family life and good citizenship. He discouraged use of wet nurses because affection flows from child to nurse and severs the emotional bonds that tie family (and thus state) together. He also advocated radical early toilet training, hitting but not beating, instilling and manipulating fear in children, and regular exposure to cold temperatures. As a result of *Emile*, some rich children were seen regularly by their parents, and evidence suggests that strong love bonds developed. For the most part, however, advantaged children were left to the care of nurses, tutors, and other servants. There was little protection from violence and other forms of abuse. *Emile* left fathers with vague and unspecified duties.

While it is well known that he abandoned his own children, Rousseau's ideas set a new standard for raising children and even today dominate the thinking of many parents. For the poor, who until late in the nineteenth century spent at least some of their lives working as servants, the intrusive approach created new pressures to abstain from infanticide, abandonment, and ambivalence. Unfortunately, most poor parents lacked leisure time to spend with their children and could not find resources to hire live-in surrogates. Nevertheless, the advent of intrusive parenting among the rich helped set the forces of law against heretofore acceptable styles of parenting.

Socialization Mode

Over the last century, deeper love feelings and more contact between parent and child have become common. Fathers participate in some child-rearing activities. Children are seen as the embodiment of the family. People have come to believe that their social instincts must be drawn out and refined, which requires less violent treatment; hitting children has given way to the use of guilt, disgrace, and fear as motivators. This approach to parenting is called the socialization mode. Parents send their children away from home for part of the day, to be educated and cared for by nonfamily members.

Today, socialization-style parenting is popular in the United States, partly because of the relative affluence and leisure enjoyed by many contemporary Americans. But other parenting styles, in their pure forms and as composites, are also currently employed. The socialization mode of parenting should produce fewer problem children than the other styles we examined. However, when ambivalence and violence are combined with what appears to be a socialization mode of parenting, children can be driven toward delinquency and other forms of misbehavior.

Helping Mode

In the last fifty years, small numbers of parents have taken the socialization mode to its extreme, where father and mother share equally in intensive, selfless parenting. Helping mode parents allow the child's needs to reign over all else in the household; employ no screaming or hitting; explain everything to their children; refrain from all discipline; let the plan of nature for the child unfold through unfettered play; and encourage relatively unrestrained ventures into adult environments. The helping style of parenting requires commitment and large quantities of time and labor from both parents; thus, does not blend well with the necessity for two adult wage-earners that most American families currently face. Yet, increasing numbers of families are aware of the helping mode, and many modern parents claim to employ it.

Figure 1.1 displays the six child treatment alternatives identified by DeMause. He asserts that the two most common forms of parenting in the United States today are the intrusive and socialization modes. Millions of American parents nevertheless practice ambivalence, abandonment, and infanticide. Perhaps the pervasiveness of bad parenting helps to explain the presence of millions of problem children in the United States today.

CHILDHOOD IN PREINDUSTRIAL ITALY, FRANCE, AND ENGLAND

Growing up, surviving childhood, has always been tough. In order to illustrate this fact, we next consider the perils that youth encountered in the past—in three civilizations that have greatly influenced American society.

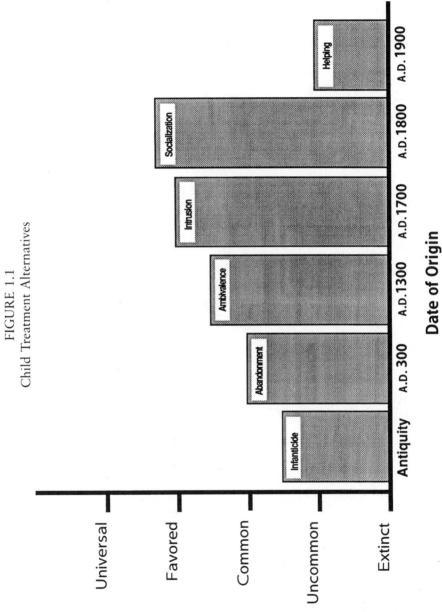

FIGURE 1.1
Child Treatment Alternatives

Italy

In the 1300s, use of adult slaves was common in the small states that today compose Italy. Slavery served to limit the need for child labor. Slaves were imported from many distant lands. Slaves were used mostly by the rich for household work. Some slaves were deployed on large farms, in mines, and at textile factories. Alongside slaves in the Italian lower class were propertyless serfs, who lived in oppressive conditions on land they worked for powerful lords. The lower class also included wage-earning factory workers—for example, the four thousand women who worked daily at the spinning wheels of a silk factory in Bologna. Italian factory workers were often women and children pushed off the farm. They worked long hours under the supervision of an owner or manager. Wages earned by women and children were usually paid directly to a husband or father.

The middle class in Italy was anchored by relatively poor rural land owners, who enjoyed some tenuous benefits of second-class citizenship. Despite holding citizenship, poor rural land owners were in hopeless competition with urban aristocrats who operated large highly capitalized farms in the countryside. Small rural land owners and their extended families worked the soil in competition with gangs of serfs and slaves; this depressed the overall value of farm products and labor. Small rural land owners lived in relative deprivation. All family members, including children, worked long hours.

The Italian upper class consisted of aristocratic owners of large land tracts, wealthy bankers, powerful government and military leaders, and high officials of the church. Powerful and wealthy persons presided over expansive urban estates. The upper class acquired country villas that rivaled their urban residences in grandeur and splendor. The upper class of Italy lived a life of extreme luxury, pretentiousness, and indulgence, rivaled only in degree by the abject poverty and oppression endured by the Italian lower class. Upper-class Italians were, in general, insecure and dangerous persons who practiced treachery, intrigue, and violent aggression, even toward their own children.

The church opened a foundling home at Milan in the eighth century. Abandoned children of legitimate birth were kept at the foundling home until they could be sent out to work or until they died. Opening of the foundling home in Milan is important because it marks the approximate date when Italian churches began to publicly advocate the safety of children. Eventually, foundling homes were opened in many of the Italian states. Children at a foundling home were taught a trade or skill; older foundlings were set free. But death rates were high at the homes; living conditions were oppressive, and enough room was available to house only a small fraction of the area's problem children.

In the tenth century, the Italian church began to alter ideas about children. Italian churches began to teach that large families were desirable and that birth control practices were sinful. Church leaders outlawed infanticide and punished some violators. Church art and philosophy idealized childhood, portraying children as saints. Church doctrine expressed love and affection toward children. At first, these changes in religious thinking affected the lives of only a few elite and middle-class children. But eventually the new religious ideas about childhood trickled down to the masses, and some ideas became embodied in law.

On the darker side, children born to slaves and to unwed mothers were generally killed at birth. Many girls and weak babies were put to death. Rural farm families kept alive healthy male offspring but few others, since labor competition from imported slaves made large numbers of children unnecessary.

In the twelfth century, Pope Innocent III opened a foundling hospital in Rome, in order to discourage mothers from throwing their newborns into the local river (Trexler, 1974). In 1500, Church policy was incorporated into criminal law when the government of Florence established fines and punishments for persons who suffocated young children. By the end of the sixteenth century, laws prohibiting infanticide were adopted throughout Europe.

There is little evidence that early laws greatly lessened the rate of infanticide and abandonment in Italy's principalities. It is clear, however, that church policy and criminal law began to push the weight of public opinion in favor of keeping growing numbers of problem children alive. Change in beliefs came slowly. Early laws were generally used to prosecute midwives and a handful of unwed poor mothers. Offenders were treated brutally by the church and courts. Punishing isolated offenders served as a reminder to other parents of what flagrant infanticide could bring. Thus, Italian states gave birth to the practice of keeping growing numbers of problem children alive. But death and abandonment remained a common fate for Italian children. For example, McLaughlin estimates that infant mortality, in the ninth through thirteenth centuries, claimed one or two of each three babies born in Italy (1974: 111).

In spite of church and government proscriptions, many Italian parents, especially those who could not find ways to send away their unwanted children, practiced infanticide. As infanticide grew less common, abandonment of children increased in popularity, and the number of those abandoned was only partially offset by the number placed into church-run foundling homes. Unwanted children could be kept at home and worked hard by ambivalent parents. Others could be sold or rented to strangers as laborers or servants. Eventually more and more unwanted children were indentured by their parents, sent to live with and work for strangers. Thus, by extending abandonment to include renting and selling of offspring, Italian parents got rid of problem children while keeping them alive. In sum, life for lower-class and middle class children in preindustrial Italy was fraught with hard work, violence, and risk of death. Even the most advantaged Italian child might be abandoned and abused.

France

Infanticide was practiced by parents of all social ranks in early France and abated slowly. Infanticide eventually lost ground because of the teachings of the church. However, even good Christians found it difficult to reconcile their religious beliefs with the reality of poverty and with the possibility that many of their children, if allowed to live, could slowly starve or be exploited by indenture.

The French church responded by opening several foundling hospitals, where children of legitimate birth could be abandoned. The first French foundling hospital was opened in 1180 at Montpellier. Babies could be deposited onto a turntable that would spin into the hospital, where employees took over and tended newborns. The abandoners could remain anonymous. Surviving babies were shipped from the hospital into the countryside, where unsupervised foster families and wet nurses cared for them. Since the death rate was high during this process, the turntable was in reality a slightly more complicated form of infanticide. Most children abandoned on hospital turntables died within eight to fifteen days (Fuch, 1984: 3).

Children who survived abandonment and foundling hospitals were kept in the countryside until the age of three or four, when they were returned to the hospitals and put to work, often alongside adult residents who were suffering from acute illness. This practice continued until the end of the nineteenth century. At about the age of seven, foundlings were sent away from the hospital to make a living elsewhere.

In 1552, the French Parliament passed a law requiring church officials to provide housing and care for abandoned children. The church responded by opening foundling hospitals throughout France. In 1556, Henry II, king of France, decreed that infanticide was punishable by death. It was nevertheless legal for parents to sell children. One foundling hospital in Paris housed 312 children in 1670. By 1772, the hospital admitted almost 8,000 castoff children per year (10). By 1800, maintaining foundling hospitals proved too costly for the church. Government agencies took over.

Thus, by 1800, the French had developed a society-wide hospital system that kept large numbers of problem children alive. Care for children in foundling hospitals was, in theory, supervised by religious women. In reality, child care was relegated to untrained, unsupervised underlings. Foundlings were fed by wet nurses when they were available. When they were not, unwanted babies were fed by less sanitary and nutritious means. French foundling hospitals were cold, dirty, overcrowded places. Older children worked hard. Babies and younger children were seldom given affection (123–26). By the 1830s, foundling hospitals became too costly for the French government to run. Consequently, admission rules were stiffened. Fewer and fewer unwanted children were taken in. Foundling hospitals eventually disappeared. In 1840, French lawmakers passed a harsh new law forbidding the abandonment of children. The French Church and federal government had set a cultural precedent, however, by briefly assuming responsibility for large numbers of abandoned children. Other European countries followed the French example, extending legal protection to at least some problem children and setting the stage for new bodies of juvenile law.

Most French children worked long hours. In the eighteenth century, French parents put their children to work at the age of three. By six years of age, children were expected to earn wages (Schorsch, 1979: 134). Parents and other adults regularly beat children, believing that physical violence was an essential part of child rearing. Hospitals and parents rid themselves of children by putting them out under the care and supervision of strangers. Children's work often involved menial labor and harsh physical abuse. Orphans could be legally put out to work until they reached twenty-five years of age, at which time they were set free.

Advantaged families sought more rewarding positions for their children in the shops of craftsmen or artisans, where a trade could be learned. Advantaged girls often worked as servants. Farm children could be kept at home and put to work. Surplus farm children were indentured to neighbors or distant strangers. Even elite French children could be sent away to work in the homes of other kin. Many indentured French children suffered sexual abuse at the hands of their guardians (Langer, 1974: 357). Lower-class children working as servants were especially at risk.

In sum, as ideas about childhood developed in France, the practice of infanticide gave way to abandonment as a common way to deal with problem children. The French Church assumed responsibility for some unwanted children. In time the French central government attempted to provide for abandoned children. Unfortunately, neither the French church nor the government was able to provide care for the large numbers of abandoned children who needed help. As foundling hospitals disappeared, French problem children were set adrift and exploited for their labor. The French, however, introduced society-wide mechanisms for eliminating infanticide and for housing unwanted children.

England

During the fourth and fifth centuries, under Roman occupation, the British provences procured ample numbers of adult slaves to meet their labor and service needs. Consequently, relatively few poor British children were kept alive. Thousands of British children were exported to Rome as slaves. Even upper class British children were raised in households where violent discipline was common. Thus, most youngsters in early England could anticipate a childhood filled with hard labor and beatings.

British law grossly favored elites and made life hard for slaves and peasants. Also, the law left women and children under the complete control of their fathers or husbands in all social classes. British law made it easy to get rid of children. The law made infanticide a family matter, with the father having final say. Children (and wives) could be rented out or sold as slaves. Babies born to slaves experienced either infanticide or lifelong enslavement. Free males could sexually exploit slave women but had no legal or economic obligations to children born out of such unions.

In the seventh century, the powerful archbishop of Canterbury issued a declaration making infanticide a crime. The church prescribed fifteen years of penance as punishment but exacted only seven years from poor parents (Kellum, 1974: 367–88). However, enforcement of child murder laws was lax and remained so for hundreds of years. In the rare cases where infanticide came to the attention of the courts, it was usually treated as a minor offense. English law exempted men from liability in child murder cases.

English tradition had established fathers as the ultimate authorities in their homes and had given to fathers the right to physically punish children in the amount and degree that they felt fit each offense ("Law Relating to Children," 1910: 138). So, before the nineteenth century, most English children remained vulnerable to violence and murder with no consequences for the offenders. For example, between 1265 and 1413, English court records show no cases of infanticide. But the same records show that 60 to 80 percent of the known deaths of children resulted from drowning—in a ditch, in a well, or in a pail of water or milk at home (Kellum, 1974: 371). Such drownings would today very likely be investigated as possible cases of parental neglect. Only a handful of English parents, the ones who murdered their children awkwardly, in public places, were prosecuted for infanticide. Almost always, the persons prosecuted were women. Almost always, courts found them not guilty. In fact, court records from thirteenth- and fourteenth-century England show that only six parents were convicted of infanticide. In one province of England, only one case of infanticide was recorded during the thirteenth century, even though three thousand cases of adult homicide reached the courts.

The English considered infanticide far less serious than many other offenses. English culture painted newborns as subhuman, and babies were thought to be highly susceptible to control by the devil. Such cultural beliefs were used to rationalize infanticide, especially in the form of overlaying, the parents' taking a baby to bed with them and smothering it with their bodies during the night. English law conveniently failed to include parental overlaying as a punishable form of infanticide. English culture subtly excused the killing of children up to the age of five by rationalizing that some too-assertive, or willful, children are likely to have more accidents than normal youngsters.

Through the fifteenth and sixteenth centuries, such attitudes underwent little change in England (Tucker, 1974). Most adults believed that children were simply another form of private property. Most parents practiced ambivalent childrearing. Tucker reports that a few elite English children were loved and liked by their parents, but even elite babies were seldom nursed by their mothers. Some elite youth emerged as literary objects, usually displaying innocence and bringing joy and happiness to their rich parents. A handful of elite children were formally educated. However, infanticide remained common throughout England in the fifteenth and sixteenth centuries. Almost all children were repeatedly beaten. Upper-class girls were generally denied access to formal education. Almost all English youth began life bound tightly in swaddling clothes, which exposed them to dangerous bacteria and caused painful rashes (232–49).

By the sixteenth century, poor children on the loose in the streets of English cities had become a significant problem, meriting legal attention (Schorsch, 1979: 137). A series of laws were passed to protect English citizens from vagrant children; one law gave local officials the authority to seize unwanted youngsters and put them out as indentured apprentices to property-owning masters.

In general, English parents had three options with the children they chose to keep alive. These options defined parenting in England and her colonies until the end of the nineteenth century. First, children could be put to work at the about age three in the home, at a family business, or on a farm. A second option, as youngsters neared seven, was to send them away to become apprentices in the homes, businesses, or farms of unrelated masters. Child abandonment was practiced by parents of all social classes. Elite children were sent to the residences of other elite families, where they served as pages under the direction of a presumably sophisticated master. Some middle-class children were placed in the shops of craftsmen, in the studios of artists and artisans, or as servants in refined households and thereby acquired marketable adult skills. Many children were abused by their masters, and a good number were violated sexually. Lower-class children were put out as apprentices. Apprenticeships lasted until age twenty-four and often involved dangerous gang labor on large farms (135). Young girls were married early or put out as prostitutes.

Advantaged parents could afford a third option: sending children away to boarding schools for formal education. Formal schooling was a luxury, of course, and became a way for rich parents to communicate to others their high social status.

The British Empire expanded and prospered throughout the nineteenth century. Ever larger numbers of unwanted children roamed the streets of English towns and cities. Vast numbers of lower class English children fell under the control of colonial governments in foreign lands as well (Illick, 1974). English government and churches responded by opening almshouses, where excess children could be quartered, and by expanding the apprenticeship system into the colonies. Using almshouses, apprenticeship, and infanticide, the English rid themselves of a good number of problem children.

By 1820, the industrial revolution was under way in England. Early industrialization required large numbers of unskilled laborers, and English children adapted well to factory work. Unwanted children were sent from farms and almshouses to factories and were worked in gangs. Once a child had been put out to a factory, no one in authority monitored how the youthful worker was treated. Rapid industrialization, and unprecedented growth in the size of industrial cities, led to increased exploitation of English children (Deardorff, 1930). Many poor English children were put to work in large cotton and textile mills. The young were used as laborers in the mines, on large farms, and in garment factories. Children worked alongside adult wage earners but earned only 25 to 50 percent of the adult wage—when they were paid. Poor English children worked sixteen-hour days, six days per week. Some youngsters were forced to live at the factories where they worked; others were allowed to return to an almshouse at night or to an exploitive home. Since birth certificates were uncommon, letters from parents or local officials sufficed to establish the age of a youth. Thus, many children under seven years of age worked in industry.

Marx and Engels saw child labor in factories as a natural

development of capitalism, since children ranked among the least protected laborers and were therefore easy prey. Political officials and business leaders pointed out that the alternatives to factory work available in England for most unwanted youth led to violence, theft, or prostitution. Thus, many English persons lauded early industrialization and the factory system as ideal solutions to problems posed by unwanted youth.

As industrialization matured, technologies, machines, and energy sources changed. Mature industry required fewer unskilled workers and employed persons who had acquired knowledge and skills that went beyond the limits of youth. Thus, as the twentieth century opened, a process began that replaced youthful industrial workers with better-trained and more highly educated adult wage earners. Consequently, unwanted children were sent back into the homes, almshouses, and small, privately owned workplaces from which they had come. The English government responded to the industrial displacement of problem children by expanding public education and by assuming responsibility for large numbers of young law violators. In order to protect children from abusive, neglectful families and from oppressive employers, English children's law was expanded, and jurisdiction over many family matters was assumed by government.

SUMMARY

This chapter offers a conceptual and historical backdrop for viewing delinquency and other problems children face. We identify six basic types of problem children, namely, delinquents, status offenders, dependent and neglected youth, and disabled and suicidal adolescents. We review six basic types of parent-child relationships. Infanticide, abandonment, and ambivalence are ancient styles of parenting. Intrusion, socialization, and helping approaches are more recent, and apparently more benign, developments. All six forms of parenting are practiced in industrial societies, although many parents today combine elements of several styles into hybrid approaches to childrearing.

Cultures offer four basic childcare alternatives. Figure 1.2 displays these in graphic form. Family care and care by a stranger are the oldest ways to care for children. During the last four hundred years, however, churches and governments have become major

FIGURE 1.2
Basic Child Care Alternatives

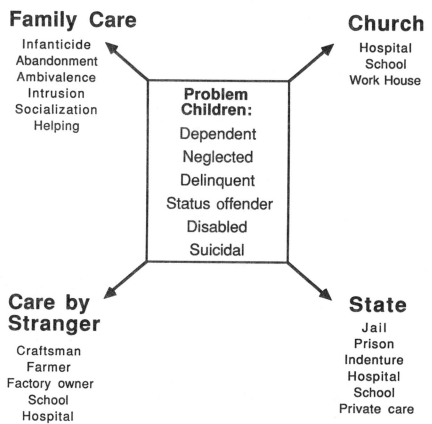

Family Care

Infanticide
Abandonment
Ambivalence
Intrusion
Socialization
Helping

Church

Hospital
School
Work House

Problem Children:

Dependent
Neglected
Delinquent
Status offender
Disabled
Suicidal

Care by Stranger

Craftsman
Farmer
Factory owner
School
Hospital

State

Jail
Prison
Indenture
Hospital
School
Private care

caretakers of problem children. Unfortunately, church and government solutions have been more limited than the scope of children's problems they confront. Church and government officials again and again have encountered more problem children than their hospitals, apprenticing techniques, and juvenile institutions can care for. In fact, church and government efforts to care for problem children can be oppressive themselves. Problem children abound in all large civilizations because large numbers of youngsters are exposed to mistreatment and other forms of exploitation. Thus, no one should be surprised to find that several million problem children currently live in the United States.

CHAPTER 2

Children's Law and Juvenile Courts in the United States

CHILDREN'S LAW IN COLONIAL AMERICA

From the 1600s on, ships carried children to America who had been stolen in Africa from their parents. Even the luckiest slave, Booker T. Washington or Frederick Douglas, for example, lived with the deadening knowledge that his life would be spent in servitude and submission and that the prosperity of his master would be drained from the souls of his children. After 1650, African Americans, adult and child alike, were bound in life-long slavery (Bell, 1992: 6; Hawke, 1988: 115–30; Turner, Singleton, and Musick, 1984: 74).

Vagrant English children were sent to the New World as apprentices. Most oppressive were apprenticeships on tobacco plantations (Schorsch, 1979: 138). Apprenticeship had changed little since medieval times. Children worked long hours, six or seven days per week. Masters were unsupervised by government or moral authority. Living conditions were poor for apprenticed children. Colonial law required that masters teach apprentices a trade and provide instruction in religion and law, but there was little enforcement. Apprenticed children were set free, after four years of service, without the benefit of literacy, a marketable skill, or a family.

The colonies soon began to generate their own problem children. In 1646, Massachusetts responded by passing the Stubborn Child Law, which provided for taking vagrant children into custody; they were to be held in jail or almshouses until they could be placed as apprentices. The Stubborn Child Law was adopted by other colonies and became, until the late 1800s, the legal standard for treatment of poor children. In accordance with English law, children's rights were considered relatively unimportant. In the 1800s, fathers (or masters) had total legal control of their children (Tiffin, 1982: 142).

NINETEENTH-CENTURY CHILDREN'S LAW

American children who violated criminal codes were treated like adults and processed through the same courts, jails, and prisons. Young convicts were first housed separately from adult offenders, in 1825, in New York City. City officials allowed the Association for the Prevention of Pauperism to open a privately funded prison for children. One year later, another private prison for children was opened in Philadelphia. By 1847, the Massachusetts State Legislature was operating a state-run juvenile prison. By 1875, forty juvenile prisons operated in the United States. Some children's incarceratories were run by private, usually religious, organizations; increasing numbers were funded and operated under state control (Bartollas, 1993: 484–85; Sutherland and Cressey, 1974: 489). In the 1800s, juvenile prisons housed persons as old as twenty-five years of age, and many children were still incarcerated in adult jails and prisons. As the authorities opened each new incarceratory, it filled up; yet the next day more problem children were found on the streets of American cities. The supply seemed endless. This situation was common everywhere in the United States, but juvenile crime was seen as a special problem by reformers in Chicago. Chicago reformers worked with law associations, judges, jailors, prison operators, churches, the school system, and police to create a new way of handling problem children.

An 1833 Illinois law restricted the numbers of young persons sent to adult prisons (Platt, 1969: 102). In 1855, Chicago opened a reform school. The State Reform School, for children who lived outside of Chicago, opened in 1867. In 1869, Illinois created a Board of State Commissioners of Public Charities to regulate private organizations housing problem children. The board came to oversee the state's interest in juvenile law. In 1876, the Women's Centennial Association opened a reform school for girls, three years before the state made it legal to imprison girls at the school (111).

Even with all of these reforms, however, in 1880, 13 percent of the inmates in Cook County almshouses were children. In the 1890s, Chicago reformers found numerous children imprisoned with adults in local jails and houses of correction. Between 1883 and 1889, Illinois passed laws compelling children between seven and fourteen years of age to attend school. School attendance laws made many more children in Illinois eligible for legal attention (127). By 1900, thirty-two states passed compulsory attendance laws. By 1918, the entire nation required regular public school attendance of young people (Tiffin, 1982: 145). The aforementioned legal changes put many children out of work and either into public school or into the arms of local police, who were newly authorized to apprehend them.

In 1892, New York courts diverted problem children from overcrowded adult courts by processing their cases separately. In 1891, reformers affiliated with the Chicago Woman's Club recommended that the Illinois legislature create a separate juvenile court system to process problem children. Their recommendations went unheeded for several years. Instead, problem children were processed through Chicago's police courts. Violators who could not pay fines were sentenced to the local house of correction. Fifty cents of their fine was cancelled for every day they spent in jail. In 1883, to accommodate increasing numbers of imprisoned children, the Chicago Board of Education converted a section of the city prison into a training school for criminal boys. Training school children were kept partially separate from adults. By 1889, the training school housed thirteen hundred boys. Average length of stay was one month. One-quarter of the boys had violated public school attendance laws (Platt, 1969: 129).

In 1899, as part of a burgeoning child-saving movement in Illinois and elsewhere across the nation, and with Chicago Woman's Club and Chicago Bar Association sponsorship, a juvenile court bill was presented to the Illinois legislature (Cravens, 1993: 6–8). It proposed the following changes in the legal processing of problem children:

- The right of the state to intervene was asserted, as a higher or ultimate parent (Parens Patriae).
- The circuit court was to create a new tribunal that would hear cases involving problem children under the age of sixteen.
- Informal, noncriminal procedures were to be employed so that the court could provide remedial, preventive, nonpunitive justice, in an individualized manner, by acting as a parent surrogate.
- The new law required that judges furnish "parent-like" care, custody, and discipline.

- The presiding judge (or any other interested person) could require a jury trial for any juvenile offender.
- The law empowered juvenile authorities to control and "treat" dependent, neglected, and delinquent children. (Bartollas, 1993: 422; Caldwell, 1970)

Illinois legislators saw no need for due process guarantees to protect problem children. Illinois reformers and lawmakers saw ño need to distinguish between dependent, neglected, and delinquent children. The Illinois juvenile code passed and resulted in stepped-up legal handling of problem children.

The first Chicago juvenile court consisted of the following persons: six probation officers (whose salaries were paid by the Chicago Woman's Club), one African American woman (who supervised all African American children), twenty-one truant officers (who worked for the Chicago Board of Education), sixteen police officers (employed by the Chicago Police Department), and forty volunteers, who oversaw children put on probation (Platt, 1969: 139–40).

Some juvenile court employees were casework oriented, focusing not on a specific crime but on the whole child, giving help, advice, and support. Other juvenile court employees operated in legalistic fashion, making arrests, filing specific charges, testifying at trials, and recommending criminal punishment for youthful of fenders (Empey and Stafford, 1991: 58–59; Tappan, 1949). Juvenile court judges alternated between legalistic handling of some juvenile cases and functioning more as a friend or counselor in others. Consequently, the same juvenile court judge could order informal, relatively nonpunitive treatment for problem children, while sentencing others to long-term incarceration. Legalistic and casework-oriented juvenile justice proliferated, without procedural safeguards, under a cloak of legislatively mandated informality and confidentiality.

TWENTIETH-CENTURY CHILDREN'S LAW

In 1903, Illinois opened a second detention home. It soon housed twenty-five hundred children per year. In 1905, Illinois assumed responsibility for paying probation officers. New juvenile court rooms built in Chicago were furnished like a living room, but they were connected to detention facilities. In the early years of the

Illinois juvenile court, more than one-half of all children who were processed violated no criminal law. One-third of the children charged were sent to the Training School, the State Reformatory, or to adult court. Two-thirds of all delinquent girls were sent to state or local institutions (Platt, 1969: 141–48).

By 1930, the Illinois Juvenile Court Act had been adopted, with minor modifications, by all but two state governments. Legal reform, however, did little to improve living conditions for American problem children. Infanticide, abandonment, and ambivalence remained common. Unwanted children fell into the hands of insensitive welfare workers or juvenile court employees (Tiffin, 1982: 41). By 1900, only twelve states had effectively legislated against child labor. American children worked "in mills, mines, factories or stores, in sweatshops or street trades" (Fuller, 1930: 418). Where child labor laws existed, they were weak and lightly enforced. By 1935, only eighteen states had passed laws specifically regulating the amount of force that could be used by parents against their children (Tiffin, 1982: 146).

Section one of Colorado's 1903 Act Concerning Delinquent Children, which is reproduced below, demonstrates how encompassing the legal conception of delinquency became:

> Section 1. "Delinquent" [is] any child sixteen years of age or under who violates any law of this state or any city or village ordinance; who is incorrigible; or who knowingly associates with thieves, vicious or immoral persons; or who is growing up in idleness or crime, or who knowingly visits or enters a house of ill-repute; or who patronizes or visits any policy shop or place where any gambling device is, or shall be, operated; or who patronizes or visits any saloon or dram shop where intoxicating liquors are sold; or who patronizes or visits any public pool room or bucket shop; or who wanders about the streets in the night time without being on any lawful business or occupation; or who habitually wanders about any railroad yards or tracks, or jumps or hooks onto any moving train, or enters any car or engine without lawful authority; or who habitually uses vile, obscene, vulgar, profane or indecent language, or is guilty of immoral conduct in any public place or about any school house. (Colorado General Assembly, 1903)

The 1903 Colorado Act Concerning Delinquent Children was the second body of state-level children's law enacted in the United States. The Act Concerning Delinquent Children, along with the

1899 Colorado Act to Compel the Elementary Education of Children, brought problem children in Colorado into public school, or under control of the juvenile court.

Variations of the Illinois and Colorado children's codes were enacted by state legislatures throughout the United States. But, since each state government is independent, juvenile courts are attached in various ways to the rest of a state's judiciary. Juvenile courts are attached to other state-level tribunals in many ways, and there is a wide variety of juvenile court configurations throughout the United States (table 2.1).

LEGAL CHANGES INSPIRED BY DISCOVERY OF CHILD NEGLECT AND ABUSE

By the middle of the twentieth century, news about neglect and abuse began to influence children's law. Parents (or guardians) are neglectful when they intentionally treat children violently or cruelly, and when they fail to provide for the physical and emotional needs of their children. Parents (or guardians) are abusive when they intentionally injure, inflict pain, or cause the death of children. Three aspects of abuse are important. These are: physical, emotional, and sexual abuse.

Although family violence has been common in the United States since colonial times, legal officials and social policy makers have only recently discovered widespread neglect and abuse (Pleck, 1987: 125–44; Schorsch, 1979). In 1946, a pediatric radiologist named Caffey reported observing big bruises and fractures of the long bones in six infant patients he treated. Caffey suspected parental abuse. Caffey believed that many of the deep bruises and fractures resulted from accidental or willful injuries to children while in the care of their parents (Smith, Berkman, and Fraser, 1980: 2). In 1949, researchers found 142,000 American children living apart from their parents. Only 1,450 of those children were in the care of legal guardians. The others were kept by informal arrangement with a relative, or stranger (Weissman, 1973: 91).

In the early 1960s, several researchers published results from studies of child abuse throughout the United States. Each study revealed hundreds of abuse cases. Most victims were under four years of age and were injured, or killed, by a parent (Shepherd, 1973: 179). Another physician, C. H. Kempe, after treating four

TABLE 2.1
Varieties of American Juvenile Court Systems

Court System	State(s)
District court, or division thereof, serves as the juvenile court	Idaho, Iowa, Kansas, Kentucky, Maine, Montana, Nevada, New Hampshire, New Mexico, North Dakota, Oklahoma, Vermont
Superior or circuit court serves	Alaska, Arizona, California, Connecticut, District of Columbia, Florida, Guam, Illinois, Indiana, Maryland, Missouri, Oregon, Puerto Rico, South Dakota, Washington
Family and domestic relations court	Delaware, Hawaii, New York, Rhode Island, South Carolina
Juvenile and domestic relations court	New Jersey, Virgin Islands, Virginia
Independent court	Utah, Wyoming
Court of common pleas	Ohio, Pennsylvania
Juvenile division of probate court	Michigan
Circuit and district courts, concurrently	Alabama
Circuit and magistrate courts, concurrently (the latter have limited jurisdiction and no authority to confine)	West Virginia
Independent juvenile court or superior court judge sits as juvenile court judge	Georgia
County court	Arkansas
Trial division of high court	American Samoa
Juvenile division of district court plus juvenile court for specific counties (only Denver County in Colorado)	Colorado, Massachusetts
Each county chooses which court is Juvenile Court[1]	Texas

(continued)

TABLE 2.1
Varieties of American Juvenile Court Systems (*Continued*)

Court System	State(s)
Independent juvenile and county courts	Nebraska, Tennessee
Judges are assigned juvenile jurisdiction, and there are separate provisions for specific counties	Wisconsin
Special juvenile courts or family courts in specific parishes; where these have not been established, district courts have jurisdiction in parishes within their districts, and parish courts and city courts have concurrent jurisdiction with district courts only within their constitutionally established jurisdictional boundaries	Louisiana
District court is juvenile court in specific counties; in counties of not more than 200,000 (and in St. Louis County), the probate court handles juvenile matters	Minnesota
Youth court division of the family court or the county court or the chancery court or certain municipal courts	Mississippi
Trial division of the high court or the district or community courts	Trust Territories
Juvenile cases are heard in district court by a judge or judges who volunteer to specialize in juvenile cases. Where no judge volunteers to specialize, the chief district court judge assigns individual judges to serve in juvenile court on a rotating basis	North Carolina

Source: Adapted from King, 1980: 5–7.
Note: This is true of other states, also that is, the size of the county or various other factors may determine which court sits as the juvenile court in given area of the state. For example, in Nebraska, in counties of 30,000 or more, if the electorate agrees, an independent juvenile court may be established.

abused children in a single day, undertook a national study. Kempe found widespread abuse of children, suggested that abuse is a major social problem, and labeled the process of abusing children "the battered child syndrome" (Kempe, 1962: 17–24).

In 1962, the U.S. Congress responded by passing amendments to the Social Security Act requiring that all political units within each state provide welfare services to all children who need them in their jurisdiction. The ammendments encouraged each state to become more aggressive in locating and helping problem children. The amendments declared that child welfare services should supplement, or replace, parental care and control in order to better accomplish the following purposes:

- To prevent or solve problems that lead to childhood neglect, abuse, and delinquency.
- To provide care and protection for homeless, dependent, and neglected children.
- To help wage-earning mothers care for their children.
- To fortify and enrich homes, or make available acceptable care for children taken from their homes. (Coughlin, 1973: 15–16)

During the 1960s and 1970s, as a result of discoveries about abuse and neglect, many state legislatures amended their children's codes. Modern children's codes require that teachers, doctors, nurses, and neighbors report all possible suspected cases of abuse and neglect to legal authorities. Modern child abuse laws protect persons who report possible abuse from civil or criminal liability, so long as they act without malice and in good faith.

The 1965 Utah Juvenile Court Act (As Amended) provides a good example of revised juvenile law (Utah State Legislature, 1969):

> Section 55-10-64. "*Child*" means a person less than eighteen years of age.
>
> "*Neglected Child*" includes: A child whose parent, guardian, or custodian has abandoned him or has subjected him to mistreatment or abuse; a child who lacks proper parental care by reason of the fault or habits of the parent, guardian or custodian; a child whose parent, guardian or custodian fails or refuses to provide proper or necessary subsistence, education or medical care, including surgery or psychiatric services when required, or any other care necessary for his health, morals or well-being.

"Dependent Child" includes a child who is homeless or without proper care through no fault of his parent, guardian or custodian.

Section 55-10-80. The court shall have jurisdiction to try the following *adults* for offenses committed against children:

Any person eighteen years of age or over who induces, aids, or encourages a child to violate any federal, state, or local law or municipal ordinance, or who tends to cause children to become or remain delinquent, or who aids, contributes to, or becomes responsible for the neglect or delinquency of any child;

Any person eighteen years or over, having a child in his legal custody, or in his employment, who willfully abuses or ill-treats, neglects or abandons such child in any manner likely to cause the child unnecessary suffering or serious injury to his health or morals;

Any person eighteen years or over who forcibly takes away a child from, or encourages him to leave, the legal or physical custody of any person, agency or institution in which the child has been legally placed for the purpose of care, support, education, or adoption, or any person who knowingly detains or harbors such child.

Revised juvenile codes such as Utah's more explicitly distinguish among abuse, neglect, and delinquency. Revisions of juvenile law also extend juvenile court jurisdiction to adults who mistreat children.

In 1974, Congress passed the Juvenile Justice and Delinquency Prevention Act. The act obligates the executive branch of the U.S. government, through its Office of Juvenile Justice and Delinquency Prevention (OJJDP), to identify and control abused, neglected and delinquent children. Goals set by OJJDP are:

improving juvenile courts, faster and more protective care programs, and shelter facilities to meet the needs of abandoned and dependent children;

providing assistance to deal with the problems of runaway youth;

developing and conducting effective programs to prevent juvenile delinquency;

improving the quality of juvenile justice in the United States;

assisting the states in providing community-based programs and services for the prevention and treatment of juvenile delinquency through the development of foster care, shelter care homes, group homes, halfway houses, homemaker and home health services, 24 hour intake screening, volunteer and crisis home programs, day treatment, home probation, and any other designated community-based, diagnostic treatment or rehabilitative service;

assisting States in developing programs stressing activities aimed at improving services for and protecting the rights of youth impacted by the juvenile justice system;

authorizing the National Institute of Juvenile Justice and Delinquency Prevention to prepare studies with respect to the prevention and treatment of juvenile delinquency and related matters. (Smith, Berkman, and Fraser, 1980: 4)

The 1974 Juvenile Justice and Delinquency Prevention Act conceptually comingles dependent, neglected, and delinquent children. The act failed to request adequate federal funding for child welfare services. Furthermore, the act has left unclear whether the federal government is prepared to pay for a nationwide child-saving program. In spite of the act, no consistent national policy currently regulates identification and treatment of American problem children. Instead, fifty state-level children's codes, a small body of federal law, federal courts, and thousands of local child-care organizations independently respond to children's problems.

MIDCENTURY REDUCTION OF JUVENILE COURT JURISDICTION

In the 1960s, New York adopted a law that reclassified many status offenders as nondelinquents. Similarly, California developed a system in which status offenders were given less judgemental labels and were afforded less punitive treatment. Ten states use generic label systems, like those in New York and California, for classifying minor juvenile offenders (Smith, Berkman, Fraser and Sutton, 1980: 39). In 1975, Florida took another route to eliminating children from juvenile court jurisdiction by erasing ungovernable behavior, truancy, and runaway from its list of delinquency offenses. Ungovernable behavior, truancy, and running away were redefined as acts of dependent children, and the Florida legislature transferred jurisdiction for them to the state-run child welfare system. In 1977, Utah and Washington followed suit by changing their juvenile codes, transferring runaways, ungovernable children, and many other types of status offenders from juvenile courts to social welfare agencies. Maine eliminated most status offense categories from its juvenile laws. State legislatures rarely allocate additional funds to social welfare agencies for expanded staff and programs. Every state legislature also made some provision enabling juvenile courts to maintain the option of retaining jurisdiction over at least some types of status offenders (38).

Some state legislatures have targeted older juveniles who commit serious crimes for automatic transfer to adult court (Bartollas, 1993: 433–35; Greenwood, 1988: 2–3; King, 1980; U.S. Dept. of Justice, 1982; National Advisory Committee for Juvenile Justice, 1984). Teenagers charged as adults face fines, probation, jail, or imprisonment. Recent revisions of the Colorado Children's Code provide a good illustration of this trend (Colorado General Assembly, 1981). The 1981 Colorado code relabels status offenders as "children needing oversight" and redefines "delinquent child" in the following way:

> Any child ten years of age or older who, regardless of where the violation occurred, has violated: any federal or state law except nonfelony state traffic and game and fish laws or regulations; any municipal ordinance except traffic ordinances, the penalty for which may be a jail sentence; or any lawful order of the court made under this title.
>
> This definition shall *not* apply to:
> children fourteen years of age or older who allegedly commit crimes of violence defined . . . as class 1 felonies; or
> children who within the previous two years have been adjudicated a delinquent child (for a felony offense), and who are sixteen years of age or older who allegedly commit crimes defined as class 2 or class 3 felonies . . . or who commit nonclassified felonies punishable by . . . life imprisonment or death; or
> children fourteen years of age or older who allegedly commit any felony subsequent to any other felony which (results) in waiver of jurisdiction by any juvenile court in this state; or
> children who are alleged to be in contempt of a municipal court, regardless of whether the penalty for such contempt may be confinement.

The 1981 Colorado Code separates out repeat offenders and serious law violators for special treatment. The code makes provisions for routine transfer of serious offenders to adult criminal court for trial and disposition. Washington's 1977 revision of its children's code included similar changes in the definition and treatment of serious delinquents. Several other states have recently followed suit.

In theory, these changes leave modern juvenile courts with a smaller population of less serious delinquents to serve, assuming that delinquents can be accurately distinguished from other types of problem children. However, one-half of the states still classify status offenders as delinquents. One-third of the states have re-labeled status offenders as dependent children (Smith, Berkman, Fraser, and Sutton, 1980: 40). Wide variations in patterns of legal classification create confusion about how to effectively identify and control distinct types of American problem children. Yet, legal officials have almost unlimited discretionary authority in deciding what label is assigned in juvenile cases (Smith, Black, and Camp-bell, 1979: 12; Bartollas, 1993: 14–17).

LEGISLATIVE ATTEMPTS TO GET TOUGH ON JUVENILE CRIME

In 1993, the U.S. Congress passed an anticrime bill that allocates $8.9 billion for additional local police officers and makes some gang-ralated crimes federal offenses. The 1993 anticrime bill also prohibits the sale of guns to persons under eighteen years of age, earmarks $3 billion for juvenile offender boot camps, and gives $400 million to inner-city schools for special programs that keep children off the street.

To date, nineteen state legislatures and the District of Colum-bia have passed tough new laws aimed at getting guns away from juveniles. Many other state legislatures are considering laws that prescribe harsh treatment for children who possess or use guns and for parents who allow their children to have guns. For example, in 1993, Colorado enacted a law that prohibits persons under age eighteen from possessing handguns, except for hunting, instruc-tion, and target shooting. The Colorado law stipulates that, if caught, juveniles possessing guns must spend five days in jail after arrest and could be required to spend up to two years locked up. Some states also make it a felony for parents to allow their children to have guns (*Daily Camera*, Oct. 21, 1993: 5B).

In Colorado, the tough new "kid gun law" has not yet gener-ated large numbers of juvenile arrests. But legislators have bud-geted several million dollars to build detention, jail, and prison space in order to accomodate the increases in arrests that are antic-ipated (*Rocky Mountain News*, Nov. 11, 1993: 37A). As stiff new juvenile gun laws spread throughout the United States, and as one hundred thousand additional local police officers are put to work, juvenile arrests will surely increase. Ironically, a recent study, spon-sored by the Justice Department, of boys in detention centers or high schools in California, New Jersey, Illinois, and Louisiana re-ports that guns are numerous and easily attainable in most cities and that "new laws controlling their sale probably would not re-duce their availability" (*Daily Times-Call*, Dec. 13, 1993: 10B).

LATE-CENTURY NEWS ABOUT ABUSE AND NEGLECT

Legal change has done little to abate abuse, neglect, and delinquen-cy. Researchers, based upon a 1975 survey of American households, estimated that 1.4 million to 1.9 million parents are violent with a child each year (Gelles, 1977). Even though official statistics under-estimate the magnitude and severity of family violence (Paulson, Strause, and Chaleff, 1982; Kempe and Kempe, 1984: 13–18), in 1985, 2 million reports of neglect and abuse in the United States were officially recorded (Children's Defense Fund, 1987: 175; Hulse and Bailey, 1986: 6–7, 60–61). In 1991, The National Committee for Prevention of Child Abuse estimated that state child welfare agencies received 1.2 million reports of neglect nationwide (*Rocky Mountain News*, Jan. 12, 1993: 4) In 1976, according to the Ameri-can Humane Association, 669,000 cases of child abuse were report-ed in the United States. In 1991, 2,684,000 abuse cases were docu-mented (Bennett, 1993: 11) In Colorado, the number of confirmed reports of child abuse increased by 44 percent during the 1980s, by 10 percent from 1990 to 1991 (*Daily Camera*, Dec. 4, 1993: 1B). Seven to ten million American children need mental health services. Thirteen million children lack sufficient food, housing, medical care, day care, and instruction.

By 1995, 75 percent of all school-age children in the U.S.—60 percent of all preschoolers—will have mothers in the paid labor force (Children's Defense Fund, 1987: xiii, 54, 56). Increased fam-ily income from wage-earning mothers may actually discourage delinquency. In spite of high abandonment rates by American fa-thers, in spite of a continued refusal on the part of many American fathers to contribute significantly to the care and socialization of their children, in spite of the chronic shortage of safe, affordable day care, in spite of a severe shortage of after-school programs, most American wage-earning mothers find ways to adequately care for their children. Most American wage-earning mothers effectively prevent their children from engaging in persistent, serious acts of delinquency.

However, there is no debating the fact that the current pattern of father abandonment and dual wage earning has created a serious deficit in before- and after-school care. Child development expert Urie Bronfenbrenner observes, "[I]f there is any reliable predictor of trouble, it probably begins with children coming home to an empty house" (quoted in Byrne, 1977: 41). Quality child care is expensive and scarce. In fact, in a recent study of 447 children ages five to nine, the Child Welfare League in Washington, D.C., reported that 42 percent were left alone occasionally or regularly. Most of the children had not been taught basic precautions and safety procedures (*Rocky Mountain News*, Jan. 12, 1993: 4; Byrne, 1977: 41). Recent news about abuse and neglect suggest that there will be no shortage of problem children in the United States for some time to come.

Homelessness is also on the rise in American society, and homeless children are especially liable to be labeled dependent or neglected. Small children are the fastest growing component of homeless America. A typical homeless family includes a parent and two or three young children (Kozol, 1988: 4). There is considerable debate about the number of homeless Americans. Government officials estimate as few as 250,000 to 350,000 homeless. The Coalition for the Homeless argues that the number is closer to 3 to 4 million persons. Jonathan Kozol suggests that there are probably 2 to 3 million homeless Americans, "and well above 10 million families may be living near the edge of homelessness in the United States" (11). While homelessness spreads, more comfortable Americans appear to be showing less tolerance for those in need. For example, city councils are passing laws that prohibit sleeping, camping, and loitering in order to force the homeless out of municipalities. According to a spokesperson for the National Law Center on Homelessness and Poverty, "[T]hey end up trying to legislate the symptoms of homelessness out of existence rather than addressing the causes" (*Rocky Mountain News*, Dec. 27, 1993: 34A).

In sum, children's law, juvenile courts, and social service agencies have not eliminated dependency, neglect, and abuse. Legislatures, courts, and social service agencies vacilitate between preserving the family in its ancient form (where fathers rule the household) and protecting victims. Many experts believe that it will take social service programs much larger than U.S. taxpayers are currently willing to support in order abate family violence (Pleck, 1987: 201–3) and other forms of abuse and neglect. We will return to other aspects of neglect and abuse in chapter 7.

RECENT COURT DECISIONS AFFECTING CHILDREN

In 1966, the U.S. Supreme Court decided *Kent v. United States,* its first case involving juvenile law (U.S. Supreme Court, 1966). Morris Kent, age 16, lived in the District of Columbia. He was arrested and accused of committing several robberies, raping a woman, and breaking into private residences. The strongest piece of incriminating evidence against Kent was his fingerprint found at the scene of the rape. Without a hearing, the juvenile court judge transferred the Kent case to a United States district court, where Morris was tried as an adult by a jury. Kent claimed insanity as a defense, and he was found guilty of robbery and housebreaking. Kent was sentenced to ninety years in prison (Wadlington, 1983: 201–9).

The Kent conviction was appealed, but it was upheld by the U.S. Court of Appeals. Kent's conviction was subsequently appealed to the U.S. Supreme Court. In *Kent v. United States* (383 U.S. 541 [1960]), the Court made the following statement:

> There is much evidence that some juvenile courts, including that of the District of Columbia, lack the personnel, facilities, and techniques to perform adequately as representatives of the State in a *parens patriae* capacity, at least with respect to children charged with law violation.
>
> There is evidence, in fact, that there may be grounds for concern that the child receives the worst of both worlds: that he gets neither the protections accorded to adults nor the solicitous care and regenerative treatment postulated for children.

The U.S. Supreme Court invalidated the waiver order by which Morris Kent had been transferred to adult court, because the order did not contain a statement of reasons. The juvenile court failed to give Kent and his attorney a hearing on the matter, and Kent's attorney was prevented by the court from providing effective help (Smith, Berkman, Fraser, and Sutton, 1980: 21).

Kent v. United States was an important ruling. For the first time in its history, the United States Supreme Court extended limited procedural and due process rights to children appearing before juvenile court judges. The *Kent* ruling forced juvenile courts to accept attorneys into their proceedings and to take more time and care with each juvenile case reaching litigation. It is interesting to note, however, what the Supreme Court overlooked in this case: When Kent was arrested, the police failed to notify his parents. The juvenile court did not learn about the Kent case until one week after Morris was taken into custody. Kent was questioned alone by the police, away from his attorney and parents. No legal official told Morris that he had a right to an attorney, and a right to remain silent. He was fingerprinted by the police. These were all violations of the Juvenile Court Act of the District of Columbia (Coughlin, 1973: 19). In terms of protecting children's rights in legal proceedings, *Kent v. United States* barely scratched the surface.

The next important juvenile case to reach the U.S. Supreme Court was *In re Gault* (387 U.S. 1 [1967]). In 1964, Gerald Gault was on probation for being with another boy who stole a wallet from a woman's purse. Gerald was taken into custody by the police in Gila County, Arizona, because a neighbor complained that Gerald and another boy made "offensive, adolescent, sex variety" remarks to her over the telephone. Gerald was held for some time in a detention home. No attempt was made by legal officials to contact his working parents. After several hearings in juvenile court, and behind-the-scenes maneuvering by a probation officer, Gerald was found guilty of "making lewd phone calls," was taken from his parents, and was sentenced to six years at the state industrial school, "unless sooner discharged by due process of law" (Wadlington, Whitebread, and Davis, 1983: 209–11). In Arizona an adult convicted of the same offense, at most, would have been fined fifty dollars and sentenced to one year in jail. An adult, if choosing not to plea bargain, would also have a right to due process. Gerald Gault got six years and no due process.

The law in Arizona prohibited appeal of juvenile court cases, so Gerald's parents took another route in order to get their son's conviction overturned. The Arizona Supreme Court ruled against the Gaults, however, asserting that the *parens patriae* principal excused the juvenile court from providing procedural safeguards for problem children. The Gaults appealed the case to the U.S. Supreme Court, contending that, contrary to rights guaranteed every citizen by the Fourteenth Amendment to the U.S. Constitution, Gerald was taken from them by the police, a probation officer and the juvenile court. In the ensuing proceedings they were denied:

> notice of the charges filed against their son;
> their right to an attorney;
> their right to confront and cross examine hostile witnesses;
> Gerald's right not to incriminate himself;
> the right to receive transcripts of all juvenile court proceedings involving their son;
> their right to appeal the decision of a juvenile court judge to higher tribunals within the state system (213).

The U.S. Supreme Court ruled in favor of the Gaults.

As part of the *Gault* case, the U.S. Supreme court also imposed three procedural requirements on juvenile courts everywhere in the nation:

> First, timely notice must be provided to parents and children of the nature and terms of any juvenile court proceeding in which a determination affecting their rights or interests may be made.
>
> Second, unequivocal and timely notice must be given that counsel may appear in any such proceeding in behalf of the child and its parents, and that in cases in which the child may be confined in an institution, counsel may, in circumstances of indigency, be appointed for them.
>
> Third, the court must maintain a written record, or its equivalent, adequate to permit effective review on appeal or in collateral proceedings.
>
> The requirements would guarantee to juveniles the tools with which their rights could be fully vindicated, and yet permit the States to pursue without unnecessary hindrance the purposes which they believe imperative in this field (228).

Juvenile courts abiding by the *Gault* requirements take more time, and tie up more labor, processing children's cases. Attorneys are admitted as full participants in all phases of juvenile litigation. For many poor children, the state now pays for an attorney. The *Gault* ruling has had great impact on legal officials everywhere. Because of its cost implications, the *Gault* case has sent legislators searching for ways to keep problem children away from juvenile court proceedings.

In *Gault*, the Supreme Court did not challenge the right of juvenile courts to intervene through the *parens patriae* doctrine. Instead, juvenile courts were encouraged to continue this, while somehow simultaneously establishing protocol that would guarantee children's rights in matters relating to arrest, personal searches, seizure of evidence, pretrial investigation, notice of charges, the use of attorneys, self-incrimination, and the confrontation of hostile witnesses (Coughlin, 1973: 21). With *Gault*, local juvenile courts were instructed by the highest legal authority in the nation to maintain their informal, parentlike, approach to resolving matters related to American problem children, while at the same time adopting expensive, time-consuming procedural safeguards that are typical of adult criminal court proceedings (Bartollas, 1993: 425).

For *In re Winship* (397 U.S. 358 [1970]), the U.S. Supreme Court reviewed a case involving a twelve-year-old New York boy, who was arrested for taking $112 from a woman's purse. The boy was charged with larceny and was brought before a New York family court. A judge found the boy guilty but acknowledged that the evidence in the case failed to establish guilt beyond a reasonable doubt. The judge ruled that guilt had been established based upon a preponderance of the evidence. The boy was sentenced to a state industrial school for periods of eighteen months that, after court review, could be extended for as long as six years. Winship's parents appealed the ruling and were defeated in state appelate court hearings. The case was appealed to the U.S. Supreme Court. The Court ruled that conviction and long-term incarceration of a juvenile based upon a preponderance of the evidence is invalid. Proof of delinquency must be established beyond a reasonable doubt. Thus, *Winship* forced even stricter requirements on judges presiding over delinquency cases (Bartollas, 1993: 426).

In *McKeiver v. Pennsylvania* (403 U.S. 528, 535 [1971], parents were appealing a declaration of delinquency made by a Pennsylvania juvenile court judge (U.S. Supreme Court, 1971). Their son had been arrested and charged with chasing, along with other gang members, three teenagers, overtaking them, and stealing twenty-five cents (Wadlington, Whitebread, and Davis, 1983, 236). The juvenile court trial young McKeiver and his parents underwent was like criminal trials of adults. In fact, in their appeal to the U.S. Supreme Court, they argued that the juvenile trial was the same, in terms of procedure followed, as an adult criminal trial, except that the McKeiver child was denied the right to a trial by jury. The McKeivers pointed out that the Sixth and Fourteenth Amendments to the U.S. Constitution guarantee all citizens charged with crimes the option of a jury trial. On this basis they asked that the Pennsylvania decision be overturned.

Attorneys representing Pennsylvania asserted that all procedural provisions prescribed by the Gault decision had been afforded the McKeivers. The Pennsylvania juvenile court judge believed that this was enough to

> insure that the juvenile court will operate in an atmosphere which is *orderly enough* to impress the juvenile with the gravity of the situation and the impartiality of the tribunal and at the same time *informal enough* to permit the benefits of the juvenile system to operate. (238, emphasis added)

The U.S. Supreme Court ruled against the McKeivers and concluded the following about juvenile court procedure:

> The Court has refrained . . . from . . . a flat holding that all rights constitutionally assured for the adult accused are to be imposed upon the state juvenile proceeding . . .
> . . . Meager as has been the hoped-for advance in the juvenile field, the alternative would be regressive, would lose what has been gained, and would tend once again to place the juvenile squarely in the routine of the criminal process.
> . . . We are reluctant to disallow the states to experiment further and to seek in new and different ways the elusive answers to the problems of the young, and we feel that we would be impeding that experimentation by imposing the jury trial . . .
> Of course there have been abuses . . . We refrain from saying at this point that those abuses are of constitutional dimension. They relate to the lack of resources and dedication rather than to inherent unfairness . . .
> Finally, the arguments advanced by the juveniles here are, of course, the identical arguments that underlie the demand for the jury trial for criminal proceedings. The arguments necessarily equate the juvenile proceeding—or at least the adjudicative phase of it—with the criminal trial. Whether they should be so equated is our issue . . .

If the formalities of the criminal adjudicative process are to be superimposed upon the juvenile court system, there is little need for its separate existence. Perhaps that ultimate disillusionment will come one day, but for the moment we are disinclined to give impetus to it. (241–43)

Thus, the McKeiver decision left juvenile court judges with considerable discretion in determining guilt or innocense, and in selecting punishment or rehabilitation for the guilty (Bartollas, 1993: 427).

Breed v. Jones (421 U.S. 519 [1975]) took another step toward regulating juvenile court procedure (U.S. Supreme Court, 1975). A California juvenile court judge found that a boy brought before him had violated a criminal statute and that he was unfit for treatment as a juvenile (Wadlington, Whitebread, and Davis, 1983: 245). The case was transferred to a California superior court, where the boy was prosecuted as an adult and found guilty. This decision was appealed on the grounds that the Fifth and Fourteenth Amendments to the Constitution protect all citizens from the jeopardy of multiple trials. Appeal went through several courts and was finally taken to the U.S. Supreme Court by attorneys representing California. The Court concluded the following:

. . . in terms of potential consequences, there is little to distinguish an adjudicatory hearing such as was held in this case from a traditional criminal prosecution. For that reason, it engenders elements of "anxiety and insecurity" in a juvenile, and imposes a "heavy personal strain" . . .

we can find no persuasive distinction in that regard between the proceeding conducted in this case . . . and a criminal prosecution . . .

We agree that such a holding will require, in most cases, that the transfer decision be made prior to an adjudicatory hearing . . . (245–52)

The U.S. Supreme Court upheld an appeals court decision, which directed a California district court to cancel the adult conviction of the Jones boy and either set him free or return him to the juvenile court for disposition (Bartollas, 1993: 428–29).

In 1978, the U.S. Supreme Court ruled in *Swisher v. Brady* (438 U.S. 204) that preliminary hearings presided over by masters (or referees), even though they sometimes result in recommendations considered by juvenile court judges at subsequent hearings, do not constitute a criminal trial and, therefore, do not place children in jeopardy of undergoing multiple trials.

In 1984, in *Schall v. Martin* (104 U.S. 2403), the U. S. Supreme court upheld preventive detention of juveniles, if there is "serious risk" that a child will "commit an act which if committed by an adult would constitute a crime." This decision gives local police and juvenile court officials permission to lock up any child who might commit a crime. It could precipitate an increase in the jailing of minor offenders.

With each ruling, the U.S. Supreme Court adds to the amount of time and resources juvenile court officials must commit to cases reaching litigation. Each U.S. Supreme Court ruling puts more pressure on state legislators to keep problem children away from juvenile court jurisdiction. Since 1966, the U.S. Supreme Court has been an active participant in regulating juvenile courts. The end result of Supreme Court involvement in children's law is hard to predict. In jurisdictions where U.S. Supreme Court rulings are obeyed, juvenile court cases now take more time to adjudicate and cost the state more money to resolve. Unless the Supreme Court reverses itself and relaxes juvenile adjudicatory requirements, more and more money will be needed to support the American juvenile court system. We return to these issues in later chapters. They are raised here to illustrate the fact that American legislatures and courts have created a legalistic and expensive environment for helping problem children (Greenwood, 1988: 1).

SUMMARY

This chapter provides a legal backdrop against which to view juvenile delinquency in the United States. Until 1899, children in the United States were subject to the same criminal laws and punishments as adults. In the late nineteenth century, reformers became aware of the large numbers of American children in adult criminal courts, jails, and prisons. American child savers lobbied government to assume responsibility for controlling and correcting problem children. Neither reformers nor government officials realized the magnitude and severity of children's problems. They failed to understand that the juvenile justice system, no matter how large it grew, would be swamped with problem children.

Reformers and their allies forged models of juvenile law that were adopted by state legislatures throughout the United States. Early American juvenile law inserted the state as a higher parent in all legal matters involving problem children. Early juvenile laws established a system of school officials, truant officers, police and probation officers, juvenile court judges, jailers, and volunteers to control abuse, neglect, and delinquency.

In 1966, the U.S. Supreme Court interceded. In a series of decisions, the Supreme Court forced American juvenile courts to change procedures for processing young violators. Children were given many of the legal protections afforded adult criminal suspects. Thus, the U.S. Supreme Court became a partner in determining American juvenile court policy and practice. Today, half of the juvenile courts in this country retain jurisdiction over all types of problem children. The other half of America's juvenile courts transferred jurisdiction over minor offenders to social welfare workers and shifted responsibility for major offenders to adult criminal courts.

PART 2

Measuring Delinquency

CHAPTER 3

Measuring Delinquency

UNIFORM CRIME REPORTS

Since 1930, the Federal Bureau of Investigation (FBI) has published an annual series entitled *Crime in the United States,* which is commonly called the *Uniform Crime Reports (UCR).*[1] Today, the *UNIFORM CRIME REPORTS* provide information about adult and juvenile arrests made by police officers working for almost ten thousand local law enforcement agencies in more than forty-six hundred American cities. The *UCR* are by far the most popular source of government information about juvenile delinquency. In 1930, the Uniform Crime Reporting program secured information from police organizations in only about four hundred cities. Even though local police were instructed by FBI personnel to use *UCR* definitions of crimes, early data are suspect. For example, there is strong indication that many crimes deemed felonies in some jurisdictions were treated as misdemeanors in others (FBI, 1982: 1; Barnes and Teeters, 1959: 75–76). The FBI nevertheless persevered.

In succeeding years, the Committee on Uniform Crime Records of the International Association of Chiefs of Police helped the FBI to develop standard definitions of the following seven crimes: (1) murder and nonnegligent manslaughter, (2) forcible rape, (3) robbery, (4) aggravated assault, (5) burglary, (6) larceny-theft, and (7) motor vehicle theft. Today, items 1–4 are called "crimes against persons," and items 5–7 are labeled "crimes against property." Collectively, the FBI named the seven crimes listed, above, "index crimes," and later renamed them "Part I offenses." Part I offenses were chosen by the chiefs and the FBI as a focus for the study of American crime and delinquency "because of their seriousness as well as their frequency of occurrence and likelihood of being re-

---

[1]See Federal Bureau of Investigation, *UNIFORM CRIME REPORTS* (Washington, DC: Government Printing Office, 1930–).

ported to law enforcement" (FBI, 1982: 1). In 1979, Congress added an eighth crime, arson, to the list of Part I Offenses. In table 3.1 each Part I offense is defined.

The International Association of Chiefs of Police and the FBI also itemized a list of "lesser" Part II Offenses, which, in their opinion, included "all crimes except those classified as Part I" (2). Today, there are twenty-one Part II Offenses monitored by the FBI. Each Part II offense is defined in table 3.2. The Chiefs of Police and the FBI did not consider elite and corporate crimes like monopolization, price-fixing, political influence buying, and worker exploitation to be serious problems. Similarly, few crimes commonly committed by middle-class Americans, for example, tax evasion, employee theft, and prescription drug abuse were listed by the FBI. Instead, the *Uniform Crime Reports* focus mainly on unlawful acts committed by inner-city poor persons, including many problem children.

The FBI, through its large Uniform Crime Reporting (UCR) field staff, and with the help of local law enforcement administrators, works hard to make the *UCR* as accurate as possible. On a monthly basis, local police agencies take from their records information about crimes uncovered and about resulting arrests. Local police data are passed on to the FBI, either directly by the local agency or indirectly through one of the approximately forty state-level UCR programs. At each step in the process, police information is edited and examined for completeness and quality by specially trained personnel. Currently, the FBI estimates that their *Uniform Crime Reports* provide crime information for the geographical area of the United States on which 97 percent of the population lives.

For Part I Offenses, the *UCR* provide information about the number of offenses known to the police, the number of offenses cleared by arrest, and the number of arrests made by police officers. For Part II offenses, the *UCR* supply only arrest data. Information is available, however, about the age, gender, and ethnic origin of persons who are arrested for Part I and II offenses.

Weaknesses of UCR Data

Using arrests of juveniles as a primary indicator of the extent and character of American delinquency has three important limitations. First, the volume of arrests of juveniles (and adults) is in part a

TABLE 3.1
FBI Part I Offenses

1. CRIMINAL HOMICIDE—a. Murder and nonnegligent manslaughter: the willful (nonnegligent) killing of one human being by another. Deaths caused by negligence, attempts to kill, assaults to kill, suicides, accidental deaths, and justifiable homicides are excluded. b. Justifiable homicides are limited to: (1) the killing of a felon by law enforcement officer in the line of duty; and (2) the killing of a felon by a private citizen. b. Manslaughter by negligence: the killing of another person through gross negligence. Excludes traffic fatalities. While manslaughter by negligence is a Part I crime, it is not included in the Crime Index.
2. FORCIBLE RAPE—The carnal knowledge of a female forcibly and against her will. Included are rapes by force and attempts to rape. Statutory offenses (no force used—victim under age of consent) are excluded.
3. ROBBERY—The taking or attempting to take anything of value from the care, custody, or control of a person or persons by force or threat of force or violence and/or by putting the victim in fear.
4. AGGRAVATED ASSAULT—An unlawful attack by one person upon another for the purpose of inflicting severe or aggravated bodily injury. This type of assault usually is accompanied by the use of a weapon or by means likely to produce death or great bodily harm. Simple assaults are excluded.
5. BURGLARY—BREAKING OR ENTERING—The unlawful entry of a structure to commit a felony or a theft. Attempted forcible entry is included.
6. LARCENY-THEFT (EXCEPT MOTOR VEHICLE THEFT)—The unlawful taking, carrying, leading, or riding away of property from the possession or constructive possession of another. Examples are thefts of bikes or automobile accessories, shoplifting, pocket-picking, or the stealing of any property or article, which is not taken by force and violence or by fraud. Attempted larcenies are included. Embezzlement, "con" games, forgery, worthless checks, etc., are excluded.
7. MOTOR VEHICLE THEFT—The theft or attempted theft of a motor vehicle. A motor vehicle is self-propelled and runs on the surface and not on rails. Specifically excluded from this category are motorboats, construction equipment, airplanes, and farming equipment.
8. ARSON—Any willful or malicious burning or attempt to burn, with or without intent to defraud, a dwelling house, public building, motor vehicle or aircraft, personal property of another, etc.

Source: FBI, 1993b: 381.

TABLE 3.2
FBI Part II Offenses

---

9. OTHER ASSAULTS (SIMPLE)—Assaults and attempted assaults where no weapon was used and which did not result in serious or aggravated injury to the victim.
10. FORGERY AND COUNTERFEITING—Making, altering, uttering, or possessing, with intent to defraud, anything false which is made to appear true. Attempts are included.
11. FRAUD—Fraudulent conversion and obtaining money or property by false pretenses. Included are larceny by bailee and bad checks, except forgeries and counterfeiting.
12. EMBEZZLEMENT—Misappropriation or misapplication of money or property entrusted to one's care, custody, or control.
13. STOLEN PROPERTY: BUYING, RECEIVING, POSSESSING— Buying, receiving, and possessing stolen property, including attempts.
14. VANDALISM—Willful or malicious destruction, injury, disfigure- ment, or defacement of any public or private property, real or person- al, without consent of the owner or person having custody or control.
15. WEAPONS: CARRYING, POSSESSING, ETC.—All violations of regulations or statutes controlling the carrying, using, possessing, furnishing, and manufacturing of deadly weapons or silencers. In- cluded are attempts.
16. PROSTITUTION AND COMMERCIALIZED VICE—Sex offenses of a commercialized nature, such as prostitutition, keeping a bawdy house, procuring, or transporting women for immoral purposes. At- tempts are included.
17. SEX OFFENSES (except forcible rape, prostitution, and commer- cialized vice)—Statutory rape and offenses against chastity, common decency, morals, and the like. Attempts are included.
18. DRUG ABUSE VIOLATIONS—State and local offenses relating to narcotic drugs, such as unlawful possession, sale, use, growing, and manufacturing of narcotic drugs.
19. GAMBLING—Promoting, permitting, or engaging in illegal gam- bling.
20. OFFENSES AGAINST THE FAMILY AND CHILDREN—Nonsup- port, neglect, desertion, or abuse of family and children.
21. DRIVING UNDER THE INFLUENCE—Driving or operating any vehicle or common carrier while drunk or under the influence of liquor or narcotics.

(continued)

TABLE 3.2
FBI Part II Offenses (*Continued*)

---

22. LIQUOR LAWS—State or local liquor law violations, except "drunkenness" (offense 23) and "driving under the influence" (offense 21). Federal violations are excluded.
23. DRUNKENNESS—Drunkenness or intoxication. Excluded is "driving under the influence" (offense 21).
24. DISORDERLY CONDUCT—Breach of the peace.
25. VAGRANCY—Vagabondage, begging, loitering, etc.
26. ALL OTHER OFFENSES—All violations of state or local laws, except offenses 1–25 and traffice offenses.
27. SUSPICION—No specific offense; suspect released without formal charges being placed.
28. CURFEW AND LOITERING LAWS—Offenses relating to violations of local curfew or loitering ordinances where such laws exist.
29. RUNAWAYS—Limited to juveniles taken into protective custody under provisions of local statutes.

Source: FBI, 1993b: 381–82.

function of *police capacity* to respond to crime and misbehavior. Simply put, many police departments do not have enough officers to make arrests for every crime that occurs. For example, a force of local officers who are spread thinly on patrol over the total area of a large, densely populated city will in all likelihood be unaware of much crime and delinquency that occurs and will, at least in some cases, be unable to make many possible arrests. A force of officers who concentrate patrol in limited geographical areas—inner-city zones, ghettos, slums, or shopping centers—are in a relatively good position to make many more possible arrests.

Second, *UCR* data are limited, or expanded, by *police willingness* to arrest. Studies of police behavior indicate that members of some departments arrest nearly every juvenile whom they catch violating the law, whereas other studies show that many police officers arrest as few as one in five children who are caught engaging in delinquency. Today, approximately one-half of all children who are caught by the police while breaking a law are actually arrested.

Third, *UCR* arrest data are limited or expanded partly because of gender, ethnic, and social-class biases in law enforcement. Preju-

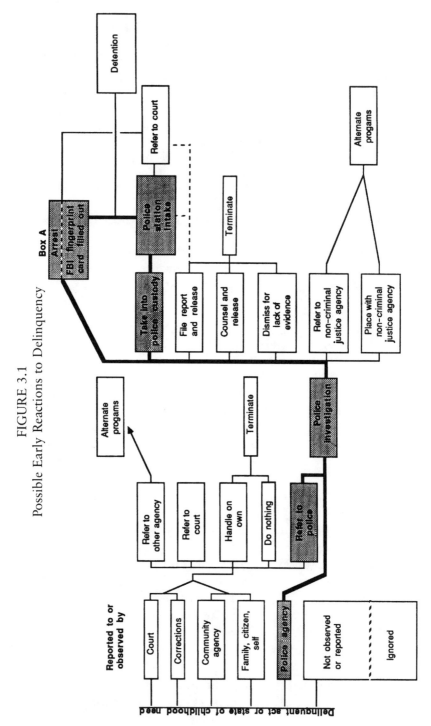

FIGURE 3.1
Possible Early Reactions to Delinquency

54

dice sometimes conditions police officers to look most closely for crime where disadvantaged males live. Similarly, ethnic and social-class preferences can encourage officers to overlook law violation which occurs in neighborhoods where advantaged children live. Thus, like other indicators, police arrest data, at best, are only partially accurate indices of the extent and character of American delinquency.

Figure 3.1 illustrates the selective nature of police arrest data by outlining many possible responses that could occur to an act of delinquency or to a state of childhood need. Boxes on the left side of figure 3.1 represent the possibility that problem children are either ignored entirely or that their problems come to the attention of agencies other than the police. Highlighted boxes connected by a broad black line, which start at the bottom-left of figure 3.1, and which proceed through the middle toward the upper-right, show the path that children must follow in order to become part of FBI arrest statistics.[2] Problem children who are ignored, youth helped by nonpolice agencies, and children processed by the police but not arrested, are unaccounted for in *UCR* data. In other words, only children who make it all the way to Box A of figure 3.1 are officially arrested.

Widespread confusion among social scientists and legal officials over what arrest statistics actually measure encourages intermingling of three somewhat distinct definitions of delinquency. A delinquent can be defined as

1. a child who commits a legally prohibited act
2. a youth who commits a proscribed act *and* who is caught by the police
3. only a youngster who breaks a law, gets caught by the police, *and* is arrested

It is important to remember that the *Uniform Crime Reports* provide information about only the third category of children.

---

[2]An arrest occurs when local law enforcement personnel fill out a fingerprint card for a juvenile, after s/he is taken into custody by an officer for law violation. Arrest can also mean that a child is cited to appear before a juvenile court, or other juvenile authorities, but is not taken into custody (FBI, 1983: 156). As late as 1950, the FBI warned that "the number of arrest records is doubtless incomplete in the lower age groups because of the practice of some jurisdictions not to fingerprint youthful offenders" (109).

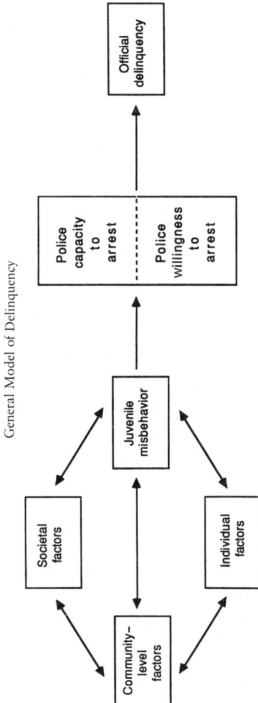

FIGURE 3.2
General Model of Delinquency

Figure 3.2 outlines a simple general model of delinquency that includes police factors along with other basic causes. On the left side of figure 3.2, three boxes represent the plausible assertion that juvenile misbehavior is, at least in part, caused by some combination of individual, community-level, and societal factors. Boxes on the right side of figure 3.2 represent the idea that only some juvenile misbehavior is transformed into official delinquency. Police capacity to arrest and willingness to arrest are primary intervening factors in determining which cases of juvenile misbehavior become part of *UCR* records.

OVERVIEW OF JUVENILE ARRESTS

Table 3.3 presents an overall picture of juvenile arrests in the United States. First, look at Row A. Row A shows that relatively few children were formally arrested in the 1940s and 1950s, and that most juvenile arrestees were *over* fifteen years of age. By 1964, however, things had changed. In 1964, nearly one million problem children were arrested, and most of them were *under* fifteen years of age. As row A shows, arrests of American problem children escalated throughout the 1970s, 1980s, and early 1990s. Recent trends again favor taking older youth into custody. Row B of table 3.3 shows that until 1974 juvenile arrests represented an increasing proportion of all arrests in the United States. Since 1974, however, juvenile arrests have been decreasing as a proportion of total arrests.

Why are so many American children arrested? Rows C and D provide information that partially explains large numbers of arrests of juveniles. Row C indicates that the juvenile population in the United States increased significantly in the 1950s, 1960s, and 1970s. Currently, there are approximately sixty-four million children living in the United States, twice as many as in 1950. In other words, there are today far more problem children to arrest than there were forty years ago. Row D reveals that the number of police employees in the United States is also on the rise. Whereas, in 1950, there were only about 150,000 police employees in the United States, today, there are almost 750,000 persons working for police agencies, and the 1993 federal Anti-Crime Bill will add another 100,000 local police officers.[3] Thus, currently, there are

---

[3] Approximately 70 percent of all police employees are sworn officers with authority to execute arrests.

TABLLE 3.3
Juvenile Arrests, 1940–1992

		1940	1950	1964	1974	1985	1992
Row A	Total arrests	**35,332**	**34,539**	**961,132**	**1,683,073**	**1,762,539**	**1,943,138**
	1–14 years old	4,103	3,533	549,114	606,548	585,745	689,877
	15 or older	31,229	31,006	412,018	1,076,525	1,176,794	1,253,261
Row B	% of all U.S. arrests*	6	4	21	27	17	16.3
Row C	Juvenile population in the U.S.†	29,735,000	30,713,000	49,396,000	50,958,000	62,318,000	64,083,000
Row D	Number of U.S. police employees‡	112,594	142,866	273,579	546,859	619,634	748,830

*Source: FBI, 1940–41: 207 for 1940; FBI, 1950–51: 110–11 for 1950; FBI, 1965: 108 for 1964; FBI, 1975: 186 for 1974; FBI, 1985: 174 for 1985; FBI, 1993a: 227 for 1992.

†Source: U.S. Bureau of the Census, 1964: 358 for 1940 and 1950; U.S. Bureau of the Census, 1965: 24 for 1964; U.S. Bureau of the Census, 1975b: 31 for 1974; U.S. Bureau of the Census, 1986a: 25 for 1985; U.S. Bureau of the Census, 1991: 12 for 1992.

‡Source: FBI, 1940–41: 95 for 1940; FBI 1950–51, no. 1: p. 19 for 1950; FBI 1965: 144–45 for 1964; FBI, 1975: 235 for 1974; FBI, 1985: 242 for 1985; FBI, 1993a: 294 for 1992.

more police officers available to execute juvenile arrests than at any other time in American history. In sum, table 3.3 shows that, as the number of juveniles increased, and as the number of police employees went up, arrests of American problem children also rose.

A NOTE ON JUVENILE VIOLENCE

As we will see, juveniles in the United States are arrested mostly for relatively minor criminal offenses, especially property crimes, and for status offenses. However, for the last thirty years, violent deaths by juveniles and arrests of juveniles for serious violent offenses— murder, rape, aggravated assault, and armed robbery—have been increasing noticeably. Increases in arrests of juveniles for violent crimes have been especially alarming since 1986. For example, between 1986 and 1991, arrests in the United States of fourteen to seventeen year olds for homicide rose by 124 percent. According to a Cleveland homicide detective, "[W]e're getting kids 12 and 13 years old involved in murders and that was very rare until a few years ago" (*Daily Times-Call*, Dec. 31, 1993: 8A). Today, in most major American cities, juveniles account for at least 50 percent of all arrests for murder and for about 40 percent of all murder victims.

According to research done by the Annie E. Casey Foundation and the Center for the Study of Social Policy, between 1986 and 1991, the violent crime arrest rate for juveniles in the United States rose by 48 percent. A Denver juvenile court judge reports, "[I]'m seeing younger juveniles, and they're more violent. We have a breakdown of the family. Kids are exposed to more violence on TV. We have a gang problem and a drug problem. It's not just one factor" (*Rocky Mountain News*, Dec. 23, 1993: 16A).

In 1990, twelve thousand American children lost their lives due to homicide, suicide, or an accident. Currently, an average of six American juveniles die violently each day. According to experts at The Centers for Disease Control and Prevention, for every teen homicide, one hundred juveniles are wounded. In the last five years, the violent death rate for African American teens increased by 78 percent. According to an epidemiologist at The Centers for Disease Control, "[E]pidemic is precisely the right word for" the steady rise in murdering and murdered juveniles in the United States (*Rocky Mountain News*, Dec. 23, 1993: 16A; *Daily Times-Call*, Aug. 1, 1993: 6B).

TABLE 3.4
Juvenile Arrests, 1940–1992

		1940	1950	1964	1974	1985	1992
Row A	Total arrests*	35,332	34,599	961,132	1,683,073	1,606,225	1,943,138
	Male	31,111	—	688,804	1,138,922	1,248,235	1,286,997
	Female	2,221	—	130,191	306,412	357,990	387,019
Row B	Female to male arrest ratio	1 to 15	—	1 to 5	1 to 4	1 to 3.5	1 to 3.3
Row C	Proportion of female to male juveniles in the U.S.†	1.1 to 1	1.1 to 1	1.1 to 1	1.1 to 1	1.1 to 1	1 to 1.1

*Source: FBI, 1940–41: 207, 211–12 for 1940; FBI, 1965: 113 for 1964; FBI, 1975: 190 for 1974; FBI, 1986: 173 for 1985; FBI, 1993: 226 for 1992.
†Source: U.S. Bureau of the Census, 1965: 23–24 for 1940, 1950, 1964; U.S. Bureau of the Census, 1975: 31 for 1974; U.S. Bureau of the Census, 1986: 25 for 1985; U.S. Bureau of the Census, 1991: 12 for 1992.

Male and Female Arrests

Table 3.4 gives us a breakdown of male and female juvenile arrests for 1940–92.[4] Data in row A of Table 3.4 indicates that it is mostly male children who get arrested. However, since 1964, significant numbers of girls have been taken into police custody. The number of female juvenile arrests increased considerably in the 1960s, and it has continued to rise through the 1970s, 1980s, and early 1990s. Today, almost four hundred thousand young females are arrested each year. Thus, while boys are more likely than girls to get arrested, the number of young females getting arrested has risen, and the male-to-female arrest ratio is dropping (see row B).

One wonders why far more boys than girls are arrested. Row C of table 3.4 shows that there are approximately equal numbers of male and female children in the United States. Do boys and girls commit different amounts of misbehavior? Are boys and girls involved in different types of delinquency? Obviously, gender role prohibitions for females play a large part, restricting opportunities for girls to violate the law. Also, American legal officials have been biased toward girls.

Historically, the police have been most interested in female status offenses, which often involve violations of appropriate gender role performance, like engaging in premarital sex, using alcohol, truancy, and acting incorrigibly. For example, in New York state, until the 1980s, *all* girls arrested, regardless of offense, were required to undergo vaginal exams. During that same time period, no exam of juvenile male genitalia was part of the routine arrest procedure (Chesney-Lind and Shelden, 1992: 127–30). Evidently, New York legal officials factored in data about sexual activity only for girls, when deciding how to handle cases involving violence, property violations and nonsexual status offenses.

Table 3.5 displays information about the offenses for which boys and girls most often get arrested. The ten offense categories for which boys most commonly get arrested are listed on the left side of table 3.5. The right side of table 3.5 shows ten offense categories that produce the largest numbers of juvenile female arrests. Arrest data show that male and female juveniles are arrested

---

[4]Please note that the total arrest estimates for 1985 and 1992 do not agree with those in table 3.3. I suspect that the FBI excluded arrest cases where no gender data were recorded.

TABLE 3.5
Offenses for which Juveniles are Commonly Arrested, by Gender, 1992

Males		Females	
Offense	Number of Arrests	Offense	Number of Arrests
Larceny/theft	242,428	Larceny/theft	101,433
All other (except traffic)	192,999	*Runaway*	*75,360*
Vandalism	*95,758*	All other (except traffic)	51,111
Other assaults	*94,428*	Other assaults	30,660
Burglary	93,925	Liquor law violations	23,636
Disorderly conduct	76,337	Disorderly conduct	21,220
Liquor law violations	59,186	Curfew and loitering	18,152
Drug abuse	58,166	Burglary	9,484
Runaway	57,488	Vandalism	8,965
Motor vehicle theft	56,731	Aggravated assault	8,695

Source: FBI, 1993a: 226.

for pretty much the same offenses. Boys *and* girls most often get arrested for larceny/theft. Similarly, male and female juveniles are frequently arrested for a grab bag of infractions called "all other offenses (except traffic)," which includes a number of status offenses, and for liquor law violations. Girls are arrested more often than boys for running away. Young males apparently burglarize and vandalize more than females. In general, however, American female and male problem children are taken into police custody for committing similar offenses. For example, Chesney-Lind and Shelden report that girls are more likely to resemble boys when arrest data for status offenses (curfew violation), larceny/theft, family-related behavioral infractions (incorrigibility or unmanageable) and alcohol-related violations are considered (8).

Arrests of Anglo and Minority Juveniles

Comparisons of arrests of Anglo and minority youth can also be done with *UCR* data. Table 3.6 presents information about arrests of children from relatively distinct ethnic groups for the years

TABLE 3.6

Arrests of Juveniles, by Ethnic Group, 1964–1992

	Ethnic Group	1964	1974	1986	1992
Row A	Anglo	671,477	1,202,572	1,119,109	1,357,661
	African American	271,057	358,865	405,771	529,534
	Hispanic	—	—	183,772	—*
	Asian or Pacific Islander	—	—	19,078	32,671
	Native American	—	—	14,570	19,590
Row B	African American/Anglo Arrest Ratio	1 to 3	1 to 3	1 to 3	1 to 2.56
Row C	Hispanic/Anglo Arrest ratio	—	—	1 to 6	—

Source: FBI, 1965: 115 for 1964; FBI, 1975: 192 for 1974; FBI, 1987: 183, 186 for 1986; FBI, 1993a: 236 for 1992.
* In 1964, 1974, and 1992 Anglo figures include data for Hispanics.

TABLE 3.7

Offenses for which Juveniles are Commonly Arrested, by Ethnic Group, 1986 and 1992

1992 Anglo		1992 African American		1986 Hispanic	
Offense	Number of Arrests	Offense	Number of Arrests	Offense	Number of Arrests
Larceny/Theft	291,308	Larceny/Theft	97,319	Larceny/Theft	35,908
All other (except traffic)	201,159	All other (except traffic)	84,229	All other (except traffic)	32,716
Runaways	114,214	Other Assaults	50,189	Burglary	16,704
vandalism	96,589	Disorderly Conduct	35,132	Drug Abuse	11,620
Burglary	92,044	Drug Abuse	34,404	Runaways	10,938
Other Assaults	89,603	Motor Vehicle Theft	29,467	Other Assaults	8,504
Liquor Laws	89,121	Burglary	27,229	Disorderly Conduct	8,473
Disorderly Conduct	72,902	Aggravated Assault	26,713	Vandalism	8,013
Curfew and Loitering	56,752	Runaways	25,199	Liquor Laws	7,212
Motor Vehicle Theft	44,148	Robbery	24,296	Motor Vehicle Theft	6,324

Source: FBI, 1987: 183, 186 for Hispanic data (which are for 1986); FBI, 1993a: 236 for Anglo and African American data (which are for 1992).

*In 1992, the FBI combined arrests of Hispanics with arrests of Anglos and reported them as "White Arrests."

1964–92. As you can see, the FBI has done a much better job of collecting arrest data for Anglos and African Americans than for other ethnic minorities. The figures in row A of table 3.6 indicate that most juveniles who are arrested are Anglo. In fact, as rows B and C show, approximately three Anglo youth are taken into police custody for every African American child arrested, and around six Anglos are collared for each one arrest involving an Hispanic child. Relatively small numbers of Asian, Pacific Islander, and Native American children are also arrested each year.

Table 3.7 looks at offenses for which Anglo, African American, and Hispanic children are arrested. On the left side of table 3.7, ten offenses are listed for which Anglo children are most often arrested. In the middle column of table 3.7, ten offenses are listed for which African American youth are most often arrested. The right side of table 3.7 enumerates offenses for which Hispanic children are usually arrested. Table 3.7 shows that larceny/theft and "all other offenses" are the most common charges filed against Anglo, African American, and Hispanic youth. In fact, larceny/theft and "all other offenses" account for over one-third of all juvenile arrests. Even beyond the top two categories, Anglo, African American, and Hispanic juveniles are arrested for roughly the same kinds of offenses, except that African Americans are more likely to be arrested for robbery. In 1992, 24,296 African American youngsters were taken into custody for robbery, compared to 15,267 Anglos arrested for robbery. In 1986, the most recent date for which these data are available, 3,626 Hispanic youth were arrested for robbery. Robbery is the only crime than nets more arrests of African American youth than Anglos. In sum, *UCR* data show that arrests of all types of American youth escalated rapidly in the 1960s and continue to rise.

Arrest data suggest that gender and ethnicity play significant roles in determining which children become official delinquents. Figure 3.3 summarizes factors that help to shape the character of official delinquency in the United States. Individual, community-level, and societal influences are represented by boxes on the left side of figure 3.3. Middle boxes represent the idea that police responses to youthful misbehavior are somewhat different depending upon the ethnicity and gender of offenders and upon police willingness and capacity to arrest.

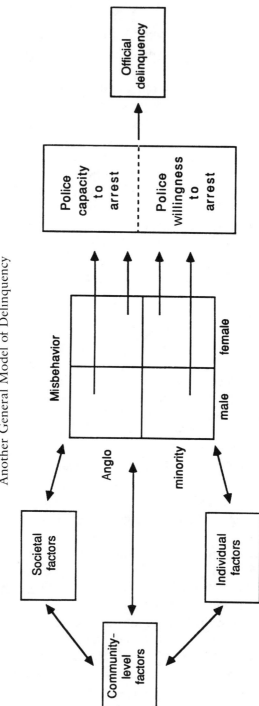

FIGURE 3.3
Another General Model of Delinquency

Police Disposition of Arrested Juveniles

UCR data can be used to determine how many children police organizations actually turn over to the courts. Table 3.8 displays information about what the police do with children who are taken into custody. Rows B and E of table 3.8 show that most children taken into custody are either handled within a police department and then released (30.1% in 1992) or are referred to a juvenile court (62.5% in 1992). Figures in row B also indicate that with each decade that has passed since 1964, police officers have handle proportionately fewer youth informally within their departments. Thus, today, local police process children more legalistically, by referring them either to juvenile court or to adult courts (see rows D and E). In the next section, we examine two survey strategies that are used by legal officials and social scientists to measure hidden delinquency.

VICTIMIZATION SURVEYS

On July 23, 1965, Executive Order 11236, issued by President Lyndon Johnson, created the Commission on Law Enforcement and the Administration of Justice (CLEAJ). This commission used hundreds of expert academic consultants, advisors, and a large full-time professional staff to examine many facets of crime and law enforcement in the United States. CLEAJ was especially interested in assessing the magnitude of crime hidden from the police. CLEAJ assumed the following:

> Although the police statistics indicate a lot of crime today, they do not begin to indicate the full amount. Crimes reported directly to prosecutors usually do not show up in the police statistics. Citizens often do not report crimes to the police. Some crimes reported to the police never get into the statistical system. (President's Commission on Law Enforcement and the Administration of Justice, 1967: 20)

In order to expose "the dark side of crime," CLEAJ hired the National Opinion Research Center (NORC) at the University of Chicago to survey a national sample of ten thousand households. A person from each household was asked whether or not s/he, or any other household member over twelve years of age, had been a victim of a Part I (except murder) crime during the past year. In

TABLE 3.8
Police Disposition of Juveniles Taken into Custody, 1964–1992

		1964	1974	1985	1992
Row A	Total Number	814,075	1,709,564	1,185,770	1,330,445
	% of total	100.1	100.0	100.0	100.0
Row B	Handled within department and released	388,898	759,137	364,487	399,856
		47.2%	44.4%	30.7%	30.01%
Row C	Referred to other police agency	21,618	40,788	13,736	14,323
		2.7%	2.4%	1.2%	1.1%
Row D	Referred to criminal or adult court	14,354	63,527	52,322	62,180
		1.8%	3.7%	4.4%	4.7%
Row E	Referred to juvenile court	381,337	803,330	732,531	831,696
		46.8%	47.0%	61.8%	62.5%
Row F	Referred to welfare agency	12,858	42,782	22,694	22,400
		1.6%	2.5%	1.9%	1.7%

Source: FBI, 1993a: 282 for 1992; FBI, 1985: 240 for 1985; FBI, 1975: 177 for 1974; FBI, 1964: 102 for 1964.

other words, victim surveys record *claims made* about victimization rather than actual behavior (Hagan, 1986: 38). Similar surveys were conducted in "high and medium crime rate" sections of Washington, D.C., Chicago, and Boston.

Findings from early victimization studies were shocking:

> [P]ersonal injury crime reported to NORC is almost twice the UCR rate and the amount of property crime more than twice as much as the UCR rate for individuals. Forcible rapes were more than three and one-half times the reported rate, burglaries three times, aggravated assaults and larcenies of $50 or over more than double, and robbery 50% greater than the reported rate (President's Commission on Law Enforcement and the Administration of Justice, 1967: 21).

CLEAJ suspected that "[E]ven these rates probably understate the actual amounts of crime" (CLEAJ, 1967: 21; see also Ennis, 1967).

Early victimization surveys did not ask respondents to estimate the age of perpetrators. Thus, it was impossible to infer the extent of delinquency from early studies. However, some researchers examined victimization claims for types of crime that are known to generate large numbers of juvenile arrests. For example, some surveys showed that larceny, the most common reason for arrests of young persons, was reported five times more frequently by alleged victims than police statistics would indicate. More recent victimization surveys ask reported victims for information about the "perceived age of offenders" (U.S. Department of Justice, Bureau of Justice Statistics, 1993a: 287, 289).

In 1973, the federal government took over responsibility for conducting victimization studies and titled the program "National Crime Surveys." Between 1973 and 1984, federal agencies surveyed about sixty thousand American households per year where a reported 136,000 occupants live. The sample of sixty thousand households was broken down into six independently selected subsamples of around ten thousand households and 22,000 occupants. Twice a year, each individual in each subsample was interviewed and was asked about the Part I criminal victimizations s/he had suffered in the preceeding six months and about characteristics of offenders. Data collected via victimization surveys were weighted and used to generate estimates of Part I crimes in the entire United States (McDermott and Hindelang, 1981: 8–9).

McDermott and Hindelang studied victim reports of offender characteristics and produced the following interesting findings:

- About one-third of the total number of reported victimizations for Part I crimes were attributable to juvenile offenders (defined as under 18) or to young adults (persons 19–20 years old).

- Most personal larcenies (pocket picking and purse snatching) are committed by juveniles or young adults.

- Juvenile involvement in robberies of persons is substantial. Youth, however, frequently do not complete crimes like robbery and personal larceny.

- Young persons rarely use guns when committing crimes.

- The vast majority of rapes are committed by adults. (1–3)

In 1985 and 1986, approximately forty-nine thousand households and about 101,000 occupants were surveyed each year looking for crime victims (U.S. Dept. of Justice, Bureau of Justice Statistics, 1986: 3; 1987: 3). The Bureau of Justice Statistics concluded that, in general, about one in three alleged victimizations are reported to the police. Approximately one-half of all alleged crimes of violence are reported, and around one-quarter of all alleged crimes of theft are known to the police (1–4). In 1990 and 1991, around forty-two thousand U.S. households were again surveyed, with approximately the same results (U.S. Dept. of Justice, 1992a, 1992b).

Of particular interest are data from the School Crime Supplement, conducted during 1989, which surveyed a nationally representative sample of students, between the ages of twelve and nineteen (U.S. Dept. of Justice, Bureau of Justice Statistics, 1993a). National estimates were derived from this survey. The estimates are virtually the same for females and males. The Bureau of Justice Statistics estimates that, in 1989, 9 percent of all U.S. students were victimized at school. Seven percent of the reported victimizations involved property crime, and 2 percent were violent (293). Six percent of the students surveyed avoided places at school out of fear. Twenty-two percent had feared being attacked at school. Around 15 percent feared attack going to and from school (295).

Only about 15 percent of the students reported the presence of gangs at school (294). Another recent national school study, the Youth Risk Behavior Survey, revealed that, in 1991, 41 percent of the males and 11 percent of the females, in the thirty days preceding their being asked, reported carrying a weapon. Twelve percent of the boys and 7 percent of the girls reported carrying handguns (319).

Victimization studies almost always find that juveniles are the most likely *victims* of alleged crimes of violence (like rape, robbery, and assault) and of crimes of theft. For example, from 1982 through 1984, youngsters between the ages of twelve and nineteen claimed to have experienced an average of 1.8 million violent crimes and 3.7 million crimes of theft annually (Whitaker, 1986: 1). In 1991, males between the ages of twelve and nineteen reported approximately one hundred violent victimizations, per thousand persons in their age group. Females reported approximately thirty-five violent victimizations for twelve to fifteen year olds, and sixty violent victimizations for sixteen to nineteen year olds, per thousand persons in their age group (U.S. Dept. of Justice, Bureau of Justice Statistics, 1993a: 264).

However, Chesney-Lind and Shelden report that "the extent of girls' victimization is much greater than many suppose, particularly when data on physical and sexual abuse are included" (24–27). They suggest that, by the age of sixteen, one-quarter of females in the United States have been sexually abused. By age eighteen, more than one-third of American females have experienced sexual abuse (26–27) A good amount of juvenile female victimization is masked by their dual status as runaways and prostitutes (34–42).

Weaknesses of Victimization Surveys

Victim surveys have three major weaknesses. First, victimization studies focus only on Part I offenses and, thus, exclude Part II and status offenses. Consequently, victim surveys provide information on only a narrow range of crimes. Second, there is no practical way to prove that thousands of respondents are willing and able to provide the information about crime that is requested by interviewers. For example, in all likelihood, and for a variety of reasons, many respondents to victim surveys choose not to tell the complete truth when they are asked by a stranger about sensitive, potentially traumatic personal experiences (Herrington, 1986: 7). Similarly, other respondents very likely do not remember, or did not accurately perceive, the details of their experiences with crime. Finally, there is no practical way to demonstrate that alleged victims of crimes can accurately estimate the age of violators. Thus, victimization data should be approached with caution.

CHILDREN'S SELF-REPORTS

Another way to study the "dark side of delinquency" involves surveying young persons and asking them whether or not they have committed crimes.[5] The best known self-report research was done by Short and Nye (1957: 326–31; 1958: 296–302). Short and Nye developed a questionnaire that included twenty-four questions about criminal or antisocial behavior. The twenty-four items were selected because Short and Nye believed that they would "(1) provide a range from trivial to serious crimes, (2) be committed by an appreciable segment of the population and (3) be admitted under favorable circumstances" (1957: 328). Short and Nye obtained responses to their questionnaire from three sources: (1) 2,350 public high school students in three connecting cities in the Pacific Northwest, (2) 596 public high school students who lived in a rural district, a rural-urban fringe district, or a suburban district in a midwestern state, and (3) 320 boys and girls who were incarcerated in Pacific Northwest juvenile institutions. The following procedures were used by Short and Nye in order to encourage complete, accurate responses to their questions: children were assured that "[Q]uestions asked were for research purposes only. Anonymity was emphasized and a sealed 'ballot box' was placed in each room so that each student could deposit his (or her) own questionnaire" (327).

Data were excluded for several types of children in the original Short and Nye sample. Eliminated from the study were (1) overconformers—children who responded "no" to three or more questions that Short and Nye believed involved juvenile misbehavior committed by all children, (2) children who admitted committing all twenty-four types of behavior on the questionnaire, each at

---

[5]Pioneering self-report studies were done by Robison in 1936; Porterfield in 1943; Murphy, Shirly, and Witmer in 1946; Schwartz in 1947; and Wallerstein and Wyle in 1947.

the highest rate of frequency, (3) children who failed to consistently complete "interlocking questions," and (4) extremely poor readers. For the reasons listed, above, Short and Nye eliminated 1 percent of the public school students from their study (including 4 percent of the girls) and 10 percent of the incarcerated children.

For final analysis, Short and Nye used answers to only the nine questions listed, below:

1. Driven a car without a driver's license or permit?
2. Taken little things (worth less than $2) that did not belong to you?
3. Bought or drank beer, wine or liquor? (Include drinking at home.)
4. Purposely damaged or destroyed public or private property that did not belong to you?
5. Skipped school without a legitimate excuse?
6. Had sex relations with a person of the opposite sex?
7. Defied your parents' authority (to their face)?
8. "Run away" from home?
9. Taken things of medium value (between $2 and $50)?

Fewer than 10 percent of the Pacific Northwest high school children admitted to running away and to taking things of medium value. Consequently, Short and Nye excluded questions 8 and 9, and they analyzed data about the remaining seven questions.

Short and Nye reported the following findings about "hidden delinquency:"

- According to reports from all three samples of children, delinquent behavior is extensive and covers a wide range of activities.
- Traffic offenses, truancy and alcohol use are most commonly reported by high school boys and girls.
- High school boys also admitted to frequent fighting, stealing, heterosexual activity and game infractions;
- Incarcerated delinquents admit to committing all seven offenses and far more frequently than high school students.

- There is considerable overlap, in terms of frequency of delinquency, between incarcerated and high school children.
- Boys report greater involvement than girls in most types of delinquency.
- Girls report high levels of running away, defying parental authority, and drinking alcohol.
- The highest and lowest status children (in terms of socioeconomic factors) admit greater involvement in delinquency than do other youth.
- Twenty-two percent of the incarcerated boys reported *less* delinquency than the most delinquent 10 percent of the high school boys. (1958: 297–302; 1957: 331).

Although somewhat dated in terms of drug use and sexual activity, findings from the Short and Nye study were widely acknowledged in the 1960s, and self-report research gained general acceptance as a valid way to measure delinquency.

Summarized below are findings from several more recent self-report studies of delinquency:

- Almost all persons surveyed claimed to have committed delinquent acts.
- Large numbers of male and female juveniles claim to have committed status offenses like truancy, drinking alcohol, driving without a license, defying parents, fornication, and running away.
- Almost as many girls as boys admit to acts of truancy, alcohol use, and running away.
- Far fewer girls than boys claimed to have engaged in sexual intercourse. Girls also claim consistently fewer total delinquencies than do boys.
- Large numbers of boys and girls claim to have committed property offenses like petty theft, shoplifting, destruction of property, and breaking and entering. Auto theft is less commonly admitted.
- In general, juveniles claim to have committed fewer crimes against persons than property and status offenses, although gang fighting and assault are commonly admitted.

- Children seldom claim to have committed armed robbery, strong arming, serious assault, or carrying a concealed weapon.

- Almost all high school students, girls and boys alike, claim that they use alcohol and cigarettes. Many children report experimentation with drugs like marijuana and cocaine, although little heroin use is admitted.

- As many as nine out of each ten acts of delinquency uncovered by self-report research are unrecorded by the police. (Empey, 1982: 105–11; Chesney-Lind and Shelden, 1992: 24–28)

Some researchers assert that minority children are more likely than Anglos to underreport criminal activity (Hindelang, Hirschi, and Weis, 1981). Other investigators find that there are few differences between the delinquency involvement of Anglo and minority children (Huizinga and Elliott, 1985).

Data from a national survey of more than three thousand high school seniors, conducted anually by researchers at the University of Michigan, suggests a high level of lawlessness in the twelve months prior to a recent survey. Twenty-three percent of the senior class of 1988 reported having gotten into trouble with the police. Almost 15 percent of the sample had damaged school property. Twenty-seven percent admitted breaking and entering. Thirty percent claimed to have shoplifted. Thirty-three percent stole items worth less than $50 (Bachman, Johnston, and O'Malley, 1989). Except for assault, the University of Michigan researchers believe that patterns of self-reported delinquency by teenagers have been relatively stable since 1975 (Osgood et al., 1989).

Between 1985 and 1987, Inciardi, Horowitz, and Pottieger conducted interviews with 611 serious delinquents in twenty Miami-Dade County, Florida, neighborhoods. One hundred of the children interviewed were females. Inciardi maintained field contact with fifty adolescent "key informants" in the area through 1991 (1993: vii, 172–73). They defined serious delinquents as children who committed, "during the twelve months prior to interview, at least 10 FBI "Index" offenses or 100 lesser profit-making crimes" (172). Their reports of delinquency are alarming. Reports of drug use among girls and boys were virtually the same, and reports of other acts of delinquency were surprisingly similar for boys and girls.

Over 95 percent of the children surveyed come from a lower- or working-class background (178). All children report "extensive histories of multiple drug use," beginning around age eight. They committed their first non-drug-related crimes at about eleven years of age. Eighty-nine percent of the girls had been prostitutes. Over 60% of the children had robbed. Ninety percent had been arrested.

In the twelve months before being interviewed, the 611 juveniles reported committing 429,136 crimes, averaging 702 violations per child (175). Almost 93 percent of the reported offenses involved petty acts, including drug-related offenses (60 percent of the total), prostitution or pimping (10 percent), shoplifting (12 percent) and stolen goods crimes (11 percent). However, 18,000 major felonies were admitted, an average of more than 29 per respondent, mostly burglaries and robberies (vii, 176). Almost 90 percent of the children reported carrying weapons most or all of the time (176).

Weaknesses of Self-Report Studies

Although findings from children's self-report studies are impressive, I recommend reading them with cautious skepticism. Five problems with self-report studies are particularly serious. First, questions asked of children in self-report questionnaires only approximate the far more specific crime categories that are used in recording arrests. Second, self-report researchers often use overlapping but somewhat distinctive lists of questions, making it difficult to interpret data from a broad range of studies. Third, it is hard to prove that children are willing and able to accurately provide researchers with potentially incriminating information about themselves (Hindelang, Hirschi, and Weis, 1981). Fourth, self-report studies usually involve small, highly select samples of children who, in all likelihood, are not comparable to the general juvenile population in the United States. Finally, most self-report studies are done on a one-time basis, limiting their use for continuous comparison with police data.

SUMMARY

Police statistics, victim surveys, and children's self-reports all indicate that delinquency is widespread in the United States. When its magnitude is combined with high rates of dependency and neglect,

American delinquency takes on the dimensions of a major societal problem. But police statistics, victimization surveys, and children's self-reports must be viewed with caution. Each method of measuring delinquency has weaknesses. Each method is limited and, therefore, yields less than ideal data.

Police statistics show that, as the U.S. juvenile population grew, and as the number of American police employees grew, arrests of juveniles rose. Patterns of police arrest are partly determined by gender, ethnicity, and social class standing of potential offenders. Patterns of juvenile arrest are also partly determined by police willingness and capacity.

Victim surveys suggest that some types of delinquency are far more frequently committed than police statistics would indicate. In general, victim surveys indicate that about three times more crime occurs than police statistics measure: there are twice as many crimes of violence and four times as many crimes of theft. Children, especially girls, and young adults report being the victims of Part I offenses more frequently than any other segment of the American population.

Self-report surveys show that most American children claim to have committed crimes and status offenses. In fact, self-report surveys imply that some unincarcerated hidden delinquents commit more crimes than do some incarcerated delinquents. Self-report surveys uncover around nine times more delinquency than arrest statistics measure. In the next three chapters we look at explanations of why delinquency emerges and persists.

PART 3

Explaining Delinquency

CHAPTER 4

Clinical and Observational Ideas about American Delinquency

CLINICAL IDEAS

Clinicians often work closely for long periods with problem children and, thus, gain a depth of information about the nature of delinquency that is seldom rivaled by researchers using other means. There are, however, several weaknesses of clinical methods. First, long-term contact with, and in-depth information about, problem children means that therapists can take on a "rooting" interest in delinquents that might reduce or eliminate their objectivity, diminishing the likelihood of obtaining valid and reliable findings. Second, clinicians work with select samples of problem children who are not necessarily representative of broader populations of juvenile delinquents. Affluent children, or children who get caught, fall into the sample of a research clinician. There is little evidence that affluent children and youth who get caught are typical of all juvenile delinquents, especially those who avoid detection and punishment. Finally, clinical researchers use concepts that have, so far, defied accurate measurement. Terms like *moral insanity, intelligence, neurosis, psychosis* and *family conflict* are provocative but difficult to define precisely enough so that other social scientists can duplicate clinical research. Thus, clinical research usually cannot pass the rigorous tests of acceptable science. This does not mean, however, that clinical ideas are useless. The first measures of good social science theory involve whether or not it produces interesting ideas and whether or not those ideas prompt other social scientists to develop even better theory (Popper, 1962: 215–50). Clinical ideas provide a rich source of information for delinquency theorists and, thus, should be considered good, if somewhat imprecise, theory.

In 1876, an Italian psychiatrist named Cesare Lombroso identified a criminal personality type that he thought was caused by a genetic throwback to more savage and primitive humans (Lombroso, 1911). In 1885, the English psychiatrist D. H. Tuke observed moral insanity in many of his patients. Tuke believed that moral insanity was caused by a weakening of some parts of the brain, resulting in paralyzed will and excessive emotionality (Malmquist, 1978: 568).

In 1909, William Healy, an American psychiatrist, published findings from a study of approximately one thousand delinquent youth who were, in most cases, repeat offenders (Healy, 1915). Healy reported several common physical, psychological, and social conditions among his delinquent subjects. Healy characterized delinquents as possessing the following qualities: displaying mental abnormalities and peculiarities, being exposed to defective home conditions (including parental alcoholism), being riddled by mental conflict, experiencing improper sex, developing bad habits, using stimulants or narcotics, failing educationally, and having negative experiences while under legal supervision (91–92).

H. H. Goddard published findings from his study of intelligence and delinquency at the New Jersey Training School for the Feebleminded. Goddard's tests indicated that all inmates had mental ages of thirteen or below, while normal people tested at ages of 16 or above (1921: 168–76). In other work, Goddard concluded that around 70 percent of all inmates are feebleminded (1914: 569).

Sigmund Freud (1856–1939) has been another influential figure in this field. While Freud wrote little about delinquency, he suggested that in each person lay the potential for law violation. Freud believed that many criminal law breakers were mentally tortured and unable to cope with the stresses of life, a condition he called "psychosis" (McCord and McCord, 1956: 9). Freud's greatest influence on the study of delinquency, however, comes from his analysis of neurosis. Freud observed that neurotics cope with stresses by committing prohibited acts, usually without getting caught or punished. Occasional stealing, fistfighting, or mooning motorists, for example, are ways that neurotic children let off steam. If undetected and kept within limits, neurotic behavior provokes little reaction from others (Hall, 1954). If a police officer, or some other control agent, finds neurotic behavior actionable, then it can become official delinquency.

Freud believed that personality develops in childhood and that each normal person passes through stages of psychosexual development (e.g., oral, anal and phallic stages). Personalities develop into three interrelated structures, id (instincts), ego (the self), and superego (the conscience). However, if basic needs are not met as children evolve psychosexually, normal personality development is impeded, and juvenile delinquency, in the form of neurosis or psychosis, can result.

August Aichhorn developed Freud's ideas to a point where they could be used by legal officials. In the early 1900s, Aichhorn operated residential facilities in Austria for orphans and maladjusted boys. Aichhorn found two types of dissocial boys in his institutions. Most common was a type of boy whose behavioral problems appeared to result from a neurotic condition. Aichhorn prescribed strict treatment for neurotic boys, because he believed that neurotic children had been overindulged earlier in life. The second type, called "psychopathic," was less common but far more disturbed. Strict treatment did not seem to work with this child. In fact, harsh treatment increased the rate and intensity of unwanted behavior. Psychopathic boys had experienced long-term, painful conflicts with their parents and had watched numerous fights between their parents. Seriously disturbed boys had been severely beaten on a regular basis. Each child hated one or more parent. None of the seriously disturbed boys had received love and support from his family. These children were aggressive, highly destructive, and violent towards weaker persons. Aichhorn found weak ego and superego development in psychopathic boys, and, in many cases, their behavior bordered on sadomasochism (Friedlander, 1947: 240–43). Aichhorn suggested gentle, nonpunitive treatment for psychopathic boys, so that they could have opportunities to learn social prescriptions and so that healthy ego and superego development could occur.

In 1925, Healy and Bronner reported findings based upon clinical records kept from 1917 to 1922 at the Judge Baker Foundation in Boston. Healy and Bronner examined after-careers of delinquents who were treated at the clinic, and they compared delinquents with nondelinquent children. Healy and Bronner reported that heredity was not a major factor in identifying delinquent children. They characterized delinquents as riddled by mental conflicts and as possessing backgrounds full of emotional problems (Bennett, 1960: 12). Healy and Bronner reported that parental conflict and poor family relationships are critical elements in producing delinquency (Friedlander, 1947: 99).

Reviewing two hundred cases of delinquency in England, Cyril Burt argued that home life was a prime factor in shaping delinquency. Burt observed that 19 percent of the delinquent children he studied lived in poverty-stricken homes, while only 8 percent of London's population was considered poor (Burt, 1929). Burt reported that emotional and moral climate was more important than intellectual, material, or physical factors. Burt believed that several factors combined to produce delinquency and that causes could vary from case-to-case. Social conditions alone rarely led to delinquency. In most cases, it was only when social forces combined with a hereditary weakness involving intelligence or temper that delinquency occurred. Burt concluded that one-half of the boys in his study were suffering from "a profound and widespread instability of the emotions" (507). Burt, however, also reported that "more than 60 special factors emerge as characteristic of, or as predominating in, the group of juvenile offenders . . . [W]e still find that as many as a dozen different factors may be operative in each case" (1935: 161). Recently, some of Cyril Burt's research on social class and ability was found to be fraudulent. Thus, his work should be considered with caution, since it is difficult to determine which research he conducted properly and which research he faked.

By the 1930s, clinicians had linked five major factors to delinquency:

- The Heredity Factor—includes size and physical constitution, intelligence, and inherited behavior patterns.
- The Organic Factor—glandular imbalance, nutrition, and illness are key elements.
- The Family Factor—parental attitudes and feelings about a child's birth, affection between spouses, affection between parent and child, broken homes, sibling rivalry, ideals and standards of the home, parental discipline, and the importance of the mother in the home are important.
- Cultural and Social Factors—include attitudes, economic status, social controls, intelligence level of the home, and companionship groups.

- The Needs Factor—emphasizes fundamental desires like the need for affection, the need for sexual response, and the need to achieve.

In the 1950s, clinicians developed detailed typologies of juvenile delinquents. For example, Bennett identified the following nine distinct types of delinquent children:

1. dull or handicapped delinquents
2. delinquents who are normal
3. otherwise normal delinquents who succumb to the problems of puberty
4. delinquents from vicious homes
5. delinquents with organic problems
6. deprived delinquents
7. neurotic delinquents
8. psychopathic delinquents
9. psychotic delinquents (1960: 17–30)

In the late 1950s, psychologist Marguerite Warren developed a system of classification, Interpersonal Maturity Levels (I-Levels) Theory, that is important because it has become a major tool used by corrections workers to classify delinquents for housing assignments and treatment strategies (Warren, 1969: 47–59 and 1976). I-Levels Theory argues that normal humans pass through seven developmental stages but that delinquents rarely progress beyond stages two to four. Children fixated at maturity level two are called "asocial passive" or "asocial aggressive." Children at maturity level three are labeled "conformist immature," "conformist cultural," or "counteractive." Children stuck at maturity level four are called "neurotic anxious," "neurotic acting out," "situational emotional reactors," or "cultural identifiers." Since one delinquent child may display a level of maturity different from that of another it is assumed that they will not respond to the same types of correctional interventions. Thus, legal systems employing I-Levels Theory group delinquent youth according to their developmental level.

In 1961, psychoanalyst R. D. Laing observed that children depend upon others who are close to them for information about self-worth, honesty, and attractiveness. Such information from close others is used by children to validate their own self-feelings and observations. If the information a child gets from close others is positive and supportive, then a stable personality develops. If a child is abused and fed negative messages, then neurosis, maladjustment, and delinquency are likely results (Laing, 1961). Laing believed that, if a child is brutalized and is subjected to trauma at the hands of family members, if messages from family are negative, cruel, and vicious, then a child can be driven insane. A painful conflict is created for children who are mentally tortured by abusive parents (or other close family members). While children need their families in order to survive, mental anguish produced by experiences with one's family may produce insanity. Laing suggested that many families that appear normal to strangers possess the potential to produce neurosis and psychosis in children.

In the 1960s, the psychiatrist William Glasser reported on his observations of incarcerated delinquent girls fourteen to twenty-one years old whose offenses ranged from incorrigibility and other neurotic conditions to first-degree murder (Glasser, 1965). Glasser had been trained by his psychiatric mentors to assume that delinquent girls were suffering from undeveloped superegos and that they lacked healthy egos. Glasser's observations, however, did not uphold these assumptions. Glasser discovered that all delinquent girls he encountered knew right from wrong and had developed some capacity to control their behavior. Glasser learned that, early in life, each delinquent girl experienced intense pressure and trauma. As a result each girl had decided to go insane by committing serious delinquent acts. The decision to go insane was accompanied by disinvolvement from normal social life. Glasser found that the delinquent girls he counseled had been denied love and support as children. Glasser prescribed a therapy that stressed providing love and acceptance for each girl, but that nevertheless enforced institutional rules, and emphasized morality. Glasser believed that delinquent girls could be reinvolved with social groups and could be taught to use acceptable means for solving problems. Glasser suggests that any child, under enough pressure, and influenced by the right set of circumstances, might go crazy and commit a delinquent act. Glasser implies that delinquency might not be solely the domain of dull, neurotic, or psychotic youth, that serious

FIGURE 4.1
Clinical Model of Delinquency

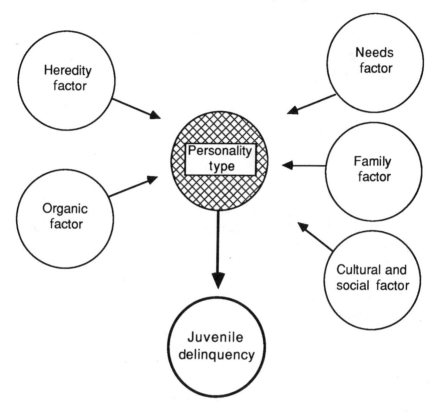

misbehavior is an alternative chosen by children who are pushed against a wall and cannot find another way out.

Figure 4.1 presents in diagrammatic form a composite clinical model of juvenile delinquency. Clinicians almost always assume that a special personality type is involved in delinquency. Factors on the left side of figure 4.1 represent the early clinical focus on biological causes of childhood misbehavior. More recently, clinicians have focused on factors like those listed on the right side of figure 4.1, namely, personal needs, family influences, cultural and social factors. Thus, current clinical ideas about delinquency encompass biological, psychological, and sociological aspects of children's lives.

OBSERVATIONAL IDEAS

The methods of observational research come from cultural anthropology. Properly conducted observational (or field) studies do not use a single method to collect a single kind of information (Zelditch, 1970). Instead, observational or field studies integrate three kinds of methods. First, a log of chronologically ordered incidents and histories is kept. Logs include information gathered first hand by a researcher functioning as an observer of, and possibly as a participant in, some of the activities of the persons who are studied. Second, observational researchers use information provided by informants who are members of the social aggregates under study. Through informants, observational researchers learn about the distribution and frequency of important incidents and about other important characteristics of human aggregates under study. Third, well-trained field researchers use records kept by groups and organizations in order to learn things about human behavior that can neither be personally observed nor reported by an informant. Observational methods allow investigators to discover subtle patterns in human behavior. Furthermore, observational methods allow researchers to view American juvenile delinquency from several points, adding much to what is known about the character of children's problems.

There are also three risks observational researchers run, and each can invalidate findings. First, a participant observer can become so involved in, and familiar with, a group and its environment that s/he loses the ability to remain objective in deciding which data to collect and record. Second, informants do not always have the information requested of them. Yet, for fear of losing credibility or attention, an informant might fabricate information and supply it to an unaware researcher. Other potential informants will possess needed information but are either unable or unwilling to share it with investigators. Third, because of the unique problems posed by gaining access to, and the acceptance of, groups in the field, observational studies run the risk of reporting findings that might not be characteristic of similar groups that were not studied. Thus, observational research, like clinical studies, cannot by itself tell all about juvenile delinquency. Yet, field investigators commit far more time and attention to the study of delinquency than do most other types of researchers. Consequently, observational data add much to our overall understanding of the nature of children's problems.

GANGS AND DELINQUENCY

Observational researchers were among the first to point out a strong connection between gang membership and delinquency. In *The Gangs of New York* (1927), Asbury describes gangs that operated in New York City in the early 1900s. Asbury observed that a few large gangs dominated New York City and that some numbered thousands of members. Each gang was headed by a captain to whom members pledged undying loyalty. Asbury reports that, by the 1920s, large gangs were replaced by numerous smaller gangs. Loyalty among members in smaller gangs was less intense, but the potential for crime and delinquency remained high. Asbury noted that crime and delinquency were on the rise in New York and pointed to the small gang as a social group in which wholesale misbehavior occurs. According to Asbury, "in the main the gangster was a stupid roughneck born in filth and squalor and reared amid vice and corruption," although he admitted that some gangsters "came from good families and were intelligent, as well as crafty" (xviii).

In the 1920s, Frederick Thrasher studied 1,313 gangs in Chicago. The gang members he observed were predominantly male, and ranged from twelve to twenty-six years of age. Thrasher used diverse sources of information including interviews, writings of gang members, reports from informants, newspaper accounts, organizational records, and research done by others. Results of his study, published in book form as *The Gang* (1927), did much to solidify the link between gang membership and delinquency. Thrasher observed that delinquency was widespread in Chicago and threatened to expand farther as urban problems intensified. Thrasher concluded that delinquency was primarily caused by peer groups and neighborhood influences. In Chicago's slums, which Thrasher typified as a series of disorganized neighborhoods located in the center of the city and bordered by railroad tracks, canals, and industrial areas, delinquency was commonplace. Slums gave children large uncontrolled areas to play in.

In slums, inadequate family life, poverty, deteriorating neighborhoods, and ineffective religious, educational, and recreational organizations are the norm. In contrast, Thrasher observed that the more affluent Chicago neighborhoods were populated by families willing, and able, to control their children. He contended that affluent neighborhoods possess attractive and effective religious, educational, and recreational organizations. Similarly, affluent neighborhoods do not suffer from physical deterioration.

Thrasher argued that children in disorganized neighborhoods have an unusually large amount of free, unsupervised time on their hands. Thrasher noted that many slum children have families whose adult members are either unable or unwilling to provide supervision and control. Without family control and supervision, slum children will form play groups as a way to acquire social acceptance and support. Play groups develop leaders and stake out turf; opportunities for fighting abound. Comradeship develops as slum boys fight off rival groups. Slum children steal, wander, and engage in acts of bravado. Over time, play groups evolve into clubs, with a name and an athletic focus. Clubs evolve into gangs.

Thrasher reported that misbehavior occurs in play groups, clubs, and gangs but that delinquency is most common in clubs and gangs. Play groups, clubs, and gangs, offer children more exciting and adventurous activities than do parents, schools, churches, and recreational organizations. Slum children, without parents to dictate otherwise, follow the gang along an ever-deepening path of prohibited, but thrilling and satisfying, social activities. Slum children are seduced by the comfort of gang tradition. Gradually, the gang becomes a dominant primary group. Poor children spend less and less time with parents, in school, or at church. Slum children begin to see police officers, teachers, and other legal agents as the enemy.

Clifford Shaw is another major figure in the observational study of American juvenile delinquency. In the 1920s, Shaw was employed by the University of Chicago. Shaw also worked for the Chicago Juvenile Court and for a residential settlement house in a Polish immigrant colony called "back of the yards." Back of the yards was "one of the grimiest, most congested slums of the city . . . there are a number of gangs . . . [S]ome indulge in gambling, moonshine, and sex irregularities as well as in athletics" (Thrasher, 1927: 18). Shaw, with various colleagues, wrote a series of books reporting his observations of problem children in Chicago's slums.

Shaw's first book, *Delinquency Areas* (1929), reported on an eight-year geographic study of truants, juvenile delinquents, and adult criminal offenders. Eight separate series of offenders, totalling sixty thousand subjects, were studied. Shaw's sample included juvenile offenders brought before Cook County Juvenile Court, delinquent boys processed by probation officers, male felons brought before the Boy's Court of Chicago, adult offenders held in the Cook County Jail, and three thousand girls brought before the Cook County Juvenile Court. Shaw, using the home addresses of offenders, plotted the location of their homes on city maps. Using these data, Shaw calculated "rates of offenders" for Chicago neighborhoods.

Six of Shaw's observations are particularly important. First, delinquency and truancy rates varied sharply from neighborhood to neighborhood. In some areas of Chicago, delinquency rates were quite high, while elsewhere delinquency and truancy rates were comparatively low. Second, delinquency rates were highest in the inner city, and they dropped consistently in outer zones. Third, where adult crime rates were high, delinquency and truancy rates were also high. Fourth, delinquency rates were highest in physically deteriorated neighborhoods where migrants live. Fifth, some Chicago neighborhoods had high rates of delinquency for thirty consecutive years. Finally, Shaw observed that the highest concentrations of repeat adult offenders lived in the center of the city, where delinquency rates were also highest (198–204).

Clifford Shaw wrote *The Jack-Roller* (1930), a book about a delinquent boy whom he met back of the yards. The boy, Stanley, was a jack roller—a boy who assaulted homosexual men and stole their money. Stanley had been arrested twenty-six times by the age of ten, thirty-eight times by seventeen, for running away, begging, truancy, bad sex habits, shoplifting, parole violation, vagrancy, and jack rolling (Snodgrass, 1982).

In time, however, Stanley became a law abider. Stanley was twelve when Shaw met him and intervened with the juvenile court. Stanley wrote a detailed account of his life, which Shaw acquired and used as data. Shaw also gathered information about Stanley from commitment, incarceration, employment, and school records.

Shaw identified several features of Stanley's life that contributed to his delinquency. First, Stanley lived in a neighborhood where most of his playmates, and the adult males with whom he had contact, engaged in constant criminal law violation. Second, Stanley had a poor relationship with his stepmother; this impelled him to run away in order to resist her authority. Shaw found evidence that Stanley's stepmother encouraged some delinquent acts. Finally, Shaw observed that Stanley's personality had developed in ways that allowed him to feel excessive self-pity and a sense of fatalism and to place blame elsewhere for his problems. Stanley felt persecuted, was suspicious, and resisted the control of others.

The Jack-Roller says much about how to identify delinquents. The most likely candidate is a boy who lives in a high-delinquency zone, whose home life is troubled, who has friends with similar problems, and whose problems extend into school. However, Shaw also notes that around 85 percent of the boys who live in slum neighborhoods were never arrested.

In sum, observational researchers emphasize the links among urbanization, poverty, disorganized neighborhoods, family breakdown, gang influences, and juvenile delinquency. Figure 4.2 presents in diagrammatic form an observational model of delinquency. Circles at the top of figure 4.2 represent the assertion that urbanization and poverty create deteriorated neighborhoods and open turf, which, in turn, contribute to family breakdown. Circles at the bottom of figure 4.2 represent the argument that, once slum families are no longer able to control children, they join play groups, clubs, and gangs, where they acquire delinquency-prone personalities and where they are provided with opportunities to commit delinquent acts.

SUMMARY

Both clinical and observational models of juvenile delinquency stress the importance of personality. But observational researchers assert that sociological factors like urbanization, poverty, neighborhood, family breakdown, play groups, clubs, and gangs are important, developing delinquent personalities in children that are prone to delinquency. On the other hand, clinicians believe that delinquent personalities develop as a result of hereditary, organic, needs-related, family, cultural, and social factors.

FIGURE 4.2
Observational Model of Delinquency

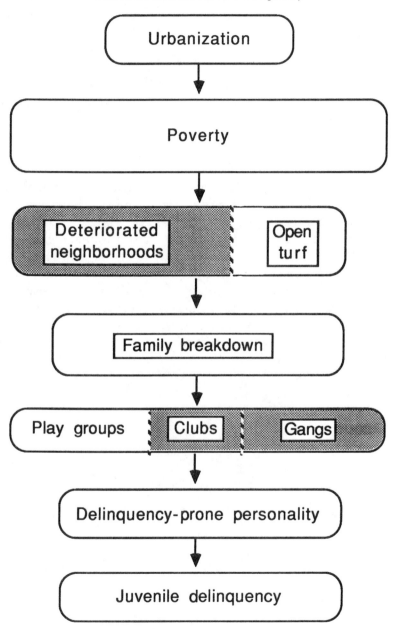

It is important to note the social class bias of clinical and observational ideas about delinquency. For the most part, clinicians and observational researchers view delinquency as a lower-class phenomenon. As we will see later, some conflict theorists argue that the lower-class bias found in delinquency theory is encouraged and perpetuated by members of more advantaged classes, through media-based ideology building processes, and through a narrowly focused, punitive criminal legal system, in order to divert public and legal attention away from their own, highly serious and much more costly, criminal activities.

We should also note the obvious gender bias of clinical and observational ideas about delinquency. For the most part, clinicians and observational researchers have acted as if female delinquents do not exist, thus leaving a large information void, and perpetuating the stereotype of females as nondelinquents. It is possible that the gender bias in clinical and observational ideas about delinquency is at least in part a derivative of biased police handling of problem children. For example, in 1940, police in the United States reported arresting fifteen boys for every one girl taken into custody, even though the ratio of juvenile males in the U.S. population to females was almost one to one. It is also possible that the gender bias in clinical and observational ideas about delinquency is at least in part due to sexism in the social science community.

CHAPTER 5

Micro Delinquency Theories

INTRODUCTION

This chapter examines a large body of micro delinquency theory.[1] While these theories explain the emergence and persistence of crime and deviance in general, our main concern here is their application to juvenile delinquency. Some micro delinquency theories date back to earlier civilizations, while others are relatively new. All of the ideas in this chapter, however, are still in vogue. Micro delinquency theorists usually address themselves to two basic questions: What causes delinquency? And what kinds of children are most likely to become delinquent? Micro delinquency theories are similar only in the basic assumption that crime and delinquency are caused by factors connected to (or existing near) individual violators. We will examine six types of micro delinquency theory: demonism, free will, physical type, modern positivism, behaviorism, and labeling.

DEMONISM

Demonism is the oldest explanation for human misbehavior. Popular belief in demons, devils, and their work can be found in all early civilizations, and it remains common today. Throughout history, most persons have been taught that two worlds exist: a physi-

---

[1] I am using the concept 'theory' loosely here. Theory, to the well-educated social scientist of today, means "abstract statements that are considered part of scientific knowledge in either the set-of-laws, the axiomatic, or the causal process forms" (Reynolds, 1971: 11; see also Blalock, 1969). Unfortunately, delinquency theories are hardly ever put forth in set-of-laws, axiomatic, or causal process forms, and for this reason many social scientists believe that delinquency theory should not be considered scientific. (See Meier, 1985, for a more complete discussion of this subject.) Instead, delinquency theories should be considered "conceptual perspectives," that is, *sets of ideas or concepts* about what causes delinquency and who delinquent children are.

95

cal and empirical world, where humans are born, live, and die after a short while, and a metaphysical world of gods, angels, spirits, devils, and demons, who have mystical powers and who are not bound by physical constraints.

For thousands of years, representatives of churches and governments have blamed social problems, including juvenile and adult lawlessness, on the work of "bad" gods, spirits, and demons. Citizens and church members learn that persons who are caught violating church or governmental law are controlled or "possessed" by a devil or evil spirit. Possessed persons are believed to be dangerous and thus are treated harshly.

Demonistic ideas about the nature of lawlessness have been, throughout recorded history, adopted by large governments, and they were used to rationalize the violent, vengeful early treatment of criminals. We see blatant legal demonism in England where, for example, as late as the 1800s, a criminal suspect was accused in the courts of violating the law *and* of "being prompted and instigated by the devil and not having the fear of God before his eyes." Similarly, in the United States, in 1862, state-level supreme court justices concluded that "to know the right and still the wrong pursue proceeds from a perverse will brought about by the seductions of the evil one" (Sutherland and Cressey, 1974: 48). Even today demonistic ideas about the causes of adult and juvenile lawlessness are held in high regard by many people.

In theory, demonism asserts that any child who violates church or government law is acting under the control and guidance of negative spiritual influences. Thus, from its perspective lawless children of all types and social classes could be treated harshly, in order to drive out an evil spirit or demon. More importantly, demonism once provided a rationale through which many poor, undefended early African, English, and later American children were culturally transformed into agents of devils. Problem children were deemed by legal and moral authority as undesirable in God's eyes and, therefore, suitable for abuse, jailing, and labor exploitation.

It was once thought that belief in demonism was growing so unpopular in American society that its connection to law violation should hardly be mentioned in academic circles (see, e.g., Barnes and Teeters, 1959: 120). But the ongoing renaissance of religious conservatism suggests otherwise. Demonism is a powerful and ancient perspective. Demonism is carried forward today as an important part of conservative religious philosophy.

FREE WILL

As early as the thirteenth century, the writings of St. Thomas Aquinas express the notion of free will (Vold and Bernard, 1979: 19–34) This doctrine emphasizes that humans are relatively free to do as they wish And that, because individuals choose what course of action they will pursue, it is imperative that church, government and family clearly distinguish good from evil. In order to encourage preferred behavior, it is necessary for church, government, and family to educate the young (and old) about the dangers of evil and about the advantages of being good. It is essential for church, government, and family to create a system of enforcement that reminds violators of their duty to the general good (Barnes and Teeters, 1959: 120–21).

As free will ideas began to merge with western political and religious philosophies, two basic types of law violators were visualized. Some law breakers were selfish and did not care about others in society; others were deranged, sick or possibly too stupid to comprehend the law. In the 1760s, free will ideas were reflected in the writings of the classical school and began to influence legal reform in Italy, France, and many other countries (see Beccaria, 1767; Maestro, 1942). Classical theorists argued that law violation is not caused by devils, demons, or spirits. Rather, humans calculate a crime by weighing pleasures derived from a criminal act against any anticipated pain or losses. If pleasure outweighs pain and loss, then crime occurs.

Reformers applied classical ideas to legislative activity and court operation in many western societies and asserted that punishment would work as a preventive and rehabilitative force only if violators knew in advance what criminal penalties could be anticipated. Strict interpretation meant that law makers should attach to each crime a prescribed punishment to be meted out to all violators regardless of social class, gender, or condition. As reform met reality, however, judges were given considerable discretion to adjust criminal punishments to the needs of the state.

As the classical school's influence spread throughout the western world, killing law violators grew less fashionable. Instead, free will advocates encouraged the use of convict labor, and the building of prisons where criminal law violators could be incarcerated on a long-term basis as a form of punishment and rehabilitation. Classical theorists believed that crimes yielding only "small pleasures" might carry a one-year jail sentence, while "high pleasure" crimes could warrant 15-year-to-life prison sentences. Repeat offenders could be given ever more harsh prison sentences. Thus, free will ideas prompted government leaders to authorize the building of vast systems of jails and prisons where, today, large numbers of adult and juvenile offenders are incarcerated.

The classical school portrays misbehaving children as selfish or unschooled. Families are expected to use harsh physical punishment on erring children as a means of discipline and instruction. Free will thinking was once used by church and legal officials to justify serving up unwanted children for institutional correction. Schools were seen as places where lessons in conformity and obedience could be taught. Regimentation and punishment-based instruction were viewed as necessary in order to keep children in line. Free will ideas are, thus, different from demonism. Rather than working under the influences of evil demons and spirits, classical theorists teach that law-violating children behave as they do because rewards and pleasures gained outweigh costs or anticipated pain.

PHYSICAL TYPE THEORIES

Throughout most of recorded history, criminals were thought to be physically different from normal law-abiding persons. By the 1870s, physical difference ideas evolved into the "positive school" of criminology (see Lombroso, 1876 [1st ed.], 1896–97 [5th ed]). Nineteenth-century positivists proposed the following ideas about crime:

1. Criminals differ from law-abiding persons in physical terms. Criminals can be recognized at birth as a separate type. Criminal types result either from an atavism, that is, falling backward genetically, or from physical degeneration resulting from an illness like epilepsy.

2. Persons possessing more than five unusual physical features (called "stigmata" or "anomalies"), such as, for example, highly developed frontal sinuses, retreating forehead, thick skull bones, large ears, greater pigmentation of the skin, or tufted and crispy hair, are certain criminals.

3. Persons with three to five stigmata may be criminals.

4. Fewer than three unusual physical features signals minimal criminal influence.

5. Concentrations of unusual physical features do not cause crime. Stigmata, however, do show which individuals have *personalities* that make them likely to engage in crime.

6. Unless given considerable supervision and support, persons with criminal personalities will be unable to keep from committing crimes. (Sutherland and Cressey, 1974: 52–53)

In 1876, most positivists believed that nearly all criminals were born criminals and could, therefore, be identified through their distinct physical traits. By 1911, Cesare Lombroso, the most famous legal positivist, conceded that, at most, born criminals accounted for approximately 40 percent of the law-violating population. In fact, Lombroso acknowledged five basic types of criminals: born criminals, criminaloids, insane criminals, criminals by passion, and occasional criminals.

Born criminals are persons who possess more than five physical anomalies. Due to genetic deterioration, or severe illness, born criminals are not able to keep from committing crimes. *Criminaloids,* like born criminals, suffer from atavisms and epilepsy, but criminaloids possess relatively fewer unusual physical features, are more lascivious, and are more prone to alcoholism. Criminaloid women are highly suggestable. Criminaloids are different in degree from born criminals. *Insane criminals* are almost always born criminals or epileptic and suffer from melancholia. Insane criminals are impulsive, obscene, and tend toward cruelty. *Criminals by passion,* except for possessing a tendency toward epilepsy, lack the unusual physical features of born criminals and, in this sense, form "a species apart." Criminals by passion have harmonious body lines and their souls are beautiful. Criminals by passion are nervous and emotionally sensitive and usually commit crimes out of love or political idealism fused with sudden passion. Passionate criminals tend toward excess, impulsiveness, and amnesia. *Occasional criminals* are sometimes called "pseudo-criminals," because they show no symptoms of atavism or epilepsy, yet they commit crimes (Lombroso, 1911).

Positivism thus offers different ideas about crime and delinquency. Early positivists emphasized genetic and biological causes of misbehavior and later pointed to "personality" as an intervening factor. Early positivism was popular in the United States. In recent years, new positivistic theories of delinquency have appeared. In the next section, important types of modern positivism are examined.

MODERN POSITIVISM

In 1913, Charles Goring, a famous English scientist published the results of his research on the connection between physical type and crime. Goring concluded that no evidence could be found to support the existence of a distinct criminal physical type. Goring's finding set positivism back for awhile. But physical type theories had grown popular in the United States.

Earnest Hooton, an American anthropologist gave positivism new life when in 1939 he published results from a study of almost fourteen thousand male prisoners in ten states and from a study of more than three thousand presumed noncriminals. Using measures of 107 physical features, Hooton asserted that his data showed criminal behavior was due almost totally to physical and racial factors. In fact, Hooton prescribed that criminals and other low-grade humans not be allowed to have children.

Ten years later, in 1949, William Sheldon, an American psychologist published results from his case studies of two hundred delinquent boys in Boston, indicating that delinquent boys have *mesomorphic* body types. That is, delinquents are either lean, hard, and rectangular, or heavy, with large wrists and hands, a heavy chest, and big muscles and bones. Mesomorphic delinquents were characterized by Sheldon as active and dynamic, assertive and aggressive. In contrast, Sheldon reported that presumably nondelinquent college students are *ectomorphs*. Ectomorphs have lean, fragile and delicate bodies, as well as introverted temperments.

Other positivists have developed ideas about the effects of chro-.

mosome abnormalities, limbic and endocrine disorders, chemical imbalances, and disabilities on delinquency. To date, little research has been done on these subjects, and there are serious questions about the propriety of methods used in early studies. Consequently, we should remember that the ideas presented in the next section are speculative, and the research supporting them, at least in some cases, is highly suspect.

Chromosome Abnormalities

Chromosomes are cell parts that house genes. Chromosomes are responsible for shaping inherited characteristics. In 1956, through use of new medical technologies, it was learned that most humans have forty-six (twenty-three pairs) chromosomes. Researchers proved that females carry two X sex chromosomes (XX) and that males carry XY, XXY, or XYY sex chromosomes. A few positivists theorized that abnormal males, especially those who carry XYY sex chromosome configurations, might be super males who are prone to aggression and violence and, therefore, are more likely to engage in criminal behavior. Prison inmate populations were studied with the super male possibility in mind. In some cases significant connections were found between XYY sex chromosome configurations and criminal activity (see, e.g., Jacobs et al., 1965; Price, Whatmore, and Clement, 1966). Other investigators report "that males of the XYY type are not predictably aggressive" (Sarbin and Miller, 1970).

Limbic and Endocrine Disorders

Nerve tissue binds the brain to the spinal column and forms an area called the "limbic system." Studies indicate that inflamations, lesions, and tumors located in the limbic area bring about disturbed conduct in humans (Shah and Roth, 1974). In children, disturbed conduct includes impulsive, explosive behavior, tantrums, and stealing. It is possible that acts of aggression, violence, and property crime are more frequently committed by children with limbic disorders. These ideas are fairly new, however, and to date no researcher has found a way to accurately estimate how many juvenile law violators suffer from limbic problems.

By the early 1900s, scientists discovered that secretions of hormones through the endocrine glands have physiological and psychological effects on humans. For example, a textbook was published that treated crime as an outgrowth of emotional disruption that was caused by unbalanced hormonal secretions (Schlapp and Smith, 1928). Another researcher reported that the juvenile delinquents he studied had two to three times as many glandular problems as nondelinquents (Berman, 1938). Other investigators, however, found less significant connections between endocrine disorders and lawlessness.

Researchers found a link between the irritability, anger, tenseness, and nervousness brought on by menstruation and female crime (Morton, et al., 1953; Dalton, 1961, 1964). However, these early studies did not use appropriate control groups for comparative purposes and thus are highly suspect.

It is possible that many American children suffer from endocrine disorders. It is also possible that children who suffer from endocrine disorders are more likely to engage in delinquency than are unafflicted youth. But, much like the connection between lymbic system disorders and delinquency, relatively little is known today about interplay between endocrine imbalances and youthful misbehavior.

Chemical Imbalances

In the early twentieth century, scientists learned that the human brain is sensitive to concentrations of some chemicals and that the brain responds to deficiencies in certain necessary chemicals. When imbalances of either type occur, perception is altered and hyperactivity results. Hyperactivity often besieges children who are alergic to foods or who receive poor nutrition. Social scientists suspect that much juvenile lawlessness is related to chemical imbalances brought on by allergic reaction to food, by food deficit, or drug consumption (Hoffer, 1975; Newbolt, Philpot, and Mandel, 1972; Pawlak, 1972; "Bad Child or Bad Diet?" 1979). There is a growing concern about the influence of diet and drugs on the behavior of young persons. Relatively little is currently known, however, about the extent of eating disorders and chemical imbalance, among American youth. Social scientists have only begun to examine these relationships.

Disabilities

Physical disabilities such as missing or crippled appendages, minimal height, extremely large ears, chronic obesity, poor skin, and occluded vision are common among delinquent children. Similarly, *mental disabilities* such as retardation and "minimal brain dysfunction" are believed to contribute to delinquency (Barnes and Teeters, 1959: 138; Thornton, James, and Doerner, 1982: 212). *Disfigurement* brought on by accident or illness also seems to be associated with juvenile misbehavior (Banay, 1943; Wallace, 1940).

Learning disabilities include listening, thinking, talking, reading, writing, or arithmetic disorders (National Advisory Committee on Handicapped Children, 1968: 4; Podboy and Mallory, 1979; Bush and Waugh, 1971; Post, 1981; Unger, 1978; Hobbs, 1975; and *Rocky Mountain News*, Aug. 13, 1988: 66). It is not known with certainty what causes learning disabilities. As in other elements scrutinized by modern positivists, little is known about the connections between learning disabilities and delinquency, or about the extent of learning disabilities among American children. Teachers, clinicians and others who work with delinquents and other types of problem children, however, report that most misbehaving and law violating youth suffer from learning disabilities.

The following set of propositions outlines possible links between learning disabilities and delinquency:

1. Learning disabled children respond poorly, if at all, to social cues and tend toward impulsive behavior.

2. Many parents and control agents probably misunderstand, and feel frustration and anger toward, disabled children.

3. If parents and control agents misunderstand and treat disabled children as problems, then such youth can grow alienated from family, school, and the rest of society.

4. Alienated children are likely to form associations with friends who share their dilemma, who are hostile toward normal society, and who are, therefore, more likely to pursue delinquent opportunities. (Murray, 1976)

There is some evidence suggesting that children suffering from learning disabilities engage in no more lawlessness than other youngsters. McCullough, Zaremba, and Rich report that learning disabled children are, however, more likely to get *caught* breaking the law. Disabled youth are also more likely to be *processed* as delinquents by legal officials (1979: 45).

BEHAVIORISM

Behaviorists developed a form of psychology that studies only activity that can be observed, measured, and reproduced (Watson 1916 and 1919; Pavlov, 1927; Skinner, 1938, 1957).[2] Behaviorists (or operant conditioners) seek to specify the actual environmental conditions that produce activity in humans (Reynolds, 1968: 2). Operant conditioners do not believe that humans are free to choose between criminal and acceptable behavior. Behavior is, instead, conditioned by experiences with stimuli in the form of rewards, punishments, and negative reinforcements. Operant conditioners assume that there are two basic types of environmental influences on human behavior. First, humans react to *contemporary stimuli,* defined as exposure to a motivator in the immediate environment. A second type of influence comes from *historical stimuli,* which are recollections of previous experiences with environmental influences (3). Contemporary and historical stimuli are categorized as rewards (positive reinforcement), punishment (aversive stimulation), or negative reinforcement (taking away something gratifying).

Put simply, behaviorist theory predicts delinquency under the following conditions:

- If children consistently receive rewards for misbehavior, it is probable that delinquency will occur.
- If, however, children are consistently punished, or negatively reinforced, for misbehavior, then delinquency is unlikely.
- Delinquency is most likely when historical and current stimuli consistently and effectively reward misbehavior and when little or no punishment, or negative reinforcement, is experienced. (Keller and Schoenfeld, 1950: 3–13)

Behaviorism thus implies that delinquency is most likely when children experience ample positive reinforcements favoring law vi-

---

[2]It can be argued that Freudian psychoanalytic theory should be included in addition to, or instead of, behaviorism. The decision to include behaviorism, and to exclude Freudian theory, is a subjective one. Behaviorism is included in this chapter because I believe that it is by far the more precise and potentially verifiable psychological theory. Freud's ideas, however, are treated extensively in chapter 4.

olation and when relatively few negative reinforcements, or punitive measures, discourage law violation. Behaviorism is an important conceptual perspective because it helps to explain how the other causes of delinquency that we have examined in this chapter could be filtered through a learning process.

LABELING

Labeling theory seeks to explain human personality development as a function of labels applied to behavior by important persons (called "significant others") in small groups. Labeling theorists propose that personality develops in the following way:

1. Newborns and infants have little personality or self-conception, defined as "a sense of personal identity, a working conception of the kind of object he or she is." (Shibutani, 1986: 163)
2. Children, however, quickly acquire the ability to interact with others and to interpret socially acquired data about themselves.
3. Personal data comes to a child via an unending series of small bits of information, called "self-images," about how others react to her/him (Mead, 1934). Self-image information comes from many persons, and is about, for example, physical appearance, possessions and whether or not others like us. (Shibutani, 1986: 162–63)
4. Most children do two things with self-image information. First, as it accumulates, they begin to see *social roles* important others want them to play. Second, children use self-images to *evaluate themselves,* in time making fairly stable decisions about, for example, how attractive they are, whether or not they are moral persons, whether or not others tend to like them and want them around.
5. Eventually, self-images accumulate and gain consistency. As self-images help a child to develop a working model of the kind of object s/he is, a relatively permanent self-conception forms.

Labeling theorists use three concepts—'primary group', 'primary deviance', and 'secondary deviance'—to explain how some children develop into delinquents while most do not (Lemert,

1951). A *primary group* is a small collective of persons with whom a child has intense long-term contact and from whom children collect influential self-image data. For example, families, playmates, workmates—even the police or court officials—can serve as primary groups for children. *Primary deviance* is misbehavior, including crime and delinquency, committed by a child but interpreted by the child and his/her primary groups as transitive and as only a small part of the child's overall normal character. For example, vandalism or drinking alcohol is primary deviance when the offending child, her/his parents, members of the community and representatives of the law see the offenses as relatively harmless and only "sowing wild oats." *Secondary deviance* is defined as unwanted behavior committed by a child in reaction to, or as a defense against, predominately negative self-image information coming from significant primary group members. In other words, secondary deviance is misbehavior committed by a child in response to "bad" or "delinquent" labels assessed by family, school, community, and the law.

The following propositions represent a labeling theory approach to explaining the emergence of delinquency:

> Normal children grow up in the midst of primary groups that provide them with ample positive self-image information.

> Normal children might break the law, but their behavior is not designated as such. When normal children commit crimes, all is forgiven, and they develop stable "good citizen" self-conceptions.

> Thus, normal children never become secondary deviants.

> Some children receive abundant negative information about themselves, especially from important family members.

> Children with damaged family relationships tend to do poorly in school and are apt to receive negative self-image data there, too.

> Children who are unsupported by their families, and who are doing poorly at school, will be prone to join gangs where deviance is encouraged. (Tannenbaum, 1938: 8–21)

> Gangs provide a structure within which negatively labeled youth can associate.

Gangs supplant family and school as the main sources of acceptance, support, and influence.

Gang members do not necessarily think of themselves as "bad kids" when they break the law. But many other members of the community see their behavior as unlawful, and, thus, some gang members will be arrested by the police.

Youngsters who get caught are exposed to a flood of negative information about themselves from the police and other legal officials.

Arrest, trial, and punishment are embarassing and painful experiences that can traumatize a sensitive child and can force her/him into a state of secondary deviance.

Children who get caught by the police are also aware that most of their playmates break the law but go undetected.

Thus, children who are processed through legal channels tend to believe that the law is applied unfairly and unevenly and that they have been singled out for punishment.

Children who are singled out by legal authority grow angry and hostile and, as a result, are likely to give up their thoughts about being normal, by adopting a "delinquent" self-conception.

A more concise presentation of labeling theory predicts behavior under the following circumstances:

1. If positive self-image information is consistently received by a child from family, school, and other significant groups, then, even though serious misbehavior might occur, secondary delinquency is unlikely.
2. If negative self-image information is consistently received by a child from family, school and other significant groups;
3. if, as a result, the child joins a gang where misbehavior is encouraged;
4. if the gang child gets caught violating a law, is arrested and processed by legal agents; and
5. if the gang child who gets caught, arrested and processed, grows angry and resentful, then secondary delinquency is likely.

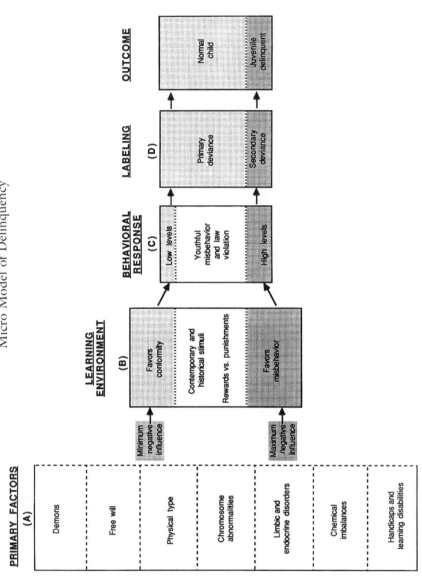

FIGURE 5.1
Micro Model of Delinquency

In other words, secondary deviants not only break the law but also accept negative labels and conform to delinquent roles. Labeling theory thus explains how children who violate the law might be undergoing personality change when they get caught and, consequently, might increase delinquent activity as a result of negative feedback from family, school, and legal authorities.

SUMMARY

Six types of micro delinquency theory were examined in this chapter. The large number of perspectives included here suggests a basic conclusion: there are many micro causes of delinquency (see fig. 5.1). Figure 5.1 shows that the genesis of delinquency in any given child can be complex and can involve numerous factors. Thus, no single factor is likely to be the main cause of delinquency.

Figure 5.1 connects micro influences as though they are operating together, making delinquency almost inevitable for some children (bottom track) and practically impossible for others (top track). The following propositions combine some of the best ideas from micro delinquency theory:

1. Factors listed in Box A of figure 5.1 operate in some combination, and at different intensity levels, on all children. Youth most damaged by the factors listed in box A are heavily predisposed to engage in misbehavior. The micro elements displayed in box A, however, do not by themselves cause delinquency.

2. Some children live in environments where law-violation is consistently rewarded, where little punishment, or negative reinforcement, is experienced, and thus their learning environment favors misbehavior (box B).

3. Children who are predisposed to misbehave, who are consistently rewarded for breaking the law, and who receive minimal punishment, or negative reinforcement, for acts of deviance are apt to respond with high levels of misbehavior and law violation (box C).

4. Some children who misbehave, and who are labeled "delinquent" by families, schools, and legal agents, accept the labels. Children who accept negative labels become secondary delinquents (box D).

Put more simply, the child most likely to become a juvenile delinquent is predisposed toward deviance, learns to misbehave, engages in high levels of misbehavior, and is negatively labeled.

We must remember that, for the most part, micro delinquency theories suffer from the same social class and gender biases that were observed when we examined clinical and observational ideas. Hopefully, as delinquency theories are improved and synthesized, these biases can be eliminated. In the next chapter we look at macro and midrange delinquency theories.

CHAPTER 6

Macro and Midrange Delinquency Theories

INTRODUCTION

In this chapter we examine a large body of delinquency theory, dividing it into macro and midrange perspectives. Although many theories that follow explain the emergence and persistence of crime, delinquency, and deviance, our main concern is with their application to juvenile delinquency. Macro and midrange delinquency theories developed largely as a reaction against various micro perspectives. Macro and midrange theorists are not primarily concerned with the psychological or biological causes of crime and delinquency or with the individual delinquent or criminal. They focus, instead, on the group, neighborhood, community, and society. Midrange theories examine causes of delinquency that lie between individuals and societal factors, such as gangs, small groups, schools, police, probation offices, and courts. Macro analysis considers more abstract and distant influences on childhood misbehavior like institutional misalignment, societal patterns of inequality, and social stratification.

CONFLICT VERSUS CONSENSUS THEORY

One additional distinction must be made. Almost all macro and midrange theorists ask the same basic question: why do some children become delinquent? They do not, however, agree about how to answer this question. Instead, there are two schools of thought on the matter. *Consensus theorists* make the following assumptions:

- Norms are strong, traditional, society-wide behavioral rules.
- Most members of society know the norms that are in force.

111

- Most members of society abide by norms because they understand that rules must be followed in order to curb individual appetites.

- In order to protect "normal" society from the influences of deviance, most societal members want crime and delinquency vigorously controlled by legal authority.

In contrast, *conflict theorists* make the following set of assumptions:

- There is much less agreement among societal members about norms and about the necessity for extensive legal control of deviance.

- Complex societies are made up of numerous minority groups, some powerful, some weak, each abiding by overlapping and conflicting norms.

- When groups come into conflict, norms embraced by the most powerful groups, especially if they seek and receive active support of government, will be forced upon all persons.

- Persons who deviate in extreme ways from majority norms will be treated as criminals and delinquents.

Some conflict theorists use stronger language. They argue that power elites use law and legal agencies as weapons, in order to mislead, dominate, and exploit the working classes (Quinney, 1970; Balkan, Berger, and Schmidt, 1980; Colvin and Pauley, 1983; Kolko, 1984).

In sum, delinquency theories described in this chapter vary along two dimensions, revealing either a macro or a mid-range focus and a consensus or a conflict approach. Thus, in the remainder of this chapter we examine four categories of theory, namely macro consensus, macro conflict, mid-range consensus, and mid-range conflict perspectives.

MACRO CONSENSUS THEORIES

In *The Rules of Sociological Method,* Emile Durkheim (1964) speculated that causes of behavior are located in the social world around humans. Further, Durkheim asserted that social behavior could be understood only by studying normal *and* pathological types. By "normal," Durkheim meant social behaviors (or conditions) that are most common. By "pathological," he meant uncommon behavior engaged in by societal members (1964: 55).

Durkheim described two types of society, mechanical and organic. In *mechanical societies,* social change is rare, the population is small, the division of labor is limited, and support for norms is ubiquitous. Durkheim believed that some deviance occurs in mechanical societies, because there are always people who will stray from normative expectations. In mechanical society, however, the number of people who deviate from important norms is relatively small, since violation of norms upsets social solidarity and provokes quick, firm, and universally supported response from persons in control. Thus, limited deviance makes civil society possible in mechanical societies by serving as a repugnant stimulus that promotes community action and control. Durkheim believed that deviance can get out of hand in *organic societies,* where the population is much larger, where technologies are rapidly advancing, and where the division of labor is complex and expanding. In organic societies, deviance can reach high levels as the numbers of norm violators and law breakers grow and come to represent a substantial proportion of the population.

In mechanical society, deviance is a small problem and can be controlled by primary processes within the family, neighborhood, and community. In organic society, secondary control in the form of legal machinery is necessary, and it operates to mediate between persons who follow the rules and large deviant minorities. Durkheim's ideas were later incorporated into a general theory of society called "structural-functionalism," which provides a broad framework for understanding the emergence and persistence of delinquency.

Structural-Functionalism

In its most general forms, structural-functionalism (S-F) attempts to explain all human behavior, conforming and nonconforming alike (Parsons, 1937; 1951: 249). S-F is based upon the following assumptions:

- Humans interact with each other in order to solve common survival problems including how to secure food, shelter, affection, social order, peace of mind, and care for the young and old.

- Through interaction *"norms* (strong society-wide rules) emerge as actors adjust their orientations to each other." Further, "these norms regulate subsequent interaction, giving it stability" (Turner, 1974: 35).

- As relatively stable problem-solving clusters of *statuses* (important ranked positions in family, education, religion, economy, and government) evolve, and as "relatively stable patterns of interaction among actors in statuses" emerge, then interactions have become "institutionalized," and a *social system* is formed (35).

- In this sense, "a social system is a system of processes of interaction between actors, it is the structure of the **relations** between the actors"(Williams, 1961: 73).

Social systems face a great deal of conflict and adversity. In order to overcome conflict, social institutions like kinship, economy, education, religion, and government tend to coordinate activity so as to encourage actors to behave in ways that support institutional survival, thus achieving a kind of dynamic equilibrium (or alignment).

Structural functionalists teach that society consists of two other structures that also tend to promote behavioral conformity: culture and personality. *Culture* is defined as a set of dominant, commonly shared values, norms, symbols, meanings, and physical objects. Cultural meanings and physical objects favored by most persons in a society are called the "cultural system" (Devereux, 1961: 30–36). *Personality* is defined as organized human motivational patterns, need dispositions, and decision-making capacities.

Culture helps to control behavior as humans pass through socialization mechanisms such as the family, school, neighborhood, and church. As humans are socialized, they are induced to prefer and to seek out certain material, linguistic, and symbolic options. In other words, actors are taught to uphold one set of values, beliefs, and ideas and to ignore or denigrate other possibilities. "It is through this process that actors are made willing to deposit motivational energy in roles, are made willing to conform to norms, and are given the interpersonal and other skills necessary for playing roles" (Turner, 1985: 37).

Structural functionalists believe that, after considerable socialization, a certain level of psychological organization is achieved in each human, resulting in motivational patterns, need, dispositions and decision-making capacities. Such psychological organization is called the "personality system."

Structural functionalism predicts high rates of acceptable behavior under the following conditions:

- In a properly functioning society, one where institutional equilibrium exists, social and cultural systems are well integrated, or aligned. When social and cultural systems are well aligned, key institutions like kinship, economy, education, church, and government share common purpose and, therefore, place demands upon individuals that are consistent, that create minimal role strain, and that result in little personal stress.

- When there is alignment between cultural and social systems, socialization of individuals is effective.

- Effective socialization leaves most humans with stable personalities, and a strong tendency to conform.

Deviance, on the other hand, is "the tendency on the part of one or more of the component actors to behave in such a way as to disturb the equilibrium of the interactive process . . . a motivated tendency for an actor to behave in contravention of one or more institutionalized patterns . . . the processes by which resistances to conformity with social expectations develop" (Parsons, 1951: 249–50). Structural functionalism predicts high rates of deviance, including delinquency, under the following circumstances:

> If social institutions are misaligned, if misalignment leads to ineffective socialization, then high rates of delinquency are likely.

Structural functional theory is diagrammed in figure 6.1. The top row of boxes in figure 6.1 represent the argument that stable-conformist personalities are produced when a high degree of institutional alignment exists and when socialization of individuals is generally effective. The bottom row of boxes in figure 6.1 represents the assertion that unstable-deviant personalities are generated by a low degree of institutional alignment, which, in turn, results in ineffective socialization of individuals. In sum, high rates of delinquency will likely occur when social institutions fail to share common purpose and direction and when the cultural system is unable to promote conformity on the part of actors (27–28).

FIGURE 6.1
Structural-Functional Model of Behavior

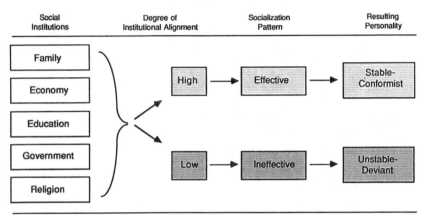

Under these conditions, socialization fails, and many persons turn to deviance. As we will see in the next section, macro conflict theory offers a somewhat different explanation for the emergence of delinquency.

MACRO CONFLICT THEORIES

Writing in the middle and late 1800s, Karl Marx did not deal extensively with crime and delinquency, although from time to time he did touch upon these subjects. Instead, Marx's focus was on the dynamics of social class struggle and on social change in western capitalistic societies (see Marx, 1967; Feuer, 1959; Aron, 1970a and b). Many contemporary social scientists nevertheless use neo-Marxist "conflict analysis" to explain the emergence and persistence of crime and delinquency (see, e.g., Quinney, 1970; Taylor, Walton, and Young, 1973, 1975; Chambliss, 1976; Balkan, Berger, and Schmidt, 1980; Colvin and Pauley, 1983). Marx wrote that the history of all society involved struggle among social classes (1967: 79). *Social class* is defined as society-wide aggregates of humans who differ significantly from other such aggregates in terms of access to scarce resources.

In industrial societies, class struggle occurs in a market economy between the proletariat and the bourgeoisie. *Proletarians* are members of the industrial lower class who lack agricultural skills, who live in large congested cities near factories, and who work for long hours as wage laborers. Members of the proletariat, although they are the larger social class, have relatively low access to scarce resources. Factories, other important means of economic production, and most other scarce resources are controlled by the *bourgeoisie* (or capitalists), a relatively small upper class. Capitalists seek, above all else, heightened profits and capital growth, which, combined with greed, induces the bourgeoisie to exploit the proletariat by holding wages as low as possible. The bourgeoisie encourages conflict and competition among groups of workers.

In time, the bourgeoisie is dominated by the most powerful industrial capitalists, who acquire the assets of all other members of the upper class and who continue to oppress wage earners in the name of profit and growth. Consequently, the proletariat maintains progressively less access to scarce resources, while the bourgeoisie grows smaller in number, becoming richer and more powerful. The bourgeoisie, of course, controls government. Members of the bourgeoisie use legal machinery to support their interests and to control members of the proletariat (Chambliss, 1969: 5; Balkan, Berger, and Schmidt, 1980: 4–10, 40–58).

Class struggle in capitalistic societies produces two kinds of crime and delinquency. First, some persons grow angry at the discrimination and oppression brought on by capitalism. They rebel and become political criminals. Second, large numbers of lower-class persons grow demoralized and despondent, succumbing to the temptations of crime and delinquency in order to ameliorate oppressive conditions.

Marxist theory suggests the following causes of crime and delinquency:

- Successful capitalism allows a political economy to dominate other social institutions.

- Capitalism forces individuals into cities, to work as wage earners.

- Motivated by greed, owners and their operatives oppress proletarians by severely resricting access to scarce resources.

- Some members of the proletarian class react to oppression by engaging in crime and delinquency.

FIGURE 6.2
Marxist Model of Deviance

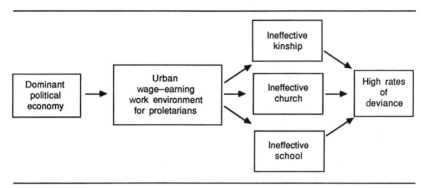

This chain of assertions is diagrammed in figure 6.2. As figure 6.2 indicates, Marxist theory views the political economy as the dominant social institution. Lower-class citizens are forced into urban industrial zones, where they sell their labor in a market for a wage. In an urban industrial environment, family, church, and school are rendered relatively ineffective, resulting in high rates of individual deviance. Another important point made by conflict theorists is that applying criminal labels to members of the working classes functions to divert public and legal attention away from elite criminal offenders—powerful individuals, corporations, and government agencies—whose lawlessness is far more serious and costly than common lower-class crime (Reiman, 1990).

MIDRANGE CONSENSUS THEORIES

Midrange consensus theory developed in the 1920s, looks within the community for causes of delinquency. Midrange consensus theory focuses upon crumbling community structures that insured conformity in earlier rural settings (Vold and Bernard, 1979: 418). Breakdown of community structures is called "social disorganization," defined as a "process by which the authority and influence of an earlier culture and system of social control is undermined and eventually destroyed" (Park, 1967: 105–10). Midrange consensus theory assumes that migration from rural areas into large urban industrial zones disrupts the lives of poor persons, leading to personal frustration and social disorganization (Cooley, 1909). Crime and delinquency result from social disorganization in poor neighborhoods.

Individual and social disorganization coexist in the same physical environment. Individual disorganization is "a decrease in the individual's ability to organize his whole life." Social disorganization is "a decrease in the influence of existing social rules of behavior upon individual members of the group." Disorganization, however, can be balanced by another process called "social reconstruction." Social reconstruction is "a production of new schemes of behavior and new institutions better adapted to the changed demands of the group" (Thomas and Znaniecki, 1920). Disorganization and reconstruction work against each other to maintain a dynamic equilibrium that can be threatened when the forces of disorganization grow too strong.

Migration of Americans, from the rural South to northern industrial cities, can be used as an example of the disorganization process. Rural migrants were forced to live in industrial cities dominated by alien rules and structures. Ideas, values, beliefs, and habits that migrants brought to the city were quickly destroyed because they conflicted with the subculture of the dominant urban class. Destruction of rural customs and beliefs impelled many migrants to develop unstable characters (Park, 1928). Consequently, experts reasoned that migrants must be supervised and assimilated through secondary control agencies like the police, courts, service agencies, and schools (Park and Burgess, 1924). In other words, poor urban neighborhoods must be held together by control agencies, because migrant families are unable to regulate the behavior of individuals. Crime and delinquency occur on a large scale when families *and* secondary control agencies fail to function (Park, Burgess, and McKenzie, 1967). The likelihood of family and secondary control breakdown increases as cities grow in size and as industrialism forces expansion and complication of the division of labor. Progress becomes "a terrible thing" as slum areas eventually fill up with "social junk."

In sum, midrange consensus theories emphasize community-level social disorganization and its impact upon neighborhoods and slum families. That is, under the strain of social disorganization, neighborhoods deteriorate, and many slum families break down, grow disorganized, and become unable to teach children values, rules and habits that constrain behavior (Faris, 1948). With family breakdown, secondary control agencies proliferate and take responsibility for more and more problem children. Below, we examine popular midrange consensus delinquency theories.

Natural Areas of Delinquency

Some theorists argue that distinct types of people occupy separate "natural areas" or "zones" of cities (Park, Burgess, and McKenzie, 1967), and others that levels of disorganization vary greatly from one area or zone to another (Faris and Dunham, 1939). Five typical "natural" zones have been identified, each residing within the next, like the rings of a tree trunk. Zones differ from each other in terms of degree of disorganization as well as in terms of the frequency of crime and delinquency (Park, Burgess, and McKenzie: 51).

The central business district (CBD) is in zone I. Stores, offices, and banks dominate activity. Relatively few persons live permanently in the central business district. Most persons live elsewhere and come to the CBD during daytime hours to work. Only a few homeless street persons sleep in the CBD.

Zone II is in transition and accomodates business, industrial, and residential activities. Like the CBD, zone II is an older section of the city where slumlike apartment housing coexists with business and industrial interests. Housing is dilapidated and occupied by the poorest inhabitants of the city, including many transients and minority persons. Streets are filled with the homeless.

Wage-earning persons live in the apartments and houses of zone III. There are fewer transients, and most adults hold a skilled job of some kind. Buildings are less likely to fall into disrepair; however, as soon as persons can afford to, they move from zones I and II into zone III, and this ongoing invasion process brings disorganization with it.

Zone IV is a residential area made up of relatively expensive apartments and single-family houses that are occupied by well-educated, highly skilled middle- and upper-middle-class couples and their children. Families stay for many years in the same house or apartment and often own their own homes. Family, neighborhood, and church are intact and strong. There is relatively little visible social disorganization.

Zone V develops beyond the city limits and consists of single-family housing and expensive apartments. People who can afford to pay high prices, and who can take the time to commute to and from the city—in other words, affluent persons and their families—live in the outer zone. Zone V families are supported by strong neighborhoods, churches, and schools.

Natural areas theory predicts that, since disorganization is high in zones I–III and uncommon in zones IV and V, crime and delinquency occur primarily in zones I–III and pose far less of a problem in zones IV and V. Natural areas theory is today one of the most popular in the social sciences. It gives credence to the idea that slum and working-class children, because of disorganized home and neighborhood environments, are likely delinquents.

Anomie

Earlier in this chapter, I outlined Durkheim's conception of deviance in mechanical and organic societies. Here we review Durkheim's ideas about "anomie." Durkheim believed that a certain amount of crime and delinquency is normal in all societies. Even in mechanical societies—where the population is small, the division of labor is simple, and norms are generally accepted—some deviance occurs, because a few people always violate important rules. In organic societies, however, where the population is large, where advancing technologies force constant change, and where the division of labor expands rapidly, deviance can take on massive dimensions.

Durkheim warned that change occurs rapidly in organic societies. He noted that when social institutions deteriorate and fail to constrain individual behavior, organic societies can reach a point of disarray, which he also called "anomie." Durkheim used the word *anomie* (which derives from an ancient Greek word meaning "lawlessness") to mean "lack of regulation" (1964, 1965; see also Vold and Bernard, 1979: 201–11).

In the late 1930s, Durkheim's ideas were applied by Robert Merton to American crime and delinquency. This variant of anomie theory is based upon the following assumptions:

- All Americans are taught to strive for success by acquiring wealth (Merton, 1939, 1968).
- American culture dictates acceptable ways that citizens can go about acquiring wealth. Acceptable ways of acquiring wealth are called "the culturally prescribed means for attaining goals."

TABLE 6.1
Individual Adaptation to Anomie

Modes of Adaptation	Cultural Goals	Institutional Means
Conformity	Accept	Accept
Innovation	Accept	Reject
Ritualism	Reject	Accept
Retreatism	Reject	Reject
Rebellion	Accept or reject	Accept or reject

- Not all people have equal *access* to acceptable means for achieving financial success.
- Not all people have equal *ability* to utilize acceptable means for acquiring wealth.
- For most Americans, pursuing culturally prescribed avenues will not produce success.

Failure to achieve economic success causes most Americans to experience anomie, which manifests itself in the form of strain and anxiety. The burden of failure falls heavily on members of the lower class, who are left with limited behavioral options (table 6.1).

Merton's adaptations describe "an individual's choice of behaviors in response to the strain of anomie" (Vold, 1958: 216). Anomie forces many lower-class persons into a state of listless *conformity*, whereby they accept the cultural goals of seeking wealth and the institutionalized means of success available to them. Some lower-class persons, however, cling to the hope for financial success and turn to deviant means in order to acquire wealth. *Innovators* commit most crime in American society. Innovators accept culturally prescribed goals and, therefore, seek wealth. But innovators understand that they will never become wealthy by pursuing prescribed avenues for success. They thus reject institutionalized means and seek new, often criminal, ways to become wealthy. *Ritualists* give up the aspiration to become wealthy but abide by all prescribed cultural norms and thereby avoid trouble. *Retreatists* reject culturally prescribed goals and institutionalized means to drop out of society as completely as possible. If retreatists become drunks or drug users, they are likely to become criminal. *Rebels* replace cultural values with new ones and invent or adopt alternative means for realizing success. Rebels, if they are politically active, or if they defy strong religious norms, can also become criminal (214–17).

Cohen (1955) sees lower-class American youth as less interested in economic success but, nevertheless, committed to gangs, because they provide attention and acceptance. Cohen reasons that children are required to attend school in order to acquire the skills necessary to achieve success and acceptance according to the dictates of American culture. Many lower-class boys do not fare well in school and feel a great deal of frustration and anger. To accomodate frustration and anger, and to obtain recognition and attention, lower-class boys congregate in gangs, where they reject the goal of achieving economic success and, instead, vent their anger and frustration through acts of violence and vandalism. Acts of violence and vandalism earn gang boys acceptance and attention among their peers. Thus, schools fail to provide for the needs of the poor. Failure, and alienation from school, forces many lower-class children to form gangs and to engage in delinquent acts.

Cloward and Ohlin (1960) argue that most lower-class children subscribe to the cultural goal of achieving success by becoming wealthy. Consequently, most lower-class children try to succeed in school. But, largely for financial reasons, lower-class children either fail in school or drop out. As school failure becomes a reality, lower-class children seek other, deviant means for achieving economic success. They join gangs as a way to meet their needs. Children who live in lower-class neighborhoods that have a successful adult criminal subculture will join adult gangs and will learn criminal trades that lead to financial success in areas such as gambling, drug dealing, burglary, robbery, and pimping.

Lower-class children who cannot join a successful criminal subculture will join a conflict subculture where fighting and other violent, destructive activities express their outrage at being rejected by normal society. Some other lower-class children who cannot join a successful adult criminal subculture will join a retreatist subculture where they reject the goal of wealth acquisition and, instead, turn to drugs as a way to handle their feelings of failure and anger.

All three modes of adaptation described by Cloward and Ohlin begin with blocked opportunities for lower-class children. But Cloward and Ohlin recognize that the deviant reaction to blocked opportunities selected by lower-class children depends upon the specialized subcultures that are available to them. Thus, some lower-class children adapt in rational, utilitarian ways, while others adapt by joining subcultures that stress irrational and violent, or retreatist, reactions to blocked opportunities.

Hirshi writes that "delinquent acts result when an individual's bond to society is weak or broken" (1969: 16). Hirschi identifies four aspects of a child's bond to society: attachment, commitment, involvement, and belief. Attachment means a child's "sensitivity to the opinions of others" is strong (16). Commitment indicates that children invest time and energy "in a certain line of activity" that favors abiding by the law (20). Involvement implies that children become engrossed "in conventional activities" and, therefore, have no time for delinquency (22). Belief refers to the argument that children believe in "a common value system within the society or group" and, thus, would not think of violating norms (23).

Matza (1964) observed that children may drift between acceptable and delinquent behavior and may never be completely law abiding or completely delinquent. Sykes and Matza (1957) outlined five techniques of neutralization which allow otherwise law-abiding juveniles to engage in periodic delinquency. Through denial of responsibility, children claim that their delinquency was an accident or that they were forced to deviate. By denying injury, children claim that their delinquency results in no real harm to anyone and, thus, that they should not be held liable for their acts. Denial of the victim means that delinquent children contend that their victims actually brought on whatever damage occurs. Delinquent children often condemn their condemnors, claiming that their victims are in actuality criminals and, thus, deserve whatever damage they receive. Finally, delinquent children often appeal to higher loyalties, stating that their allegiance to a gang or other group requires misbehavior of them.

Differential Association

Edwin Sutherland asserted that deviance, especially crime and delinquency, is a group phenomenon and that deviant behavior is learned in exactly the same ways as conforming behavior (1939: 4–9). Sutherland developed a differential association theory that emphasizes inputs made by important persons in small groups and those persons' influence on the formation of deviant behavioral tendencies. Differential association theory is popular among social scientists and legal officials, especially in the United States, because it serves as a conceptual bridge connecting group and individual influences with more broadly conceived cultural and structural factors. Differential association theory has some basic propositions

- Delinquent behavior cannot be explained by the exclusive consideration of general needs and values as possible causes.
- Instead, delinquent behavior is learned by all of the mechanisms that are involved in any other learning situation.
- Delinquent behavior is learned in interaction with other persons in a process of verbal and nonverbal communication. Most learning about delinquency occurs within intimate personal groups. Associations with people in groups that favor law violation, or with people in groups that favor obeying the law, may vary in frequency, duration, priority, and intensity.
- Learning about delinquency includes mastering techniques of law violation, internalizing unfavorable definitions of legal codes, and acquiring motives, drives, rationalizations, and attitudes that favor law violation.
- Persons become delinquent because they learn an excess of definitions favoring law violation. (Adapted from Sutherland and Cressey, 1974: 75–77)

An interesting extention of differential association theory asserts that almost everything juveniles do can be divided into either tight or loose social occasions (Sanders, 1981: 81–95). *Social occasion* is defined as "an affair, undertaking, or event bounded by time and place within which many situations and gatherings form, dissolve and reform." *Tight occasions* are formal, allow close supervision by adults, and strictly define appropriate behavior. High school team football practice and a cheerleader tryout are examples of tight occasions. *Loose occasions* are informal, lack adult supervision, leave appropriate behavior undefined, and allow for a wide variety of activities. A street fight, an evening spent petting in a parked car, and an afternoon of hanging out at a shopping mall are examples of loose occasions.

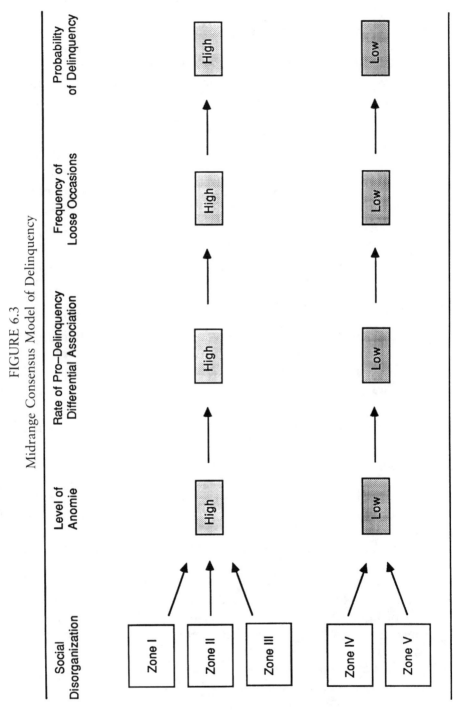

FIGURE 6.3
Midrange Consensus Model of Delinquency

Loose occasions encourage delinquency, because children at loose occasions will encounter vaguely defined, exciting, sometimes dangerous situations where delinquent responses are likely to occur. Thus, juveniles who spend most of their time at loose occasions are most likely to engage in delinquent acts. In sum, differential association theory emphasizes intimate peer relationships, and loose occasions, as causes of delinquency. Differential association theory lacks the social class bias of most other midrange and macro delinquency theories, and it leaves open the possibility that any child who is unsupervised by responsible adults can get into trouble.

Figure 6.3 brings together the various factors that midrange consensus theorists point to as causes of delinquency. The leftmost column represents the assertion that the type of neighborhood a child lives in is important. In other words, disorganized neighborhoods (zones I–III) put children at risk, whereas better organized, more affluent neighborhoods (zones IV and V) protect children from crime and delinquency. The top row of boxes in figure 6.3 lists midrange factors that are likely to increase the probability of delinquency. Children in disorganized neighborhoods are more likely to suffer from high levels of anomie, to associate with children who do not respect the law, and to attend loose occasions. The bottom row of boxes in of figure 6.3 shows midrange factors that protect children from delinquency. Sheltered life in affluent peripheral neighborhoods insulates children from anomie, from prodelinquency associations, and from loose occasions, thus reducing the probability of delinquency. In the next section, we examine midrange conflict theories that offer somewhat different explanations for the emergence and persistence of delinquency.

MIDRANGE CONFLICT THEORIES

Midrange conflict theories are based upon the following assumptions:

- In complex societies many different subcultural groups must interact with each other.
- Conflict occurs because most subcultural groups teach their members somewhat different conduct norms.

- Intergroup interaction, thus, generates conflict. (Sellin, 1938: 27)

Members of different groups experience two kinds of *primary cultural conflict*. First, when groups share borders, and when the law of one group is forced upon another, conflict is likely. Second, when one group migrates into the territory of another, then the laws of the most powerful group will likely dominate, leading to conflict. *Secondary cultural conflict* is also possible. Secondary conflict occurs when a group grows so large and complex that it divides into subcultures and when each subculture teaches its members overlapping and contradicting norms (105).

If primary or secondary conflict exists, then law fails to reflect the values and beliefs of all societal members. Instead, legal authority tends to represent the views and interests of a dominant subculture. Crime and delinquency result when members of some groups live under the constraints of a dominant subculture but continue to behave in accordance with conflicting norms of another subculture. In the next section, group conflict ideas are incorporated into a theory of crime and delinquency.

Group Conflict Theory

Group conflict theory proposes the following:

- Humans are always group-involved.
- Society is made up of many groups that are "held together in a shifting . . . equilibrium of opposing group interests and efforts."
- Groups engage in a "continuous struggle to maintain, or to defend, the place of one's own group in the interaction of groups" (Vold and Bernard, 1979: 283–84)
- Group conflict is, thus, a basic social process.

In the extreme, group conflict ultimately results in victory by one group over another. Victory is especially likely when one group is very weak and another strong. But many times struggle goes on for a long time, or it reaches a stalemate. Conflicting groups will seek to use political channels in order to gain advantage over their rivals, since politics is "primarily a matter of finding practical compromises between antagonistic groups in the community at large" (287). Groups that are most successful in the political arena will have laws passed that defend their interests and that prohibit encroachments by rivals. Thus, "the whole political process of law making, law breaking, and law enforcement directly reflects deep-seated and fundamental conflicts between interest groups and their more general struggles for the control of the police power of the state" (Chambliss, 1969: 288). Delinquent children are seen as a minority group, banding together into gangs because they cannot reach goals through legal means. Thus, many poor urban youth are forced to form gangs in order to gain strength in numbers and a modicum of protection from legal authority (289–90). Since police, in general, protect the interests of affluent adults, constant conflict is inevitable between law enforcement officials and juvenile gangs.

Turk sees struggle in society occurring mostly between authorities and subjects (Chambliss 1966, 1969). The goal of the authorities is to balance coercion of, and cooperation with, subjects so that neither control technique is overused. When coercion and cooperation are effectively used by the authorities, subjects grow conditioned to their roles in society and learn to accept inequalities. It is only when cooperation breaks down that authorities resort to brief interludes of conflict in order to force subjects into yielding to the demands of a more powerful group. When authorities and subjects are committed to cultural and social norms that disagree, the likelihood of group conflict is high. Group conflict is most likely when authorities and subjects are well organized, when each has a well-developed language and philosophy of action, and when each knows relatively little about its adversary.

Assuming that conflict is high between subjects and authorities, three additional factors determine how many subjects will be turned into criminals and delinquents. First, if all levels of the law (legislators, police, prosecutors, judges, and corrections personnel) find a prohibited behavior, or attribute, highly offensive, then many subject offenders will be arrested, prosecuted, convicted, and corrected. Second, when authorities have a great deal of power and subjects are relatively powerless, authorities can increase arrests, since they face minimal costs in processing large numbers of subject offenders. Third, large numbers of criminals and delinquents will be generated when subjects make conflict moves that are unrealistic and thus decrease their chances for success.

William Chambliss (1984) uses a two-level form of conflict analysis to explain how some children who engage in delinquency get arrested and negatively labeled, while other children who engage in delinquency go undetected and avoid arrest. Chambliss observed that:

- Boys who regularly violate the law, but avoid getting caught, are anglo upper-middle-class gang members.
- Children who avoid getting caught are active in school affairs and benefit from the support of stable families.
- In contrast, boys who get arrested and punished for law violations are lower-class gang members (126).

At the *societal level,* biased laws result from basic contradictions that are built into the structure of a capitalist political economy. Chambliss asserts that capitalism results in a basic dilemma: masses of citizens aspire to consume material goods, but only some are sufficiently employed to earn the wages they will need to satisfy their material desires. All other workers (and potential workers) cannot earn enough money to buy the goods that they have been conditioned to need. Thus, the potential for social conflict is built into the American capitalist political economy and becomes a primary concern of law makers and law enforcers. Since members of upper social classes have considerable access to scarce material resources, while persons in the lower classes fall short of meeting their material needs, class conflict in the United States is inevitable and constant.

When class conflict turns into riots and other forms of civil disobedience, the state passes laws aimed at eliminating strife. Similarly, courts and the police use existing laws to justify action perceived as necessary in order to eliminate conflict (30). Legislators, police officers, and court officials pass and enforce laws that go beyond an immediate crisis, laws that are aimed at assuming greater control of groups that cause conflict. In this way, the state defines more and more behaviors of the poor as delinquent or criminal in order to prevent future conflict. Criminal law enforcement does little, however, to prevent subsequent conflict between poor persons and legal officials, since the basic dilemma of unequal access to scarce material resources is never addressed.

In order to study interaction among the police, schools, and gangs, Chambliss recommends that macro explanations of delinquency be supplemented by conflict analysis that uses *surface variables* (131–34). According to Chambliss, some gang boys get arrested while others do not because they differ in terms of visibility, demeanor, and bias.

Lower-class gang boys live closer to the center of the city and must hang out there because they lack transportation. The city center is also used by many other community members and is heavily patrolled by the police. Because of this, transgressions of lower-class gang boys are often *visible* to the police. Lower-class gang boys make themselves even more visible by hassling people whom they encounter and by frequent fighting. On the other hand, upper-middle-class gang boys have access to automobile transportation, which they use to stay mobile, often never visiting one part of the city more than once. Similarly, affluent gang boys tend to hang out in bars or pool halls located at the edge of the city, where population density is low and where the police patrol far less frequently. Most delinquency committed by upper-middle-class gang boys goes unnoticed by the police. Affluent gang boys also tend to fight infrequently, and they tend to hassle citizens less often than do their poorer counterparts. Thus, upper-middle-class delinquency is less visible than lower-class forms.

Upper-middle-class gang boys who get caught by the police utilize apologetic, penitent *demeanor* to convince the police that they are basically good and are only sewing a few wild oats. Affluent gang boys pretend to comply with school rules, thereby hiding truancies from school officials. Lower-class gang boys, in contrast, react to the police, and to school authorities, by displaying disrespect, hostility, and disdain.

Police officers, school authorities, and most citizens seem to be *biased* against lower-class gang boys. Offenses committed by poor children are usually seen as far more serious than the misbehavior attributed to affluent youth. The defiance and hostility of lower-class children is taken as an indication that they are deeply entrenched in a delinquent lifestyle and that they deserve to be treated like delinquents.

In sum, social class conflict sets the stage for delinquency by impelling the state to outlaw many common behaviors of poor children. This fact does not in itself, however, explain surface con-

FIGURE 6.4
Macro and Mid-Range Model of Delinquency

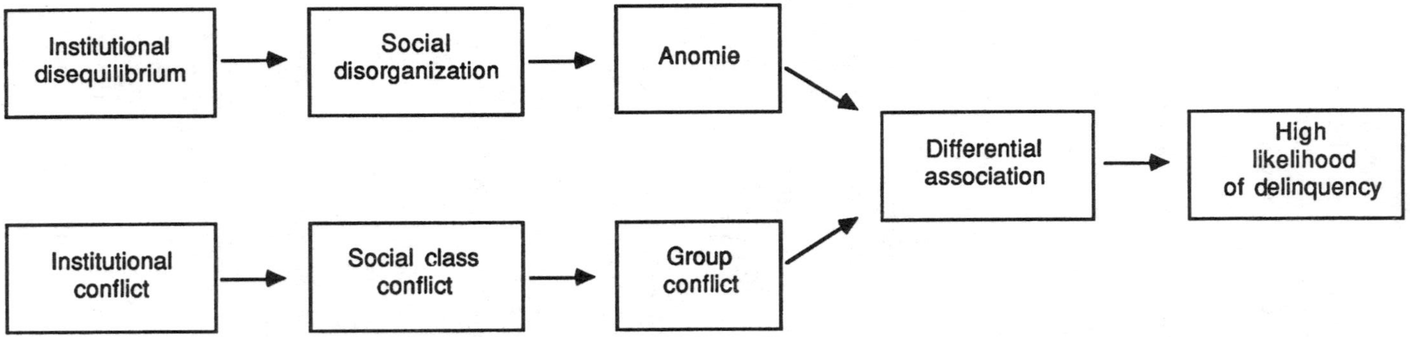

| Institutional disequilibrium | → | Social disorganization | → | Anomie | → | Differential association | → | High likelihood of delinquency |

| Institutional conflict | → | Social class conflict | → | Group conflict | → | Differential association |

flict that occurs between poor children, on the one side, and citizens, police officers and school officials, on the other. In order to understand surface conflict, one must consider variables like visibility, demeanor, and bias. Such concepts can help to explain how some control agents overlook much deviant behavior committed by affluent children, while treating transgressions of lower-class children as delinquency.

SUMMARY: INTEGRATING AND EVALUATING DELINQUENCY THEORIES

Figure 6.4 brings together in diagrammatic form important elements of macro and midrange delinquency theory. Figure 6.4 serves two purposes. First, it shows the parts of macro and midrange delinquency theory that a more general conceptual scheme could include. Second, this figure allows us to develop a few tentative general propositions about the genesis of delinquency, at least from the macro and midrange sides of the puzzle.

The top and bottom rows of figure 6.4 represent two unresolved sets of assertions about the macro and midrange environment of delinquency. Consensus theory (top row) predicts the following:

> If institutional disequilibrium is high, then serious social disorganization results, leading to widespread anomie, differential association, and consequently, a high likelihood of delinquency.

Conflict theory (bottom row), on the other hand, asserts that:

> If institutional and social class conflict occur, group conflict and differential association will result, making delinquency highly likely.

In all likelihood, both sets of assertions are valid in many respects and misguided in others. At this time, only one conclusion is certain. Chapters 4, 5, and 6 demonstrate that there are many causes of delinquency and that no single explanation is likely to encompass all of the factors that can come into play.

There is a developing tradition of integrating delinquency theories. Delbert Elliott and his coworkers were among the first to combine assertions from several delinquency theories into an integrated causal model (Elliott, Ageton, and Canter, 1979; Elliott, Huizinga, and Ageton, 1985). Colvin and Pauly (1983) offer an integrated structural-Marxist delinquency theory. Hagan (1986) combines variables like social class, parental workplace experience and children's willingness to take risks into a theory of delinquency. Wilson and Herrnstein (1985) have been developing a theory of criminal law violation that draws upon some biological, psychological, and sociological factors. Krohn (1986) has been assembling a theory that includes assertions from differential association and social control perspectives. It is possible that these efforts to integrate delinquency theory will bear fruit in the future. However, there is currently little agreement among experts about which of these integrative efforts is most promising (Gibbons and Krohn, 1991: 213–14).

I believe that there are currently too many competing ideas about what causes delinquency to combine into a single theory. Our efforts might prove more productive if we develop comprehensive delinquency theories at the micro, midrange, and macro levels before attempting to proceed with general theory building.

As with micro delinquency theory, midrange and macro delinquency theories have, for the most part, perpetuated deep-seated social class and gender biases. According to Chesney-Lind and Shelden, traditional delinquency theory is characterized by the "absence of interest in gender" (1992: 70). Chesney-Lind and Shelden note that ignoring female delinquency is ironic, because much traditional delinquency theory is applicable (62–70). I agree and, in chapters 4, 5, and 6, have presented traditional delinquency theory as gender neutral, so that the ideas described therein can be applied equally to boys and girls, to young women and men.

PART 4

Delinquency and Social Organization

CHAPTER 7

Kinship Networks, Family Life, and Delinquency

INTRODUCTION

This chapter examines connections among kinship networks, family life, and delinquency. Families are primary groups that share living quarters and organize important aspects of daily life. Families are formed through marriage, birth, and adoption (Turner, 1985: 295; Shibutani, 1986: 207). Kinship networks are systems of families. Kinship binds society together. For most of recorded history, humans have lived in the midst of large kinship systems involving hundreds, even thousands, of individuals (Nanda, 1987: 234–35).

Kinship and family are prime determinants of delinquency. It is in the home that children's values, personality and self-concept begin to develop (Durkheim, 1961; Hirschi, 1969; Kratcoski and Kratcoski, 1990: 113; Shibutani, 1986: 206–7). Effective delinquency prevention comes "from a warm, loving, stable family, [where] the child learns that people are friendly, worth knowing and can be depended upon." Delinquency is most likely "when a family is cold, despairing, rejecting, or neglectful, [because] the child learns distrust, hostility, or downright hatred of people" (National Conference on Prevention and Control of Juvenile Delinquency, 1974). Warm and cold families exist in every social class and in all types of ethnic groupings, although factors such as family income and place of residence can heavily limit, or enhance, a child's life chances (Shibutani, 1986: 207; Barnes and Teeters, 1959: 177–85).

There are many possible connections among kinship networks, families, and delinquency. No single family-related factor, by itself, causes juvenile delinquency. Figure 7.1 illustrates the most important links. The outer ring of figure 7.1 displays aspects of culture,

FIGURE 7.1

Links among Kinship Networks, Families, and Delinquency

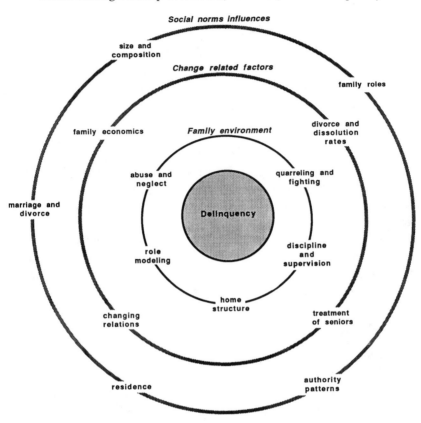

called "social norms." Social norms set general societal standards for family size, operation, and location. Modern family norms do not directly cause delinquency. Modern norms push families along a developmental path that renders them poorly equipped to care for children. Urie Bronfenbrenner, a child-development expert, illustrates this point with his contention that "what's destroying the family isn't the family itself but the indifference of the rest of society. The family takes a low priority" (in Byrne, 1977: 41). Indifference toward the family is reflected in contemporary societal norms. The middle circle of figure 7.1 lists social change-related factors. Children in the United States grow up in the midst of constant and rapid social change. Many recent changes in American society, especially those pertaining to economics and important relationships, leave families without sufficient human and monetary resources to properly care for children. According to Bronfenbrenner, "increasing numbers of children are coming home to empty houses. If there's any reliable predictor of trouble, it probably begins with children coming home to an empty house" (41).

The inner ring of figure 7.1 outlines features of family environment that propel children toward delinquency. While factors listed in the two outer circles of figure 7.1 indirectly hinder families, environmental influences are primary determinants of delinquency. Yet, in order to understand why family life fails to constrain behavior, more distant factors must be considered. Parents who are subjected to intense pressure from outer influences are likely to vent anger or practice indifference on their children. Thus, connections among kinship systems, families, and delinquency exist on three levels, and each level must be considered in order to understand the others.

KINSHIP NORMS AND DELINQUENCY

Kinship networks and families are ancient structures that organize social life. Because of their importance, much analysis has occurred focusing on kinship norms that regulate five basic aspects of family life. While there is no body of social science research that links kinship norms to delinquency, I nevertheless believe that modern kinship norms encourage patterns of family life that make widespread delinquency possible. In this section we examine norms related to family size and composition, place of residence, allocation of authority, family roles, and marriage and divorce practices.

Family Size and Composition

Throughout most of human history, social norms dictated that kinship networks be made up of several large extended families, where persons filling different statuses—like husband, grandfather, grandmother, wife, child, uncle, aunt, and so on—lived together in the same household (Eshleman, 1991: 19). The duty of rearing children was shared by many persons in different statuses. Parents, especially mothers, were usually active in raising their children. But uncles, grandparents, single aunts, older offspring, and childless wives also helped care for children. In extended families it was a rare child who escaped learning the language, values, beliefs, morality, and habits of the family, since supervision was provided by many members, and there were few places to hide (Nanda, 1987: 225–28). In urban industrial environments, where most persons in the United States today reside, kinship networks and extended families are social and economic liabilities. In industrial society most persons live in nuclear family units, where mothers, alone, carry much of the burden of raising and supervising children (220–24). Increasingly, families in urban industrial societies send both parents out into the workplace to earn wages in order to survive. With both parents out of the home working for a wage, there is less time for the care and supervision of children and few kin to go to for help. Today, many American children are left alone and untended, creating the possibility of their engaging in delinquency (Hirschi, 1969: 237–39).

Place of Residence

When couples marry in traditional societies they are usually required to live either near the husband's relatives (patrilocal norm) or near the wife's relatives (matrilocal norm). A consequence of strong patrilocal or matrilocal residence norms is that most children in traditional societies live among several large families that belong to the same kinship network. Thus, in traditional societies many members of the kin group see to it that children behave. Little room exists for escaping supervision by older family members. Thus, conformity on the part of children is likely.

In urban industrial societies, like the United States today, there is far less pressure from either side of the family to live nearby (neolocal residence norm) (Nanda, 1987: 228–29). Most newlyweds in the United States live where they must in order to gain employment. Neolocal residence norms tend to break down large kinship networks and to erode the size of families. As neolocal residence norms dominate, relatively fewer families, and family members, remain together to help with the care and supervision of children. Neolocal residence norms ensure that many children are left uncared for and, consequently, are exposed to the influences of delinquency (Byrne, 1977: 45; Turner and Musick, 1985: 118).

Allocation of Authority

In all societies, rules develop that dictate that certain kin and family members have the legitimate right to make decisions for all others. In most traditional societies, elder males make critical decisions for kinship networks. Fathers usually make important decisions for their family units (patriarchal norm). Sometimes men on a woman's side of a kin network will make critical decisions (matriarchal norm). Either form of traditional authority can be used to teach children about the rules of social life and to help the young acquire a set of habits that promote good citizenship.

In many contemporary American families authority is egalitarian, that is, shared by husband and wife. An egalitarian authority norm creates the potential for disagreement between spouses about issues involving control and supervision of children. Thus, egalitarian authority makes it more likely that children will be confused about which parent's rules apply to their behavior. Confused children tend to misbehave, and are prime candidates to engage in delinquency (Turner and Musick, 1985: 119). I am not advocating here that one or the other parent should rule over the household. I am making the point that, as family norms change, confusion can result, leading to misbehavior.

Family Roles

In every family, rules exist that organize labor so that basic work can be done. In traditional agricultural societies there is a relatively clear division of labor in most families. Able men are expected to provide food, shelter, and family defense. Traditional men also administer physical punishment to children, when deemed necessary. Little else is expected of traditional men, especially in terms of parenting children and doing household chores.

Traditional women, on the other hand, are expected to give birth to children, to provide food through agricultural pursuits around the home, to make and repair clothing for the family, to maintain a domicile, and to help with the care and training of children (Eshleman, 1991: 13). Under these circumstances, most children learn the rules of society and conform to the basic requisites of their family. Traditional family roles leave little room for the deviant child.

In contrast, modern family life increasingly involves parents who work for wages outside the home. Parental energies are spread more thinly today, leaving many children uncared for and unsocialized (Bartollas, 1990: 263; Byrne, 1977: 43; Turner and Musick, 1985: 131, 246). Stress and pressure brought home by parents from the workplace can cause anger and violence. In families where men or women act like emotional bullies, home life becomes "a tyranny ruled over by its meanest member" (Van Waters, 1925: 64; also see Chesler, 1978). I am not advocating that one or another parent stay at home in order to care for children. I am noting that changing norms often lead to stress, confusion, and misbehavior.

Marriage and Divorce Practices

In order to insure survival, traditional kinship networks and extended families closely control marriage and divorce. For example, in most cases traditional males and females are not free to choose whomever they wish as a marriage partner. Rather, the kin group dictates that some relatives are off limits (incest taboo). Traditional kinship networks also exclude members of some other kin groups from consideration (exogamy), while often specifying that a spouse should be chosen from a preferred kin group (endogamy) (Nanda, 1987: 205–20).

Divorce is tightly controlled by kinship networks, since dissolution threatens the kin group's existence. Divorce is difficult to obtain in traditional societies, especially for women. Making divorce hard to obtain serves to keep families intact, guaranteeing that kinship groups will remain large. Difficult divorce also assures that a full array of family members will be available for helping with the maintenance and supervision of children. Thus, norms resulting in low divorce rates minimize delinquency by providing more family members for the care and control of children (Bartollas, 1990: 262–63). However, where families are oppressed by an emotional bully, strict divorce norms can mean that violent families remain intact, rendering children exposed to the unsettling influences of a bad family life.

In industrial societies, males and females are relatively free to choose marriage partners and base their choices upon feelings of love and personal preference. Kin have little say over what happens when industrial-age courtship occurs. Divorce becomes relatively easy to achieve, and broken families are common. In one way, easy divorce takes pressure off of some children, because a tyrannical parent can be exorcised. But, following divorce, many children are exposed to unfriendly and potentially dangerous parent surrogates. Thus, high rates of divorce can create wholesale problems for children.

In sum, in terms of family norms, industrial urbanism creates an ever-changing environment for children (Fischer, 1984). Families lack important child care capabilities. Home life occurs away from kin in urban isolation. Family authority breaks down. Divorce and family dissolution loom everywhere. Yet, somehow most American parents teach their children to abide by the law. Most American children conform, in spite of it all (Barnes and Teeters, 1959: 178).

RAPID SOCIAL CHANGE AND DELINQUENCY

Social change is "a succession of differences in time in a persisting identity" (Nisbet, 1970: 302). Social change, in economics, politics, kinship and family, education, and religion, occurs continuously in modern mass societies like the United States (Shibutani, 1986: 308). Rapid, constant social change disorients people and tends to pit generations against each other. In Shibutani's words, "In a changing society members of each generation tend to develop a somewhat different perspective, for they are subject to dissimilar influences during their most impressionable years" (309). Social change renders old ways of solving problems, old assumptions about how the world works, obsolete (Stetson, 1991: 6). Thus, rapid, constant social change also contributes indirectly to widespread delinquency by disorienting and confusing parents and children.

Economic Status of Families

Americans endure gross inequality in the distribution of income, and life has been getting worse for the poor (Phillips, 1990; Duncan and Rodgers, 1991: 548). According to Huey, "the nature of entrenched American poverty is changing for the worse—getting meaner, harder" (1989: 125) Between 1974 and 1988, the proportion of American children who are considered poor rose from 15.1

to 19.6 percent, an increase of 2.5 million children (Barancik, 1989). In 1991, according to the U.S. Bureau of the Census, 14.3 million American children lived in poverty. In other words, today almost 22 percent of all children in the United States are poor (Bennett, 1993: 6). U.S. citizens are compartmentalized into lower, middle, and upper social classes (Turner and Musick, 1985: 174–77). Heightening income inequality diminishes the ability of less advantaged parents to care for their children. In 1988, the best paid 20 percent of the U.S. population earned 44 percent of total income available (up from 41 percent in 1974). In contrast, the least well paid 20 percent of the U.S. population, the poor, supported their families on only 4.6 percent of total income available in 1988 (down from 5.5 percent in 1974). Approximately 51.4 percent of total U.S. income in 1988 went to the middle 60 percent of American families (Barancik, 1989; U.S. Bureau of the Census, 1983a: 747; 1986b).

In 1973, there were 23 million poor Americans. In 1987, there were at least 32.5 million Americans living in poverty. Thirty-seven percent of the poor are single mothers and their families (Huey, 1989: 126). In 1988, 29 percent of Anglo women, 52 percent of African American women, and 55 percent of Hispanic women headed families with no husband present and lived below the poverty level (Eshleman, 1991: 34). These data indicate that affluent American families have ample resources to use in caring for their children. However, poor and many middle-class parents must provide for their families with less and less income.

Divorce and Dissolution

Dissolution is the breaking up of families, whereas divorce involves legally ending a marriage. While there are no authoritative statistics to confirm this, it is generally believed that dissolution is today far more common than divorce among Americans. It used to be difficult to get a divorce, but over the last thirty years, divorce law has been increasingly simplified. Until recently, divorce law and court procedures were complicated and involved adversarial procedures during which damage to one spouse had to be proven in court. Over the last thirty years, however, state legislatures have liberalized the laws so that in most places it is today possible to obtain a no fault divorce, one requiring only that spouses agree to legally terminate their marriage. Loosening rigid divorce laws made it possible for Americans to seek the divorce option in un-happy marriages. Public beliefs shifted toward a more tolerant view of divorce. As a result, many American families are now in constant flux.

The United States has the highest divorce rate in the world (Manis, 1984: 309). Well over one million American marriages end in divorce each year. For every two marriages in the United States there is one divorce (Bennett, 1993: 13). Between 1960 and 1980, the ratio of divorced Americans to married people living with their spouses doubled (U.S. Bureau of the Census, 1983b: 51). About 55 percent of all U.S. divorces involve children.

Dissolution and divorce are hard on parents and children for several reasons. Separation and divorce are often more painful than marriage partners expected. Spouses who break apart have usually gone through long periods of anger, hostility, and quarrel-ing with each other and with their children. Family breakup im-poses extreme financial hardship, especially for women and chil-dren. Divorce and dissolution leave parents with a sense of incom-pleteness and feelings of guilt, frustration, and failure. Divorce and dissolution leave parents and children feeling ambivalent about each other (Freudenthal, 1959; Wallerstein and Kelly, 1980; Wal-lerstein and Blakeslee, 1989). Finally, divorce and dissolution make possible the introduction of adult live-ins to the household. Sometimes surrogate parents fit in well. Stepparents or other types of adult live-ins, as well as biological parents, however, can be violent or sexually exploitive toward children. Surrogate parents, as well as biological parents, may also fall short as positive role-models. Thus, divorce and family dissolution are major problems for a growing number of women and their children and, no doubt, contribute significantly to the delinquency problem.

Family Relations

The husband role has changed little for most males (Manis, 1984: 299; Vanek, 1983: 226). American men are expected to work as wage laborers. But they do little housework, child care, and shop-ping (Vanek, 1983: 226). Modern wives, however, are expected to fill traditional female family roles *and* to work outside the home as a wage laborer. Modern women who accept their dual roles have about one-half as much time for housework as did their traditional counterparts, and labor as many as ninety-five to one hundred hours per week (Turner and Musick, 1985: 247). Women who complain and who assert that their husbands should take on some of the domestic and child care work are likely to meet with resistance. Children are often caught in the middle of arguments over adult family relations.

Almost all American children are legally required to attend public school, giving wage-earning parents some relief from child care responsibilities. But public education means that nonfamily persons contribute significantly to the training of children. What is learned by young persons at school does not always agree with what is taught by parents in the home, thus introducing another source of family conflict. Similarly, as women earn wages, their power and authority tends to escalate somewhat inside the family. If parents with roughly equal authority disagree about what children should be taught and about how children should be cared for, then family conflict can run high. In other words, the potential for strained relations between husband and wife is high in industrial society, and, therefore, many American children live in the midst of severe family conflict.

Contemporary parent-child relationships are also difficult. Perhaps the biggest problem comes from the fact that the home is about the only place where industrial-age children are allowed to show intense emotions and to seek affection and support. Unfortunately, modern parents are all too often unable to meet the basic emotional needs of their children because their own lives are demanding. In the contemporary American nuclear family there are no other adult members to help parents out when children need attention, affection, and support. Therefore, many children go without help from their family (136–37). Finally, since children change tremendously from birth through adolescence, modern parents also face a stiff challenge in recognizing and in adapting to the needs of their children as they grow. With no other adult family members to give assistance, many American parents very likely "lose touch" with older children.

In traditional societies older persons are valuable members of kinship networks and families. Seniors often own the group's material property and possess considerable power and authority. Much has changed. In the United States, where families must frequently change residence so that working adults can remain employed, senior members are a financial and social liability. Today, most of the twenty-five million or so older persons in America live by themselves, away from their children and grandchildren (138). Isolation causes many elderly persons to feel lonely, bored, and worthless. Many seniors suffer failing health and poverty in the absence of family support. For children, however, the cost of segregating seniors may be just as great. Many children who grow up away from their grandparents live without necessary love, care, and supervision.

DELINQUENCY AND FAMILY ENVIRONMENT

In this section we look at family-related factors that exist in the immediate environment surrounding children. Factors such as residence in broken homes, quarreling and fighting, parental abuse and neglect, poor role modeling, and inappropriate discipline and supervision are believed to be primary causes of delinquency and thus have attracted the attention of the majority of researchers studying delinquency.

Broken Homes

A child's home life can be either physically or psychologically broken (Barnes and Teeters, 1959: 181). A *psychologically broken* home is one where quarreling and fighting dominates, where regular verbal abuse of children and parents occurs. *Physically broken* homes are those where one or both parents are missing. Most early social research focused on physically broken homes and indicated that many delinquent children are the products of broken families. Since a physically broken nuclear family offers, at best, only one parent to assume all child care responsibilities, researchers and legal officials suspected that broken families would, at least in many cases, leave children relatively unschooled, uncared for, unsupervised, and, consequently, likely to engage in delinquency. We should note here that the *presumption* by legal officials that children from physically broken homes were *more inclined to be delinquent,* might play a large part in explaining why misbehaving children from physically broken homes were more frequently arrested and processed by juvenile courts (Platt, 1969).

At the turn of the century, a study of thirteen thousand delinquent children revealed that 34 percent were from broken homes (Breckinridge and Abbott, 1912: 91–92). The 1912 finding was interpreted to mean that delinquent children are the products of physically broken homes, even though 66 percent of the delinquent children in this study lived in homes where both parents were present. In 1926, another researcher studied a group of delinquent children who were incarcerated in New York juvenile prisons and compared them to a sample of allegedly nondelinquent children who attended public school in New York (Slawson, 1926). Slawson uncovered further evidence that presumably supported the link between broken homes and delinquency. He reported that 45 percent of the incarcerated children and only 19 percent of the possibly nondelinquent children came from broken homes.

Other researchers, however, found less difference between the levels of delinquency engaged in by children from broken versus intact homes. For example, using a control sample of presumably nondelinquent Illinois school boys and a sample of delinquent children who had been referred in either 1929 or 1930 to the Cook County, Illinois, juvenile court, Shaw and McKay (1932) found that, when differences in age, nationality, and place of residence were taken into account, roughly 36 percent of the school boys and 42 percent of the youth referred to the court were living in broken homes. Most early research, however, indicated that many delinquent children do come from physically broken homes. For example, a summary of studies conducted between 1929 and 1958 reported that children processed by officials for delinquency are almost twice as likely to come from physically broken homes as are youngsters who never get caught. Also revealed was a pattern whereby girls and younger boys who are caught breaking the law are the most likely of all children to be living in shattered homes (Peterson and Becker, 1965), a finding about girls that has been upheld by other studies (Monahan, 1957, 1960; Toby, 1957a; Morris, 1964).

Hirschi (1969: 262) found little difference between the levels of delinquency reported by boys living without a father and boys whose parents were at home. Hirschi did discover that boys who lived with step- or foster-fathers were far more likely to commit delinquent acts than were boys from unbroken homes. Researchers studying middle-class children found no connection at all between delinquency and broken homes, except that in some cases youths from intact homes were actually more delinquent than the children living in broken homes (Hennesey, Richards, and Berk, 1978).

In sum, research seems to indicate that incarcerated children and, in general, girls who get caught, are more likely than other types of children to come from physically broken homes. It is difficult to determine the degree to which these findings are shaped by legal system bias toward children living in physically broken homes. The available data are inconsistent and far from conclusive. While most research suggests that many law-violating children live in physically broken homes, some also demonstrates that many delinquent children live in homes where both parents are present.

Quarreling and Fighting

In the 1940s, a psychiatrist gave psychological tests to one hundred young criminal offenders, and the results showed that many felt hostile, aggressive, and sexually confused as a result of long-term exposure to family tension. In cases where negative emotions were repressed, these young people were often subject to illness and, even when they worked hard to remain law abiding, finally resorted to crime (Abrahamsen, 1949). Abrahamsen concluded that emotionally and sexually undeveloped parents create tense home environments. Tense family life twists the emotions and sexual outlook of children, thus, perpetuating intergenerationally what Abrahamsen calls a "contagion of undevelopment." Abrahamsen noted that immature parents, those whose emotions and ideas are distorted, can hardly expect to produce even-tempered, law-abiding offspring. Instead, the product of home tension is all too often an extremely hostile, confused, and alienated child—a child who is likely to get into trouble with the law.

Other social scientists indicate that quarreling, or any form of conflict between parents, is more closely associated with delinquency than whether or not both parents live at home (Nye, 1957; McCord, McCord, and Thurber, 1962). Some analysts report that many misbehaving junior and senior high school students endure a high level of conflict at home (Norland and Shover, 1977; Norland et al., 1979). It is interesting to note, however, that the study of junior and senior high school students also identified highly delinquent male and female students who experienced little family conflict.

In sum, the available data seem to indicate that quarreling, fighting, and other forms of conflict in the home damage children.

Family tension promotes childhood illness and delinquency. Yet, many children in homes where conflict abounds obey the law, or at least avoid legal detection. Similarly, many children who live in homes where conflict is relatively uncommon nevertheless violate the law on a regular basis. In other words, social scientists are barely scratching the surface in terms of learning about the effects of family conflict on children's behavior. While it is generally understood that fighting and quarreling at home can devastate a child and can propel her/him into a downward spiral of misbehavior, much is left to be learned about the process.

Parental Abuse and Neglect

Considerable evidence indicates that neglect and abuse of children is widespread in American society and that many neglected youngsters become delinquents. For example, according to the U.S. Department of Justice, children who have been abused and neglected, when compared to other children, are arrested at younger ages and twice as often (*Denver Post*, Dec. 18, 1993: 7B). Abused children are usually categorized by state law as either dependent or neglected. A *dependent* child is without proper care or is homeless, but through no fault of his/her parents, guardians, or custodians. *Neglect* occurs when proper child care is lacking because of abandonment, mistreatment, or abuse. Neglect is due to the fault or habits of parents, guardians, or custodians.

Abuse has recently emerged as a special type of neglect to which social scientists and politicians are paying considerable attention. *Child Abuse* is defined as serious trauma experienced by a young person for which there is no apparent reasonable, justifiable explanation. Child abuse can be emotional or physical. Many children endure both types of abuse. Child abuse often involves sexual exploitation (Justice and Justice, 1976; Helfer and Kempe, 1976; Kempe and Kempe, 1978; Strauss, Gelles, and Steinmetz, 1980).

Child abuse is found in all types of families and crosses social class boundaries. However, incidents of child abuse involving lower-class parents are more likely to become part of the public record. Elite and middle-class persons are less often caught abusing children. When middle-class and elite child abusers do come under legal scrutiny, their children can be labeled "accident prone" and can be referred out of the legal system to a medical doctor, counselor, or psychiatrist. Thus, child abuse in America, especially if we believe the public record, is a problem blamed mostly on lower-class parents (Bennett, 1993: 11).

A simple stereotype of the abusing parent includes four elements. First, most child abusers were physically, psychologically, and often sexually mistreated as youngsters. Second, abusing parents know relatively little about the phases of psychological development that normal children pass through. Third, abusive parents are relatively socially isolated and are significantly alienated from community and society. Finally, abusive parents experience considerable stress, are likely to break down emotionally, and are prone to venting anger and frustration on their children (Steele and Pollock, 1968: 103–45; Newberger, Newberger, and Hampton, 1983: 262–68; Kempe and Kempe, 1978).

Experts agree that dependency, neglect, and abuse go hand-in-hand with delinquency (see, e.g., Children's Defense Fund, 1987: 177; Kempe and Kempe, 1984: 188–96; Hunner and Walker, 1981; National Advisory Commission on Juvenile Justice Standards and Goals, 1976; American Bar Association, Institute of Judicial Administration, 1977). Specific connections are hidden by the fact that most dependent, neglected, and delinquent children remain undiscovered by social scientists and legal officials. All abused children, however, are placed under tremendous stress. Stress can lead to depression, heightened aggression, or to a diminished capacity to feel emotions.

Discipline and Supervision of Children

Researchers have reported that parents who either are overly restrictive and punitive or are too lax and lenient raise children who get caught breaking the law. Also, they have maintained that parents who threaten punishment and other forms of discipline but fail to follow through raise delinquent children (Nye, 1938; Glueck and Glueck, 1950). Findings like these were widely accepted until recently when researchers began to assert that restrictive discipline actually keeps many children from getting arrested (McCord and McCord, 1958; McCord, McCord, and Zola, 1959; Jensen and Eve, 1976).

Investigators believe that close parental supervision prevents delinquency. In a study of "good boys," for example, researchers reported that parents continually knew where "good boys" were and that parents kept close tabs on who "good boys" were associating with (Reckless, Dinitz, and Murray, 1956). Close parental supervision can prevent delinquency in two ways. First, parents who stay close to their children and who participate in activities with them set a course of action that is within the prescriptions of law. Thus, children who are closely supervised by their parents have less opportunity to break the law. Second, children who are closely supervised by their parents will come to believe that adult family members know what they are up to, even when no one in authority is around. Thus, fear of getting caught is heightened in closely supervised children.

Close supervision of children is not always possible in urban industrialized societies, where youngsters have considerable access to transportation. Sanders' (1981: 129–36) work illustrates the problems that parents face in supervising children. For example, he reports that shoplifting is a group activity among big-city youth. Many urban children tell their parents that they are setting out into the city on law-abiding business only to steal with friends for profit, pleasure, and enhanced social status.

In sum, parental discipline and supervision probably work best as delinquency prevention mechanisms when children are young and can be closely tethered to the home. Hirschi reports that as parents spend more time working outside the home, the incidence of delinquency among their children increases. Unemployed parents, who spent more time supervising their children, had offspring with the lowest delinquency rates (1969: 237–39). In urban environments, however, as children grow older, and are gripped by "youth subculture," they venture farther and farther away from home where parental discipline and supervision become all but impossible to maintain.

Role Modeling and Teaching Respect for Authority

To be accepted by most groups and organizations, children must learn basic prescribed values, norms, and roles. Experienced persons such as parents, older family members, neighbors, and teachers must serve as guides and instructors while children awkwardly fill new roles in recurring social situations, a process of learning called "socialization." Persons who teach children about values, norms and roles are called "role models" (Shibutani, 1986: 155–57). Role models tolerate and correct the mistakes of younger persons who usually fill relatively simple roles in groups until they can learn to enact more complex and varied roles.

Basic socialization of youth into the community takes several years to achieve, and thus successful role-models must be committed to meeting their children's needs for a long period of time. Role models encourage some types of behavior by praising and materially rewarding children. Role models discourage other types of behavior through administering punishment and withdrawing attention. Role models can teach children either to conform to and obey the law or to resist authority and defy rules. Today, many parents and neighbors either cannot or will not socialize children, leaving education and training of the young to public school teachers, police officers, social workers, and court officials. Most urban children, nevertheless, learn enough to perform a handful of simple adult roles. Unfortunately, many other children are caught in a trap where positive role models do not exist.

Effects of role modeling on children were examined by McCord and McCord (1958) who collected two sets of data on a sample of 253 lower- and lower-middle-class boys (in 1935, when the study began, and again in 1955). The McCords reported that 45 of the boys in their 1935 sample had been raised by criminal fathers. Of the 45 boys raised by criminal fathers, 25 had, themselves, been labeled "criminal" by 1955. Thus, many persons who became criminals were raised by criminal fathers. But 20 children whose fathers were presumably criminal role models conformed to the law or otherwise avoided legal sanction.

Sixty-nine boys in the study were raised by alcoholic or sexually promiscuous fathers. Of this group, 30 had been labeled "criminal" by 1955. Again, however, 39 boys raised by alcoholic or sexually promiscuous fathers had conformed enough to avoid criminal conviction. Of the 139 boys in the sample with noncriminal fathers, 49 had been convicted of crimes by 1955, leaving 90 children who escaped criminal conviction with noncriminal fathers.

The McCord study suggests that boys with criminal fathers are somewhat more likely to be found guilty of a crime than are boys with fathers who avoid conviction. Boys who were most likely to become criminal had criminal fathers who rejected them and passive or rejecting parents who employed inconsistent patterns of discipline. However, not all boys raised by criminal fathers and

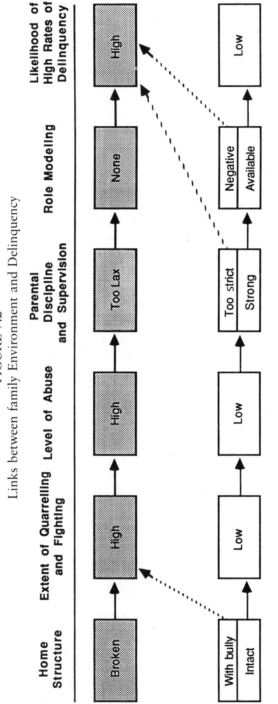

FIGURE 7.2
Links between family Environment and Delinquency

inconsistent, passive, or rejecting parents were convicted of criminal law violation, a finding that might be partly explained by another study that indicates that many criminal parents actually pressure their children to obey the law (Sykes and Matza, 1957). Other researchers report that children who receive conflicting input from their parents tend to interpret the law as they choose (Jaffe, 1969). Also, children who respect and admire their parents tend to feel the same ways about other adults in authoritative positions (Hirschi, 1969). Children who are attached to their parents and who are loved and nurtured by family members are less likely to become delinquent than are youth who are isolated from, and rejected by, family (Jensen, 1972), even when influences outside the home encourage law violation (Linden and Hackler, 1973; Hepburn, 1977).

SUMMARY

There are many possible connections among kinship networks, families, and juvenile delinquency. Recall that figure 7.1 outlines the most important of these links. The outer ring of this figure identifies social norms that push families along a developmental path that renders them poorly equipped to care for children. The middle circle of figure 7.1 lists social change-related factors that contribute to high rates of juvenile delinquency.

Figure 7.2 identifies links between family environment and juvenile delinquency. The top row of boxes shows aspects of family environment that increase the likelihood of delinquency. In other words, physically broken homes (or intact ones with a bully), high levels of quarreling and fighting, high levels of abuse, parental discipline that is too lax (or too strict) and no (or negative) role modeling dramatically increase the chances of a child's becoming delinquent. The bottom row of boxes shows the features of home life that keep children out of trouble with the law. Intact homes, minimal quarreling, fighting and abuse, strong discipline and available positive role models discourage delinquency. We should remember that no single family-related factor, by itself, causes delinquency.

CHAPTER 8

Schools and Delinquency

INTRODUCTION

When families fail problem children in industrial societies, those children often turn to friends and schools for help. Dedicated teachers and administrators throughout the United States provide love, acceptance, care, guidance, and instruction for millions of children who would otherwise go without. Teachers, administrators and schools thus prevent or minimize a good deal of delinquency. We should also note that problems at school may be caused by children themselves and/or problems at home as well as by negative forces at school (Chesney-Lind and Shelden, 1992: 189; Inciardi, Horowitz, and Pottieger, 1993: 137–49, 198).

However, many problem children experience schools as harsh, forbidding, and meaningless places, where alienation and lack of caring abound (Donmoyer and Kos, 1993b; Weis and Fine, 1993; Wollons, 1993). In this sense, schools can encourage misbehavior and delinquency. Critics argue that American schools function primarily as rigid, biased credentialling mechanisms, where some students are favored and given credentials allowing entry into preferred occupations and where others are discouraged, denied access to important credentials, and thus relegated to the bottom of the occupational ladder (Illich, 1975; Foster, 1993; Gandara, 1993).

In this chapter we explore connections between schools and juvenile delinquency. Education and schooling are not always the same thing (Wells, 1921: 948). Education involves acquiring survival skills as well as social skills. *Education* can be defined as "the deliberate or purposeful creation, evocation or transmission of knowledge, abilities, skills and values" (Silberman, 1970: 6). *Schooling*, on the other hand, is what happens in schools. Children are educated by many means other than schools. In fact, for most of human history, formal education was not essential; members of agricultural societies learned necessary survival and social skills at home within their kinship networks. As large religious and political organizations evolved, education expanded considerably in the form of schooling. Schooling involves hiring tutors or teachers to instruct and supervise children. Schooling requires that children convene outside the home for instruction in a special place called the "classroom" or "school." Churches and governments have utilized schools throughout history to teach children skills and to disseminate knowledge, values, and motivations that insure cooperation and good citizenship. Although reserved for a minority of children until recently, formal education is quite old and has been found, for example, in large mass civilizations like that of Egypt as early as 4000 B.C. (Turner, 1985: 371).

Formal education is neither enjoyable nor rewarding for many children. In fact, today, nearly seven hundred thousand American high school students drop out each year, accounting for $240 billion in lost earnings and unpaid taxes. African American and Hispanic children drop out of school, in proportionate terms, far more often than Anglos (Donmoyer and Kos, 1993b: 7). There is some evidence that a higher proportion of girls than boys who are engaged in serious delinquency drop out of school (Inciardi, Horowitz, and Pottieger: 139). Millions of other American children stay in school but attend sporadically and fail to learn much of consequence (Donmoyer and Kos, 1993b). African American students are expelled at four to five times the rate for Anglos. African American students are two to three times more likely than Anglos to be labeled "learning disabled" (Mitchell, 1993: 396).

Why do so many children fail at school? Why do such large numbers of students find school uninteresting and worthless, especially when it comes to solving personal and job-related problems? Friedenberg a vocal critic of schooling in the United States, argues that adults in American society loathe adolescence and believe "that it cannot be allowed to proceed without massive intervention" (1963: 4). Holt, another critic of American schooling, asserts that the young must be induced "to abandon their barbarism and assimilate the folkways of normal adult life." Thus, adults "are inclined to tolerate a shade more brutality in school . . . than the law allows." Schools in the United States "remain about what they always have been, bad places for children or . . . anyone to be in . . . there is still a lot of cruelty in them" (1969: 23).

A less extreme perspective is offered by Weis and Fine, who point out that, for the most part, American educators silence voices of dissent at school, purportedly in order to prevent controversy and discomfort. Thus, many children who disagree with their teachers, with school policies, or with prohibitions against meaningful discourse are likely to grow alienated and become problematic (1993: 1–6).

Lerman (1993) identifies yet another dimension of student *and* teacher disenchantment. Lerman explains that the U.S. economy is changing, offering proportionately fewer jobs for unskilled workers and requiring higher skill levels as a condition of employment. Lerman argues that most schools in the United States stress acquisition of abstract academic capabilities rather than concrete, job-related, tool-oriented skills. Thus, non-college-prep students often see no meaningful connection between schooling and success on the job, leading them to develop indifference, if not hostility, toward teachers and the curriculum.

Links among schools, problem children, and juvenile delinquency are complex, and they can be placed into three categories. First, the organization of schools, though an abstract and subtle influence, can create social conditions that encourage many children to misbehave and thus can expose children to heightened risks of becoming delinquent. Second, the organization of classrooms, which also exerts an abstract and subtle influence, can likewise encourage many children to misbehave and to engage in delinquent acts. Both school and classroom organization may encourage delinquency indirectly, by creating social conditions that alienate children, make possible withdrawal from school, and result in widespread misbehavior. It is difficult to scientifically establish links between delinquency and school and classroom organization. Consequently, delinquency researchers have, for the most part, ignored these influences. Instead, delinquency researchers devote most of their energy to studying a third type of link between schools and delinquency, namely characteristics of students themselves. In the following pages we will examine all three types of educational influences.

School Organization and Delinquency

Schools in industrial societies develop organizational logic that helps produce learning problems, misbehavior, and delinquency

(Boocock, 1972: x–xi; Polk and Schafer, 1972; Donmoyer, 1993). Almost all American children between the ages of seven and sixteen are required by state law to attend school. Thus, whether or not they want to, approximately forty-five million American children attend public or private schools (Grant and Snyder, 1986: 8, 36). In order to accomodate millions of children, public schools are organized into large, bureaucratized systems. For example, the largest school system in the United States, that of New York City, enrolls more than 900,000 children, employs more than 46,000 teachers, and operates almost 1,000 schools. Even the tenth largest school system in the nation, that of Fairfax County, Virginia, enrolls more than 120,000 students, employs more than 6,600 teachers and operates more than 170 schools (60–61). Educational policy in large school systems is set by administrative personnel who have little day-to-day contact with students and teachers. This means that children in urban areas have little control over what happens to them at school.

In terms of power and authority, students are at the bottom of the the organization structure of primary and secondary schools (fig. 8.1). In fact, the bigger and more bureaucratized a school becomes, the more likely that critical decisions about education will be made by principals and other administrative employees instead of by teachers and students (Goslin, 1965: 30). The bigger and more bureaucratized schools become, the more likely that

FIGURE 8.1
Organizational Structure of Elementary and Secondary Schools

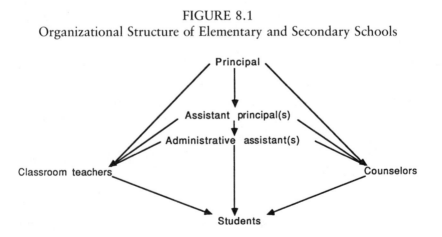

administrators will value above all else the maintainence of order and control among students (Boocock, 1972: 174).

Counselors and teachers must conform to the directives of the administration if they are to keep their jobs. Many counselors and teachers are given handbooks that specify the following acts as unacceptable behavior for students: being truant, tardy, stealing, fighting, scuffling, necking or petting, smoking, running in the corridors, defacing or damaging school property, driving cars and motor bikes, setting off false alarms, throwing snowballs, smoking across from the school, loitering on streets near the school, and misbehaving in the homeroom, classroom, or elsewhere on campus (Schafer, 1972: 149). In other words, counselors and teachers are required to look for a wide range of behavioral infractions that could earn children deviant status in the school. Thus, many teachers and counselors fill two roles, serving both as educators of children and as law enforcement officers. School administrators pass down to teachers and counselors a logic of education that forces the categorization of children into bright, dull, culturally deprived, and troublesome groups. Children so labeled fit readily into tracking systems, where students are segregated from each other, and where some are given "deviant" labels (Polk and Schafer, 1972: 4). Many students grow alienated from the bureaucratic structure of schools and form subcultural groups as a means of defense (Inciardi, Horowitz, and Pottieger, 1993: 150–71). Student subcultural groups may support and encourage behaviors that schools find undesirable for children, thus setting up a dynamic where some young persons learn to deviate while they attend school.

Since the late 1960s, students have gone to court to attempt to win basic legal rights. School officials in these cases cite state-level education law and the common law principle of *in loco parentis*—that school authorities should act in place of parents while children are at school—as reasons for establishing relatively harsh rules and regulations about, for example, punishment and suspension, freedom of speech and expression, and dress and hair styles (Goldstein, 1969: 373; Reutter, 1970; Grossberg, 1993).

In 1969, the U.S. Supreme Court ruled that students do not relinquish their constitutional rights to freedom of speech because they are at school. The Court further ruled that wearing black armbands was a political statement and was, therefore, protected by the First Amendment (*Tinker v. Des Moines Independent School District* [383 U.S. 503]). In 1975, the U.S. Supreme Court ruled that students could not be suspended unless school officials first employed fair fact-finding procedures (*Goss v. Lopez* [419 U.S. 565]). Also in 1975, the Court warned school officials that they could be sued and held liable for damages if they denied students constitutional rights (*Wood v. Strickland* [420 U.S. 308]). In the same year, however, the Court ruled in favor of *in loco parentis,* declaring that corporal punishment is allowable and is not cruel and unusual punishment as defined by the Eighth Amendment (*Ingraham v. Wright* [430 U.S. 651]). More recently the U.S. Supreme Court held that students could not be forced to salute the flag in violation of their religious beliefs. Several state-level court decisions, in 1969 and 1970, awarded students the right to determine for themselves appropriate hair and dress styles (Bartollas, 1993: 312).

Court decisions, described above, in theory awarded students many rights guaranteed to adults by the United States Constitution. Some school administrators and other experts believe that, by awarding students constitutionally guaranteed rights, courts seriously impede school officials in their quest to fight violence, property crime, drug use, and disruptive behavior at school (Cohen, 1985: 80–81; Rubel and Goldsmith, 1980; *Daily Times-Call,* Jan. 5, 1994: 9A). However, it is also possible that many school officials in the United States are not aware of court decisions awarding students rights or that many educators choose to ignore laws made by the courts because enforcement is lax where they work. To date, school officials still retain the right to use corporal punishment, expulsion, and many other negative sanctions in response to student misbehavior (Donmoyer and Kos, 1993: 192; Inciardi, Horowitz, and Pottieger, 1993: 137–49, 198).

Classroom Organization and Delinquency

Schools are divided into classrooms where the bulk of each child's journey away from barbarism is supposed to occur. For most children, the classroom "is a first initiation into the austerity of duty. Serious life now has begun" (Boocock, 1972: 123). There are two basic status positions inside the classroom, teacher and student. Teachers control classrooms by creating seating arrangements and work groups, by rewarding students for conformity and achievement, and by punishing for dissent and failure (Goslin, 1965: 24–5; Glasser, 1969: 1–13; Cummins, 1993; Fine, 1993). While teachers have relatively low ranking in the status hierarchy of the school, and while many decisions about education are made for teachers by administrators, the classroom activities of teachers are loosely monitored. Durkheim observed that teachers have "indisputable authority" (in Boocock, 1972: 126). In disputes with students, Boocock notes that "the teacher nearly always wins" (128).

Silberman argues that in order "to survive in school, as in other 'total institutions,' students are forced to develop a variety of adaptive strategies and attitudes." Survival, in the form of completing each disjointed classroom task, becomes the primary goal (1970: 146–47). Good students in all types of schools can become docile, passive, and overly dependent on their teachers for direction. For example, Donmoyer observed, after teaching in a Harlem school *and* a school in an affluent suburb, that many students at both schools were disadvantaged. The Harlem children often lived lives, at home and in school, dominated by lack of structure and chaos. However, children in the affluent suburban school suffered from *too much structure*. Successful students all too often accept and assimilate, without criticism or question, whatever teachers give to them. Children who do well in school learn to be patient while enduring countless interruptions to the classroom routine. Successful students are able to deal peacefully with adults in authoritative positions. Dominant middle-class values dictate that children compete against each other. School children withstand constant testing and evaluation, which can be used to their disadvantage (Boocock, 1972: 126; Haney, 1993).

Good teachers overcome many of the structural obstacles to education by earning the respect and attention of students and by finding "ways to soften the dullness and harshness of the daily grind" (Boocock, 1972: 129). Good teachers, however, are relatively rare. Even though they are "decent, intelligent and caring people," most schoolteachers go about their classroom activities in a state of mindlessness that precludes their thinking "seriously about educational purpose" (Silberman, 1970: 11; also see Foster, 1993). Many teachers are overly concerned about preserving discipline, control and order in the classroom (Boocock, 1972: 129).

Glasser argues that failure in school is the inevitable result of classrooms where teachers and students are not allowed to feel loved, and are unable to develop feelings of self-worth (1969: 14). In classrooms devoid of love, where few opportunities are available to develop a sense of self-worth, teachers are likely to retreat into a mindless commitment to rule enforcement and task achievement. Students react by forming peer cultures that often work against educational goals and by utilizing neutralizing, apple-polishing, or withdrawal tactics (Boocock, 1972: 128).

A good example of this phenomenon is offered by Fine (1993), who studied a group of adolescent females, their perspectives on sexuality and allowable sex education in their schools. Fine reports that "evidence of sexuality is everywhere within public high schools" but that "official sexuality education occurs sparsely" and "sexuality is managed inside schools" (77). Fine identifies four dimensions of sexuality, namely, sexuality as violence, sexuality as victimization, sexuality as individual morality (stressing premarital abstinence), and sexuality as desire, pleasure, or entitlement. She reports that discourse about sex as desire, pleasure, or entitlement remains "a whisper inside the official work of U.S. public schools" (79). Whenever desire, pleasure, or entitlement is discussed, usually out of protest or as an interruption to a superficial planned lesson focusing on male heterosexuality, teachers quickly remind students, especially females, of the negative consequences that can result from premarital sex. Fine observed that, in order to avoid being ridiculed and harassed, sexually active children (especially females), young persons who had little or no sexual experience, and homosexual and lesbian children, rarely participated in classroom discussions about sexuality.

Fine reports that sexual meanings voiced by adolescent females are rarely simple and are "informed by peers, culture, religion, violence, history, passion, authority, rebellion, body, past and future, and gender and racial relations of power" (81). She concludes that if young women cannot adequately discuss desire and other elements of sexuality at school without fearing punishment, they will do so elsewhere. Fine warns that "while too few safe spaces exist for adolescent women's exploration of sexual subjectivities, there are all too many dangerous spots for their exploitation (82–83). She fears that silencing of children's complex thinking about sexuality is so pervasive in U.S. schools that it might very well constitute a form of serious and debilitating discrimination, especially against females (99).

FIGURE 8.2
Model of Educational Influences on Childhood Behavior

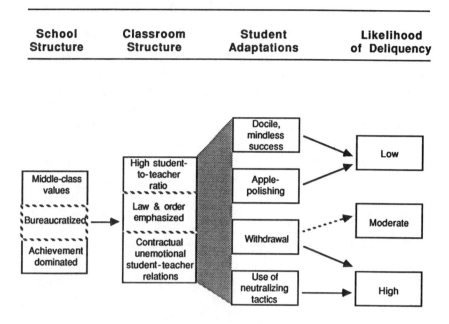

School Structure	Classroom Structure	Student Adaptations	Likelihood of Deliquency

Figure 8.2 diagrams a set of hypothesized effects of school and classroom structure on childhood behavior. The leftmost column of this figure represents the assertion that American schools are bureaucratized and that achievement orientation and other middle-class values are emphasized. The next column of boxes to the right asserts that classrooms, because of high student-to-teacher ratios, are organized around the themes of law and order. Relationships are unemotional and contractual. The third column of boxes lists possible student adaptations. Many alienated but nevertheless successful students adapt by becoming docile and mindless, and by apple-polishing. Less successful children withdraw or employ neutralizing tactics; this increases the likelihood that they will engage in delinquency.

STUDENT CHARACTERISTICS AND DELINQUENCY

We saw in the last section that school and classroom organization create learning environments that push many children toward misbehavior. In this section we examine the effects of achievement, social standing, alienation, peer subculture, truancy, expulsion, and dropping out on childrens' school experiences.

Achievement

Achievement in formal educational systems is usually defined as performing satisfactorily (or better) on tests and as earning passing (or higher) grades for courses taken. School failure, on the other hand, involves performing poorly on tests, receiving low or failing grades for courses, and being held back when successful children are advanced to the next grade-level (Haney, 1993: 46–56). Kvaraceus reported that school children who receive low grades are treated like failures (1945: 140). Schafer and Polk observed that, for many children in the United States, failure in school begins early and occurs regularly. Failure accumulates, and at some point in a child's academic career, usually in junior or senior high school, provokes negative reactions from teachers, administrators, and successful students. Schafer and Polk noted that children who fail in school *and* who are treated negatively by important others at school are likely to engage in delinquency (1967: 230). Research sponsored by the President's Task Force on Juvenile Delinquency revealed that boys failing in school are seven times more likely than successful boys to be recognized by authorities as delinquents (1967: 51). Liazos (1978) affirmed the connection between school failure and high delinquency risk.

In fact, school failure seems to be closely associated with delinquency wherever and whenever the connection is studied (Empey and Lubeck, 1971; Gold and Mann, 1972; Kelly and Balch, 1971; Polk, Frease, and Richmond, 1974; Polk and Halferty, 1972; Polk and Richmond, 1972; Inciardi, Horowitz, and Pottieger, 1993). However, school failure alone does not explain why all children become delinquent. For example, all of the studies cited above found children who were failing in school but who were not recognized by authorities as delinquents. Also, some children who do well in school engage in delinquency.

Social Standing

Children bring two types of social standing to most school experiences. First, each schoolchild is evaluated by others in terms of her/his family social class level. Most American families fall into either lower-, middle-, or elite-class categories. Since elite children are usually segregated from other American youth, most public school students are part of middle- or lower-class families. Albert Cohen (1955) reported that working class boys are forced to attend schools operated by middle-class teachers who uphold middle-class educational values. Cohen pointed out that working-class children are at a considerable disadvantage when competing against middle-class students. Cohen concluded that working class youth who fail at school reject middle-class values and form delinquent subcultural groups. Toby (1957b) found that misbehavior in lower-class school children was at least partly due to the family's inability to offer encouragement to do school work and to family failure to help children acquire verbal skills.

Polk and Schafer observe that schools, in order to identify and reward above average and excellent students, must develop corresponding mechanisms for discouraging and punishing children who are labeled "below average" or "failing" performers. Decisions about whether children receive success or failure labels in school are made by teachers and administrators, partly on the basis of individual performance on tests and on grades earned. However, teachers and administrators also excercise social class and ethnic biases when evaluating children (Polk and Schafer, 1972: 23). Lower-class and minority children who perform poorly or who fail are stereoptyped by teachers, administrators and successful students as dumb and as having limited potential. Students who are labeled as "poor performers" or "failures" are locked out of subsequent opportunities for achievement and success at school and are pushed into deviant roles (Schafer, 1972: 153; Sapon-Chevin, 1993).

The second type of social standing that children acquire is school social status. School social status is based upon teacher, administrator, and student assessments of each child's intelligence level, task performance capabilities, social skills, physical attractiveness, and family social class level. Polk and Schafer believe that "school experience is emerging as a fundamental determinant of adolescent status" and that "the manner in which a youngster is identified within the status system in the school exerts a basic influence on the development of deviant careers" (Polk and Schafer, 1972: 21–22). In the United States public schools serve the needs of many different types of children (Schafer, Olexa, and Polk, 1972:

35). American educators developed and implemented tracking systems within schools in order to separate children into different
ability groups. Kelly and Pink (1982) report that educators begin
stereotyping and tracking students early in elementary school. The
track a child is on becomes a major determinant of school social
status. Most common are two track schools where students are
separated into college prep and non-college-ability groupings. Some
schools have as many as six tracks for children (Damico and Roth,
1993).

Schafer, Alexa, and Polk studied the academic tracking of 1,154
students in two midwestern high schools and found that 83 percent
of the children from white-collar homes and 48 percent of those
from blue-collar homes were assigned to the college prep track.
Seventy-one percent of all Anglo children but only 30 percent of the
African American youngsters were assigned to the college prep track
(1972: 36–37). They concluded that "children from low income
and minority group families more often find themselves in low-
ability groups and noncollege-bound tracks than in high-ability
groups or college-bound tracks" (34; also see Haney, 1993: 72–73).

Once children are placed into a low-status ability group at
school they are stereotyped as dumb and as having limited potential. Thus, it is not easy for a child to escape a low-ability track
(Fine, 1993: 98). Consequently, tracking systems assure that non-
college-bound students have constricted opportunities for achieving success at school. Under the restraints of tracking, many non-
college-bound youth are likely to suffer from alienation, weakened
motivation, and feelings of failure. Rebellious behavior can result.
Non-college-bound children are more likely than college-bound
students to misbehave at school and to engage in delinquency
(Hargreaves, 1967; Kelly and Pink, 1982; Schafer, Alexa, and
Polk, 1972).

Alienation

Alienation, defined as "withdrawal of human energy from the
roles, statuses, and norms of the social order" (Nisbet, 1970: 55),
can take two forms in school children. First, there is alienation of
the individual, in which a child grows upset by and anxiety ridden
over frustrating, painful, and unfair features of the school (Shibutani, 1986: 326). For example, a minority child who is regularly
forced to interact with racist teachers or any child whose teacher is

unfair may feel pain, frustration, and anxiety (Foster, 1993; Gandara, 1993). A child who responds by withdrawing energy from school activities is suffering from individual alienation. Glasser (1965) notes that children who are severely exploited can experience a form of extreme personal alienation. For example, a child who is sexually abused might partly escape from the experience by withdrawing from reality and by engaging in prohibited behaviors.

In its second form, alienation manifests itself as a characteristic of groups of children within a school. Shibutani observes that frustrated, anxiety-ridden, dissatisfied individuals often find each other, communicate, and "stimulate one another in a circular manner, thus reinforcing one another's feelings" (1986: 326). Collective or group alienation creates for some schoolchildren an emotional climate of heightened anxiety and extreme dissatisfaction.

Several facets of public school life can have an alienating effect on children. School performance seems to be a very important determinant of alienation. In general, children who perform poorly on tests and who earn poor grades tend to be more alienated from their teachers and from school than do students who test well and earn better grades. Unsuccessful, alienated school children tend to commit more acts of delinquency than do successful, presumably more involved, students (Empey and Lubeck, 1971: 96–97; Hindelang, 1973; Hirschi, 1969: 113–32; Reiss and Rhodes, 1961; Inciardi, Horowitz, and Pottieger: 121–23, 137–43).

Another major cause of alienation in children appears to be the perceived irrelevance of schooling. Alienated children who misbehave believe that school is not helping them to prepare for the future (Hirschi, 1969: 170–83; Stinchcombe, 1964: 70). Schools teach abstract skills. Children want schools to teach more relevant job-related subjects (Lerman, 1993). Paul Goodman asserts that American schools cannot be more relevant because "there get to be fewer and fewer jobs that are necessary or unquestionably useful; that require energy and draw upon some of one's best capacities; and that can be done keeping one's honor and dignity." Goodman concludes that at the root of alienation among adolescent students is the fact that when schooling is over there will not be enough meaningful, useful, and honorable jobs to go around (1960: 17). Weis, in a more recent study of male Anglo working-class students, observed the same process (1993: 237–58). If Goodman and Weis are correct, then students who perceive that the future job market holds little for them could have trouble committing enough energy to school to succeed.

Large public schools also offer cold, impersonal, and segregated learning environments. Violence and theft are endemic to large schools. Thus, the very structure or social climate of the American public school can alienate students. Similarly, children who are forced into passive, docile student roles feel more like inanimate objects than like important participants in learning. No doubt, some children who are treated like objects withdraw energy from school. Whatever causes alienation, once children withdraw energy from schooling they are headed for trouble. Alienated children very often form deviant groups. Alienated students cut class and flirt with expulsion. Alienated students are likely to drop out of school.

Peer Subcultures

By the time children are in school for a few years, their living environments have changed tremendously. Most important, as children grow older, their habitat, or area of travel, expands considerably and includes more and more social environments that operate beyond the control of adult authorities. Also important is the fact that school children in industrial societies pass back and forth between three somewhat connected social groupings: families, schools, and peer subcultures (Gold, 1970).

Most children live at home with their families throughout elementary and secondary school. Throughout childhood, family members exert an important influence on behavior. Children also spend several hours a day at school, where they are under the control of teachers and administrators, and where they are influenced by another set of values and role-expectations. Children form a third type of group called "peer subcultures." Subcultures are groups "whose members share values and beliefs and abide by norms that differ, to varying degrees from those held by the majority" (Turner, 1985: 71; see also Miller, 1958a; Yinger, 1960). Peer subculture provides children with a source of approval, status, and acceptance that can rival families and schools in importance. Peer subculture provides children with opportunities to express compulsive independence from parents, teachers, and other adult authorities (Goldstein, 1991). In Parsons's words, "on the one hand the peer group may be regarded as a field for the exercise of independence from adult control; hence it is not surprising that it is often a focus of . . . adult-*disapproved* behavior; when this happens, it is the seed bed from which the extremists go over into delinquency" (1951: 206–7).

Peer subcultures operate in all junior and senior high schools. Their orientation toward the dominant culture of teachers, administrators, and parents ranges from passive compliance to outright rejection and hostility. Boocock (1972) asserts that, due to societal trends, such as increasing ethnic segregation and widespread group conflict, students are divided into two distinguishable types of groupings (239). First, there are successful groups, which are reasonably compliant and identify closely enough with their teachers to embrace the school norms that require achievement-motivation, behavioral conformity, and academic performance. Even successful peer subcultures will support some values, beliefs, and behaviors that conflict with adult authority. For example, drinking, drug use, situational violence, and premarital sexual activity are often condoned and encouraged by groups of students who are otherwise relatively successful in school. Adults encourage the formation of successful peer subcultures by infiltrating and organizing activities. Cub Scouts, Girl Scouts, Big Brother, school athletics, and theatrics all serve as examples of adult-controlled peer subcultures.

A second type of peer subculture consists of children who fail socially and academically, students who reject the basic adult goals of achievement motivation, competition, performance, and success (Gaines, 1991: 3–12). Some failures are "active rebels, who disrupt the smooth functioning of the system and who are viewed in a very negative way by most school personnel." Other school failures are "passive withdrawers, who simply mark time in school until they are old enough to drop out" (Boocock, 1972: 239). Parsons notes that the distinction between college-goers and noncollege-goers could be a primary source of selection into successful or failure peer subcultures (1968: 208). In general, successful peer groups allow and encourage student identification with teachers, while failure subcultures do not. For example, Schafer, Alexa, and Polk discovered in their study of midwestern high school students that children assigned to a low-achiever track were also involved in a student subculture that "stressed and rewarded antagonistic attitudes and behavior toward teachers and all they stood for." Conversely, students put on a high-achiever track were supported by friends who encouraged cooperation with teachers. "The result was a progressive polarization and hardening of the high- and low-stream subcultures . . . and a progressively greater negative attitude across stream lines, with quite predictable consequences" (1972: 48).

Alienated children, especially failures, tend to form peer subcultures that encourage and support delinquency. Thrasher (1927) observed this connection and noted that gangs become important to unsuccessful students because it is there that some understanding, acceptance, and freedom from adult authority can be achieved. Karacki and Toby (1962) report that peer subcultural values and activities hold more importance for failing students than do prescribed school values and activities. A survey of students conducted by Polk and Richmond revealed academic failures spend more time than successful students with nonschool friends, off campus, engaging in activities not involving school personnel (1972: 65–69). Gold indicates that the least delinquent boys he studied were academically successful and had nondelinquent friends, while the most delinquent boys were failing in school and associated with other delinquents (1970: 125).

How can schools be made more attractive to larger numbers of students? Lerman (1993) argues convincingly that educators in the United States must do far better at preparing children for future jobs that will pay well but will also require high levels of skill. He suggests that American schools abandon traditional college prep and vocational education tracking strategies and, instead, implement a nationwide apprenticeship program, offering students on-the-job training as a significant part of the school curriculum. On-the-job training would eliminate the problems of outdated philosophies and obsolete equipment that plague school-based vocational education programs. On-the-job training would expose children to positive role models who might be able to neutralize some negative peer influences.

Chesney-Lind and Shelden describe basic components of effective educational programs: (1) understanding teachers, (2) effectively combining basic education with teaching of practical skills, (3) using discussion groups, and (4) providing meaningful rewards for desired behavior (189). Donmoyer endorses "a rich array of approaches." However, he notes that educators in the United States, when implementing reform aimed at maximizing "the likelihood of school success for at risk students," usually restrict themselves to "five ideal types of programs and practices: . . . supplemental programs . . . whole-school restructuring programs . . . therapy programs . . . intervention team approaches . . . and community/home/school partnership programs" (1993: 212).

Grassroots programs that provide good teachers with monetary rewards and make available money for special activities and programs might help. For example, over the last eight years, a wealthy Colorado resident has given teachers at two Denver schools $120,000, to be used for faculty awards, for activities aimed at increasing parental involvement in school, and for dealing with the issue of violence (*Denver Post,* Dec. 18, 1993: 20A). On a grander scale, a wealthy American couple recently donated $500 million to the federal government, to be used to "stem the violence eroding the nations schools." They hope that their donation helps to "establish schools that are centers of excellence where children will want to learn and their parents will want to be involved; places where teachers will be able to teach" (*Daily Times-Call,* Dec. 26, 1993: B5). No specifics have been announced about how the money will be spent.

Truancy, Expulsion, and Dropping Out

'Truancy' is a legal concept that is defined by compulsory school attendance laws. In Texas, for example, *truancy* is defined as "conduct which violates the compulsory school attendance laws" (Miller et al., 1976: 55). All states have compulsory school attendance laws that obligate children to be present in school for most of their childhood. Most states categorize truant children as youth in need of supervision; this means that students who cut school can be arrested, incarcerated, and otherwise processed by legal authorities.

Many American children start missing class as early as elementary school, often with the support and cooperation of parents and guardians (Inciardi, Horowitz, and Pottieger, 1993: 140–41). By junior high, absenteeism is widespread, and it continues at a high rate throughout high school. Officials view cutting school as a serious act. Several surveys reveal that school administrators consider truancy and dropping out to be critical problems (Duke, 1978: 325–330; "2.4 Million Children," 1976; Wright, 1978).

Missing school is common in the United States. Grant and Snyder estimate that approximately 10 percent of American pupils who are enrolled in school fail to attend on a daily basis (1986: 30–31). Consequently, many big-city teachers must find ways to effectively supervise and instruct students where an average of six to eight are absent each day from a class of thirty-five (Glasser, 1969: 146). Veteran ditchers are so devoted to skipping class that they give every reason imaginable to explain irregular attendance (148). Irrelevance and boredom, the demands of an exciting life outside school, and family and employment obligations are favorite justifications for skipping class.

Many students who are illegally absent from school know how to play the game, fabricating allowable excuses for their deviance. Students who play the game flirt with acquiring a delinquent label, but a large number go undetected by school and legal authorities. Many students, especially lower-class and minority children, will not or do not know how to mask truancy. Youth who are flagrant about cutting school and who get caught are often labeled "deviants." Troublesome truants are shunted off to segregated classes, into isolated specialized schools, or on to the juvenile court system (Polk and Schafer: 270). Many investigators report that high proportions of delinquents skip school on a regular basis (Thrasher, 1927; Healy and Bronner, 1936; Glueck and Glueck, 1950; Ferguson, 1952; Reckless and Dinitz, 1972; Walberg, 1972; Inciardi, Horowitz, and Pottieger, 1993: 140).

Expulsion (or suspension) is a mechanism used by school administrators to rid themselves of children who would otherwise cause problems (Birman and Natriello, 1980: 170; Inciardi, Horowitz, and Pottieger, 1993: 198). *Expulsion* is defined as a labeling process that disqualifies misbehaving children, including habitual truants, from attending school (270). Some students are embarrassed and punished by expulsion; others are delighted. Youth who are expelled from school and who do not have full-time employment run a high risk of being labeled "delinquent." Expulsion exposes many rejected children to a form of culture shock that predisposes them toward misbehavior (Sexton, 1967: 96). As many as two hundred children are expelled each year from a large school (Bartollas, 1990: 304). In the words of one school administrator in charge of discipline, "I see my job as the pilot of a hijacked plane. My job is to throw the hijacker off, even if that means bodily" (in Fine, 1993: 97). Reflecting a nationwide trend, Colorado students are being expelled in record numbers, due largely to a new state law requiring mandatory, often long-term, expulsion for students caught on campus with drugs or weapons (*Daily Times-Call*, Dec. 29, 1993: 3A).

Dropping out also puts children at high risk of being labeled "delinquent." Dropouts are persons who do not graduate from high school and who are not enrolled in school. In 1980, approximately 13 percent of all American children aged 5–17 years were not enrolled in school (Grant and Snyder, 1986: 30–31). In 1983, approximately 2 percent of all fourteen and fifteen year olds and 7 percent of all sixteen and seventeen year olds in the United States had dropped out of school (76). Currently, approximately seven hundred thousand American children drop out of high school each year (Donmoyer and Kos, 1993: 7). Principals of affluent schools predict that around 7 percent of their children will drop out. Principals of lower-class schools project that as many as 44 percent of the students will leave without a diploma (Brookover and Erickson, 1975: 367). Students in lower achievement tracks are more likely to drop out (338). Yet there is evidence that most dropouts have the ability to finish high school (Sexton, 1967: 95; Stevenson and Ellsworth, 1993). A national study of American children indicated that many leave school due to financial problems forcing their desperate need to get a job (Boocock, 1972: 40–41). Dropouts who find employment usually end up with jobs featuring low pay, poor working conditions, and intermittent layoffs. Many dropouts remain unemployed (Goslin, 1965: 52). Unemployed dropouts have "a good chance of becoming delinquent" (U.S. Dept. of Health, Education and Welfare, Office of Education, 1967: 278). Children also drop out of school because of irrelevent curricula; uncaring and negative teachers, counselors, and administrators; and insensitive school policies (Stevenson and Ellsworth: 260).

A number of studies give some sense of how dropouts are perceived (National Advisory Council on Supplementary Centers and Services, 1975: 2; Boocock, 1972: 291; Brookover and Erickson, 1975: 271; Stevenson and Ellsworth, 1993: 260–62). According to these studies, dropouts are generally stereotyped as failures who

- feel hostility toward adult authority
- are underachievers

- lack motivation
- cannot function in the classroom
- are often tardy
- exhibit high absenteeism
- are unable to establish future career goals
- do not participate in school activities
- experience serious financial problems
- lead a stressful home life

A study of approximately twenty-six hundred high school students indicated that the rate of delinquency among children who drop out is much higher than it is for those who remain in school. Delinquent behavior appears to increase immediately after children drop out of school, but it eventually subsides as youngsters find employment and marry (Elliott and Voss, 1974). Approximately 85 percent of the children imprisoned in the United States are school dropouts (Boocock, 1972: 316). Reflecting a national trend, increasing numbers of Colorado children are dropping out of school. According to a Colorado education commissioner, "we have more and more kids who just don't see school in any form as the answer to their needs" (*Denver Post,* Dec. 15, 1993: 1A). In the words of Richard Riley, U.S. Secretary of Education, "too many youth see no connection between their education and their lives outside the classroom" (*Daily Camera,* June 12, 1993: 7A).

In summary, figure 8.3 brings together in diagrammatic form links among school organization, classroom organization, student characteristics, and juvenile delinquency. On the left side of the figure, the first two circles list features of school and classroom organization that predispose children toward misbehavior. These factors by themselves, however, do not cause delinquency. In the middle of figure 8.3, a top row of circles displays the factors that insure a low likelihood of juvenile delinquency. A bottom row of circles shows the factors that prompt deviant adaptations to school life. Figure 8.3 shows that delinquency is caused by a combination of determinants, including school organization, classroom organization, and the personal qualities of students. Please remember that this figure, like others like it throughout this book, *hypothesizes* links among human organization, social behavior, and juve-

FIGURE 8.3
Links between Schools and Delinquency

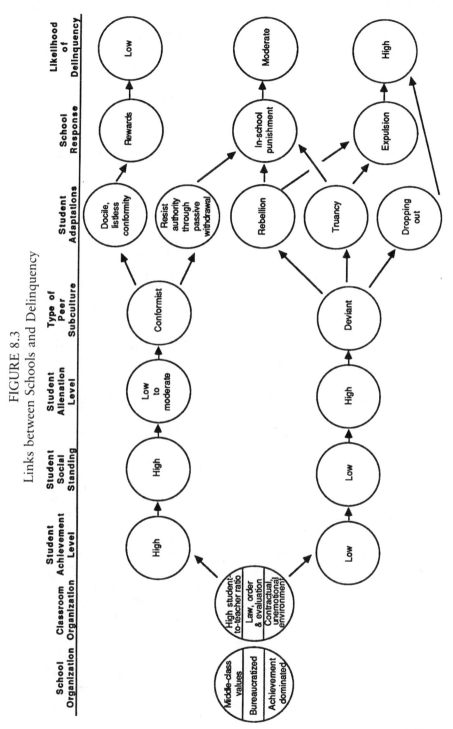

nile delinquency. Connections made herein are suggested by research results, but they are *not* hard and fast for every child and thus require much more validation through research.

CRIME IN AMERICAN SCHOOLS

In the 1970s, the U.S. Senate, through its Subcommittee to Investigate Juvenile Delinquency, provided a rare glimpse of the extent of property crime and violence in American schools. The U.S. Department of Health, Education and Welfare (now called HHS) was commissioned to prepare a comprehensive report on the subject. The report, *Violent Schools—Safe Schools: The Safe School Study Report to Congress* (1977), states that many large American schools are anything but safe. For example, in 1976, investigators documented $600 million in destroyed property, twelve thousand armed robberies, nine thousand rapes, and one hundred murders on school grounds (1–3). Teenagers spend approximately one-quarter of their time at school. Thirty-six percent of the physical violence and forty percent of the robberies they experience occur at school. The risk of being a crime victim at school is highest for poor and minority students. *Violent Schools—Safe Schools* reported that forty-three percent of all violent acts occur in hallways and stairwells, sixteen percent in restrooms, thirteen percent in classrooms, and nine percent in cafeterias.

A second study, *The National Crime Survey*, also documents widespread illegal activity at school. In 1981, two million larcenies, two hundred thousand assaults, twenty-two thousand robberies and twenty-seven hundred rapes were experienced by children while they were on school grounds (Flanagan and McLeod, 1983: 320–21). School violence and property crimes are committed by enrolled students and by large numbers of trespassing non-students. Crime on campus poses such a large threat that many students stay away from school out of fear.

Of the 611 serious delinquents interviewed by Inciardi, Horowitz, and Pottieger in their Miami area study, 436 were still in school (1993: 138). Practically all serious delinquents still in school, and almost all dropouts, reported regularly being high on drugs at school and frequently cutting classes (140–41). Gender differences were minimal. Some serious delinquents point out that school is an ideal place to sell drugs. The typical school reaction to illegal behavior, when children get caught, is expulsion or suspension (144).

School crime also victimizes teachers (Bennett, 1993: ii). A survey by the National Education Association (1982) reports that in 1981 approximately 29 percent of all American teachers had property stolen from them, and 5 percent were assaulted while at school. As a consequence of crime in their schools, many big-city public school teachers grow wary of contact with students and withdraw from campus life to the fullest allowable extent. Wary, withdrawn teachers make poor role models and offer little resistance to delinquency. Some argue that teachers and administrators are afraid to violate the constitutional rights of students by punishing them for misbehavior (Cohen, 1985: 80–81; Rubel and Goldsmith, 1980: 73–77; Bennett, 1993: ii).

However, teachers, administrators, and legal officials in many school districts throughout the nation are fighting back. For example, largely due to recent cooperative efforts among teachers, school administrators, and legal officials in Colorado Springs, students caught fighting, or breaking other laws, can be expelled from school, charged by the police, and further punished by local court officials, usually via fines, probation, or incarceration (*Daily Camera*, Nov. 13, 1993: 10A). The Safe Schools Act of 1993, which is currently being considered by the U.S. Congress, would allocate $75 million to fight school violence. Some of the money would pay for security guards and metal detectors in order to fortify schools. Other funds from the Safe Schools Act would be used for prevention programs emphasizing conflict resolution and peer mediation (*Daily Camera*, June 12, 1993: 7A).

SUMMARY

In this chapter we learned that high rates of delinquency are encouraged by many aspects of school and classroom organization. In industrial societies, education becomes highly formal and is organized into large school systems. Industrial age schools are massified and bureaucratized. Educational decisions are dominated by politicians and school administrators. Teachers have little power, except over students, who are at the bottom of the authority ladder. Teachers usually work in isolated classrooms with large numbers of students. Tense contractual relations evolve. Law, order, competition, and constant evaluation of student performance are major classroom themes. Consequently, many students and teachers become alienated. In order to survive in school, many successful children grow docile and give mindless allegiance to the rules. Students often adopt apple-polishing, withdrawal, or neutralizing tactics.

Research reveals strong links between delinquency and low achievement, low social standing, high alienation, membership in deviant peer subcultures, truancy, expulsion, or dropping out. In contrast, students who avoid delinquent labels earn acceptable or higher grades, possess moderate or high social standing, experience low or moderate levels of alienation, belong to conformist peer groups, evade getting caught for truancy and remain enrolled in school. Finally, recent evidence indicates that American public schools have become major staging grounds for using and selling drugs, stealing, and committing violent crimes.

Although there is little doubt that schools and delinquency are closely linked, we should remember that social science research techniques are subject to considerable error. For example, social researchers might very well draw different conclusions about the links between schools and delinquency simply by using data provided by police and courts, rather than by using self-report data. Therefore, the specific connections drawn between schools and delinquency in this chapter must be considered speculative, and only partially substantiated by social research.

CHAPTER 9

Police Organizations and Gangs

INTRODUCTION

If families and schools fail children, it is often friends and the police who step in to fill the breach. Police forces in the United States, especially those in suburban and big-city areas, process four overlapping categories of problem children: delinquents, status offenders, neglected youth, and dependent youth. Most police work with children is done out on the beat or at the station. Police handling of several types of problem children requires that enormous discretion be allowed. Police organizations and officers help large numbers of problem children find needed care, support, and direction. In so doing, the police prevent much delinquency (Goldstein, 1991: 227–28, 41; Lipson, 1982; Norman, 1972; Pursuit et al., 1972).

Unfortunately, police officers also possess the potential to encourage wholesale delinquency (Trojanowicz and Morash, 1987: 193; Miller, 1958b). In order to fully understand connections between police organizations and delinquency, it is necessary to consider many facets of police work. Consequently, in the following pages, we examine the history and structure of community-level police organizations, the police and gangs, and police options with juvenile offenders.

HISTORY AND STRUCTURE OF COMMUNITY-LEVEL POLICE ORGANIZATIONS

As late in American history as 1790, American citizens had little need for professional police, because there were few large cities, and most persons lived in rural settings where family and church effectively enforced the law (Perry, 1975: 27–28). Before the nineteenth century, only a few volunteer legal officials, like constables and sheriffs, helped colonial governments deal with problem chil-

181

dren. Early American volunteer police helped as many problem children as possible and ignored a good many others. The most unruly children were taken into custody and indentured out to masters. Children who violated serious criminal laws were treated just like adult offenders. Child care, however, was only a small part of early American police work. Constables, volunteer watch personnel, and sheriffs first pursued murderers, thieves, robbers, peace breakers, vagrants, nightwalkers, persons who drank, swore, and lied, and those not in church on Sunday. Afterwards, problem children could be helped (Inciardi, 1987: 159).

By the mid-1800s, cities like New York, Boston, and Philadelphia had outgrown volunteer policing. Populations of big cities are too heterogeneous to follow the behavioral prescriptions of family, church, and volunteer police. Big American cities of the late 1800s were hotbeds for labor and race riots. Property crimes shot upward. Violence and vice skyrocketed. Large concentrations of problem children appeared in city centers. In response to urban problems, big cities formed municipal governments in order to organize and manage professional police organizations (Perry, 1975: 29–31). Out west, the sheriff and deputies provided basic, range-style law enforcement for rural populations and offered few services for children (Inciardi, 1987: 160–62).

Urban and Suburban Municipal Police Departments

In 1833, Philadelphia first experimented with a small professional police department. Boston, in 1837, introduced a successful form of professional policing. In 1845, New York City began operating a refined version of the Boston policing experiment, employing eight hundred officers, and providing law enforcement year round, twenty-four hours per day. From its birth, the New York City Police Department was a military organization, controlled and managed by a municipal government afloat in corruption. A chief of police, with a handful of assistants, directed in relative secrecy the activities of hundreds of officers, who patrolled New York neighborhoods armed with vague laws, authority to use force, the right to make arrests, and the opportunity to bring criminal charges against troublesome persons. Modern policing, New York style, appeared to meet the immediate needs of municipal political leaders, and it was pronounced a success. By 1865, municipal governments in large cities, including Baltimore, Chicago, Cincinatti, Newark, and New Orleans, were operating police departments patterned after the original in New York. By 1870, modern policing had spread to most large American cities. At the turn of the century, almost all urban zones were patrolled by professional police (Inciardi, 1987: 165; Perry, 1975: 32–33).

Patrol work has always been the largest part of policing. In the early days of municipal policing, patrol was done on foot by a cop who got to know almost everyone on the beat. In the early twentieth century, however, as municipal policing spread to new American cities, law enforcement adopted automobiles and two-way radio equipment. These innovations significantly enlarged patrol areas but placed physical and emotional distance between officers and members of the community. As urbanization and suburbanization continued on into the middle and end of the twentieth century, New York style policing, modified by emerging transportation and communication technologies, spread to approximately ten thousand American communities, employing more than five hundred thousand officers and almost two hundred thousand civilians (FBI, 1991: 237).

Municipal police departments today serve as a major buffer between problem children and the courts. It is the police officer on patrol who has first legal contact with most American problem children, especially with youth who are reported to authorities by concerned citizens, victims, schools, and families. In terms of organizational philosophy and juvenile gang intervention strategies, most municipal police departments fall somewhere along a continuum that, at the one end, emphasizes gangbusting—outlawing, suppressing, arresting, prosecuting, convicting and punishing young, gang-connected, drugged-up sociopaths—and, at the other end, stresses prosocial approaches—focusing on counseling adolescents, teaching literacy and job skills, providing medical services, and helping with food, employment, and housing (Goldstein, 1991: 135). In keeping with the current trend in American society, at all levels of government, toward the increasing criminalization of marginal persons, most police departments find gangbusting irresistible (Goldstein, 1991: 135; Walker, 1994: 278). However, almost all police departments also offer prosocial programs for at risk children (Goldstein, 1991: 41). For example, the Denver Police Department deploys specially trained officers in Crack and Gang Task Forces and totally cooperates with the District Attorney's Office in prosecuting gang-related offenders. At the same time, the Denver Police Department offers education programs in schools and other places throughout the city (Denver Police Department, 1992: 2).

In terms of structure, there are two basic types of municipal police departments, those with and those without special juvenile, youth, or gang units. Figure 9.1 shows the formal structure of a medium-sized police department (serving a city of approximately sixty thousand residents and employing around one hundred officers) that has no special juvenile, youth, or gang unit. Today, most small and many medium-sized police departments do not have special juvenile units. Instead, police departments with fifteen or more employees are encouraged to designate at least one officer as a youth specialist (National Advisory Commission on Criminal Justice Standards and Goals, 1973: 223). Some small and medium-sized police departments provide extra training and education for youth specialists. Others do not.

FIGURE 9.1
Formal Structure of Medium-sized Police Department
without Juvenile Unit

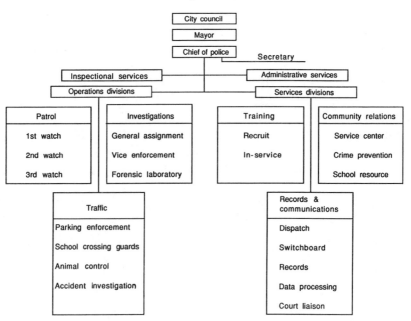

Figure 9.1 shows that medium-sized police departments are broken up into several divisions and units, although it is important to keep in mind that approximately 80 percent of all officers are assigned to patrol and investigative functions, where maintaining public order (which includes traffic control) and fighting crime are primary concerns. In other words, even a medium-sized American police department has become a complex military bureaucracy where secrecy, authority, force, and contractual relationships dominate activity. In police departments that have no special juvenile units, most encounters with problem youth involve patrol officers and investigators who also handle large quantities of peace keeping and adult criminal work.

MODERN AMERICAN YOUTH GANGS
AND THEIR MEMBERS

In chapter 4 we briefly reviewed the history of gangs in the United States and examined why children join gangs. Here we focus on modern youth gangs and the children who are attracted to them. There is evidence that gangs have proliferated over the last ten years. Gang violence, drug trafficking, and disruption of public education by gang members are also on the rise. Gangs are most problematic in big cities like Los Angeles, Chicago, and New York. However, through migration and imitation, gangs have moved beyond our biggest cities. Gangs are appearing in small and medium-sized communities throughout the United States (Cummings and Monti, 1993).

There is no standard definition for *gang* or *youth gang*. Gang members almost always identify themselves by adopting somewhat distinctive linguistic, dress, and physical appearance styles. Gang members often communicate through tatoos and graffiti (Community Youth Gang Services, 1993: 1–12). Ethnic or gang language can be frustrating for parents, teachers, and legal officials (*Denver Post*, Jan. 6, 1994: 2A, 9A). Experts point out that as much as 70 percent of a gang's language can be subject to day-to-day change (Community Youth Gang Services: 9).

In the most general sense, *gang* can be defined as a collectivity of humans who band together for mutual protection and in order to pursue common interests. This general definition of gang qualifies a broad range of children for consideration as gang members. For example, youthful members of athletic teams, theatrical groups, or well-established clubs, as well as groups of lower-class or working-class delinquents, could be considered members of gangs. While there is much disagreement, even among academic and legal experts, about whether or not gang members always engage in criminal behavior, today it is generally assumed that "the link between gang membership and delinquency appears indisputable" (Thornberry et al., 1993: 56).

Thus, modern youth gangs are most often defined as "groups that are organized to some extent around delinquent conduct" (56). Gangs are usually organized around ethnic identification, a common interest like motorcycles, or hate. The biggest gangs in the country are Crips and Bloods, but hate goups have great potential for growth (Denver Police Department, 1992: 2; Anti-Defamation League of B'nai B'rith, 1988: 1; Weis, 1993: 251).

Gangs claim members ranging in age from nine to thirty (Goldstein, 1991: 23). Many gangs, for example, bikers, big-city Bloods and Crips, are dominated by members over eighteen years of age (Denver Police Department, 1992: 2). Other gangs, especially those organized around hate, "are composed overwhelmingly of teenagers—many as young as 13 and 14 years of age—who have had no previous involvement in organized hate groups" (Anti-Defamation League of B'Nai B'rith: 1).

Males outnumber females in gangs by a factor of twenty to one (Goldstein, 1991: 23). But, according to the Denver police, "females are becoming more and more visible with their involvement in gang activity. Most gangs have female auxiliaries. They hold the Crack and the weapons for their gang boyfriends. They are also used for intelligence gathering" (Denver Police Department, 1992: 2). Chesney-Lind and Shelden agree that females have never been as involved as males in gangs (1992: 44). Goldstein points out that probably less than 5 percent of gang-related crime can be blamed on female members. Girls become gang members later than do boys. Females quit the gang more quickly than do males (1991: 23). However, there is mounting evidence that females in gangs "often engaged in the same behaviors as the boys, such as smoking pot, drinking, fighting, committing theft, and partying" (Chesney-Lind and Shelden, 1992: 45)

Goldstein observes that, over the last twenty years, "gang violence in the United States gradually changed for the worse . . .

violent offenses . . . are three times more likely to be committed by gang members than by nongang delinquents" (1991: 32). There are many reasons for the steady, horrific upswing in youthful gang-related violence in the United States. Perhaps Leon Watkins, the founder of "Brotherhood Crusade" in Los Angeles, protecting and supporting victims of gang violence, explained it best. He believes that the affluent sector of American society has for the most part abandoned disadvantaged, especially urban dark-skinned, children. He points out that the gap between the haves and the have-nots has grown so wide that many dispossessed children lose sight of a hopeful, prosperous future. Consequently, a number of at risk children are angry, often violent. They are needy and willing to band together for protection and action (Street Gangs, ZDF, 1990).

There are numerous causes of gang violence. Foremost is the fact that many adults in American society, in all social classes, in all walks of life, model for children disturbing and dangerous themes of masculinity. For example, Connel points out that in men's team sports children are taught to achieve goals and solve problems through "a combative, dominance-focused masculinity." Elsewhere at school, constant testing and the academic curriculum teach children "a rationalized masculinity" typical of people in business, administration, the professions, or politics (1993: 204). The existence and dominance of a rationalized masculinity in the affluent classes helps explain the widening gap between well-off Americans and the millions of at risk, alienated children who live in the United States. Combative, dominance-focused masculinity seems to be a main ingredient of much violence.

Guns contribute to heightening youth violence. In spite of the spate of gun trade-in or buy-back programs springing up throughout the country, inhabitants of the United States are well armed. There are at least two hundred million privately owned guns in the country (Goldstein, 1991: 35). Almost all American police organizations employ a wide range of firearms. And, currently, American manufacturers produce about three million new guns each year (*Daily Times Call*, Jan. 9, 1994: 5B). Guns are readily available, through legitimate and illegitimate sources, everywhere in the United States. While there is still a demand for older firearms, most people who regularly use guns prefer newer, lighter models that fire more powerful ammunition, more frequently. Thus, over the last twenty years, many firearms used by the police *and* criminals have grown lighter and more lethal. Children, especially gang members, not only use guns, but also sell them, often generating significant income.

Drugs contribute to heightening violence. Drugs sometimes give children false courage and fuel violent impulses. Drugs are readily available everywhere in the United States. Many children, including gang members, sell drugs (Inciardi, Horowitz, and Pottieger, 1993: 28–49, 85–89). Big gangs, like the Crips, Bloods, and bikers, generate a good deal of revenue from weapons and drug sales (Denver Police Department, 1992: 2). Much criminal violence results from disputes over drug use and sales (Goldstein, 1991: 34).

There are many other contributors to heightening violence in the United States. For example, a primary cause of violence is territoriality. According to Goldstein, "gangs continue to mark, define, claim, protect and fight over their turf" (34). Media depictions of violence must also be given their due. For example, Goldstein reminds us that "prime time television in the United States . . . showed an average of 9.5 acts of violence per hour" (29). In sum, while there is still considerable diversity, American gangs have grown "more violent and more drug involved" (7).

HATE GANGS

Hate gangs are known by many names: neo-Nazis, Skinheads, KKK, the Aryan Youth Movement, War Skins, and so on. Over the last twenty years, hate gangs have increased their youth outreach activities and are attracting many new young members (Anti-Defamation League of B'nai B'rith, 1988: 1; Denver Police Department, 1992: 2). Weis suggests that many school-age Anglo working-class boys in the United States are likely recruits for the New Right, which includes hate groups. According to Weis, "the very real fact that the form of schooling offered these young men will not enable the vast majority . . . to break into anything other than the contingent economy, leaves them quite bitter . . . The anger seeps out in a variety of ways" (1993: 251). Anger, under the direction of hate gangs, is often translated into violent acts of racism and sexism.

GANGS AND THE POLICE

Because large numbers of problem children must be sorted and processed on a daily basis, many big-city police departments have special juvenile or gang units. Figure 9.2 outlines the formal structure of a large municipal police department with a juvenile division (serving more than one-half million residents and employing several hundred officers). A youth and women's division is shaded at the bottom of the figure. Juvenile or gang units may also be formed within investigations or detective divisions of big-city police departments (Chicago Police Department, Special Functions Group, 1988). Juvenile or gang units often operate independent of other police divisions and enjoy a considerable degree of discretion in resolving cases. In fact, a study of police departments in the Los Angeles area revealed that most police chiefs knew very little about juvenile procedures in their departments and showed minimal interest in juvenile matters. Thus, juvenile and gang specialists operated with lax administrative control (Klein, Rosensweig, and Bates, 1975: 85). In some big departments, almost all children who need police attention are immediately shifted from patrol or investigation officers to a member of the juvenile or gang unit. In other police organizations, only children who are taken into custody and transported to headquarters are transferred to juvenile specialists. Policy on this matter varies greatly from city to city. Some police departments require juvenile or gang unit officers to undertake special training and education. Others do not. Some police departments hold juvenile specialists in high regard. Most do not (Empey and Stafford, 1991: 310).

The actual duties of juvenile specialists vary from department to department. In general, juvenile specialists are expected to protect children; prevent delinquency; uncover delinquency, dependency, and neglect; and collect evidence that can be used to resolve cases. Unlike police generalists, juvenile specialists are often able to conduct lengthy meetings with problem children and their families, where informal resolution can be achieved.

Gang-related problems are epidemic in large and medium-sized American cities. For example, in the Los Angeles area, more than four hundred street gangs operate with a total membership of between forty thousand and sixty thousand young persons (Coffey, 1990: 354). Street gangs have been active in Los Angeles for more than a century. But there has been a recent explosion in gang membership. Gang activity, especially involving Hispanic (traditional turf gangs) and African American (Crips and Bloods) youth, has spread to all lower-class and many middle-class living areas. In response to criminal violence, drug use, property crime, and vandal-

FIGURE 9.2
Formal Structure of Large Police Department with Juvenile Division

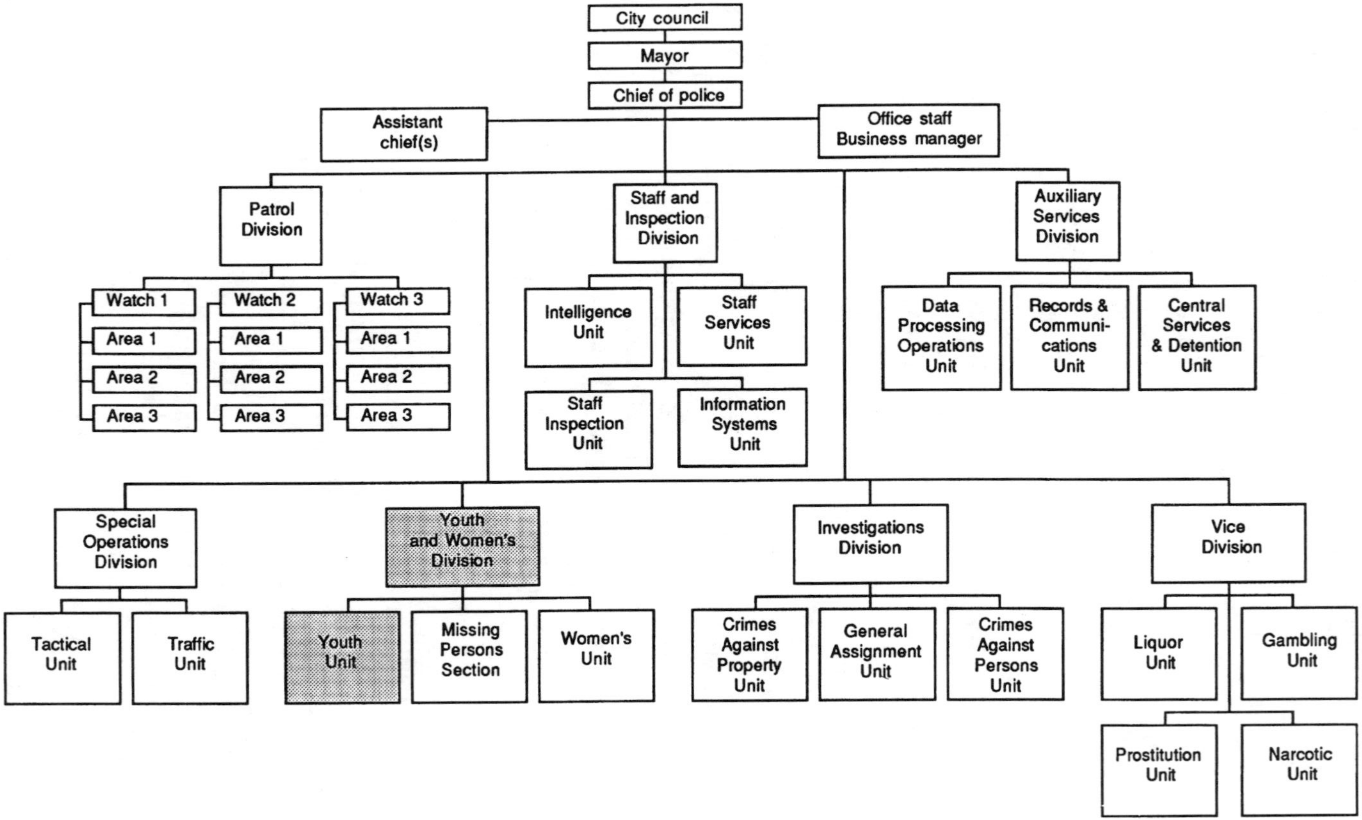

ism perpetrated by gangs, the Los Angeles County Sheriff's Department, along with the District Attorney's Office Hard Core Unit, the Probation Department's Specialized Gang Supervision Unit, the California Highway Patrol, and the Community Youth Gang Services organization, created Operation Safe Streets (O.S.S.), and Gang Enforcement Teams (G.E.T.). Today, seventy deputy sheriffs work without uniforms on permanent assignments in ten Los Angeles areas where street gangs are most active. O.S.S./G.E.T. members, released from other police duties, investigate gang-related crimes, collect evidence, incarcerate and help prosecute members of targeted gangs. O.S.S. operates a computer system that monitors activities of Los Angeles area gangs and their members. O.S.S./ G.E.T. officers identify marginal gang members, attempting to establish rapport, respect, and trust with them and eventually trying to discourage gang participation. O.S.S. also operates a Street Gang School that enrolls law enforcement personnel from all over the country. O.S.S./G.E.T. allows police officers from other agencies to ride along with them while they execute their duties. O.S.S. officers speak on a regular basis at citizen meetings, where anti-gang objectives and activities are explained (352–58).

The Chicago Police Department combats approximately 125 active street gangs with a Gang Crimes Section of the Patrol Division. The Gang Crimes Section employs more than three hundred police officers. Gang Crimes Specialists investigate gang-related crime, observe and monitor gang activities, and provide support for traditional patrol officers (Kratcoski and Kratcoski, 1990: 227). Many other medium-sized and big-city police departments have special gang units. Most claim success in reducing gang-related crime.

In sum, as the number of problem children has grown in American cities, and as the number and sophistication of firearms available to urban and suburban youth has increased, the gang problem has grown worse. Today, the gap between the affluent segment of American society and poor problem children has grown so wide that many juveniles see gang membership and suicidal behavior, in the form of criminal violence, weapons sales, stealing, drug use, and sales, as their best opportunity to lead a "good life." These conditions make police work with gang members dangerous, unceasing, and full of disappointment. Unfortunately, all too often the police response to gang membership and activities is gangbusting (Goldstein, 1991: 41). In response to gangs, police officers often model combative, dominance-focused masculinity and corresponding problem solving strategies for at-risk children.

Whether or not a gang or youth unit is present, however, medium-sized and large police departments are complex organizations with several divisions and units. Figures 9.1 and 9.2 show that, even under the best of circumstances, care of problem children is a relatively small part of municipal policing. According to the American Bar Association (in Goldstein, 1976: 35), police officers are responsible for the following types of work:

1. preventing and controlling serious crime;

2. aiding victims of criminal violence or helping individuals who are threatened by violence;

3. defending constitutional guarantees like freedom of assembly and speech;

4. supervising the movement of vehicles and people;

5. aiding persons who do not properly care for themselves, including drunks, drug users, citizens suffering from mental disorders, seniors, those with physical disabilities, and *youngsters;*

6. mediating conflicts between citizens and government agencies, resolving disputes involving individuals or groups;

7. detecting situations involving individuals or groups that could become serious problems; and

8. building and nurturing a sense of safety in the community.

Thus, American police departments are structured to respond first to crime fighting, order maintenance, and traffic concerns, only secondarily to the needs of children. Most problem children are ignored by police officers. Only 2 to 5 percent of American police officers are juvenile specialists. In fact, in the 1980s, some big-city police departments actually eliminated their youth divisions in reaction to tightening budgets.

POLICE OPTIONS WITH JUVENILES

Police officers and their departments take one of two general approaches toward handling problem children. Some adopt a prosocial, or social work, posture toward children. Social work oriented officers emphasize counseling and finding informal ways to help children with their problems. Other officers and departments prefer gangbusting or handling problem children legalistically. Gangbusters, or legalistic officers, stress conducting criminal investigations and processing offenders formally, through arrest and court referral. Although every police department in the United States employs social work oriented officers, legalism or gangbusting is by far the more common approach (Goldstein, 1991: 41).

Step one in police screening of problem children is to determine whether they are status offenders, delinquents, dependent, or neglected. The most important factors in categorizing children are the nature of the offense and the situation of the child (Black and Reiss, 1979; Miller et al., 1976: 179). For example, children who are noticeably failing to thrive and who have committed no criminal or juvenile offenses are usually classified as neglected or dependent. Neglected or dependent youngsters can be taken into custody or referred to shelter care, to court intake, or to social service agencies for processing. When shelter care is unavailable, dependent and neglected children are sometimes locked up in facilities with delinquents. At the other extreme, children who are suspected of committing serious crimes, have records of prior police contact, or violate probation or parole are usually categorized as delinquents (Ariessohn, 1972; Ferdinand and Luchterhand, 1970; McEachern and Bauzer, 1967). Most young persons who are categorized as serious delinquents are taken into custody and incarcerated.

Children whose criminal or juvenile offenses are less serious, and whose dependency and neglect less obvious, are much more difficult to categorize. Most police officers recognize the need to separate less serious offenders into two categories: (1) youth who appear able to respond well to street-level rehabilitative efforts and (2) children whose offenses are relatively minor but who seem likely to engage in future serious delinquency. Demeanor and parental involvement are major factors in distinguishing minor, salvageable offenders from possible future delinquents. Children who are abusive, rebellious, uncooperative, and unrepentant are most likely to be seen as future delinquents (Hohenstein, 1969; Lundman, 1974; Lundman, Sykes, and Clark, 1980: 147–48; Miller et al., 1976: 180; Piliavin and Briar, 1964; and Werthman and Piliavin, 1967: 56–98). Similarly, police officers who are generally suspicious of and harsh with law-violating youth will treat many children like future delinquents (Goldman, 1969; Pepinsky, 1976). Youngsters whose parents are unavailable when an officer calls or looks for them, or whose parents are unable or unwilling to offer effective help, are likely to be treated as potential serious offenders (Miller et al., 1976: 179–83).

There are five basic options available to police officers as they process juvenile offenders. First, most delinquency, dependency, and neglect will be ignored by officers who concentrate on what they perceive as more urgent and important aspects of the overall police mission. Officers also rationalize, and thus ignore, much youthful misbehavior as sewing wild oats or as transitive behavior, that is, as acts committed by good children under unusual and mitigating circumstances.

Second, street-level police officers may respond to delinquency by calling in a special youth officer and washing their hands of the matter. In theory, youth specialists are better trained and have more time and the social work orientation needed to rehabilitate delinquents. In reality, juvenile officers are overworked and tend to function as double agents, vacillating between a social work approach and their more natural inclination and mandate to function as criminal investigators. Youth specialists have the luxury of holding quasi-judicial hearings with juveniles and their parents; there problems can be discussed and informally resolved. Street-level police, on the other hand, must come up with quick solutions to childhood dilemmas.

Third, police officers counsel and release many problem children, usually into parental custody, but sometimes without establishing contact with parents. "Counsel and release" can mean many things. Most likely, the officer will deliver a stern lecture, offer some advice and a warning to a child, and then terminate contact. Some officers work out informal, voluntary restitution or disciplinary programs with children, parents, and victims. Other police officers verbally and physically abuse children in order to administer a perverted but immediate form of retribution. If parents are available, capable, willing, and cooperative during police processing, if victims are willing, and if guilt is voluntarily admitted, children will usually be counseled and released for minor offenses. Should officers suspect underlying dependency or neglect, young persons can be referred to social service agencies. In general, where parents are present, capable, and willing, and where communities provide fruitful alternative services and programs, officers will make every effort to resolve youthful misbehavior without further legal processing. In 1992, more than 30 percent of the children taken into custody were counseled by the police and shortly thereafter released, almost always to their parents (FBI, 1993a: 282). In order to be counseled and released after arrest, juveniles must voluntarily admit guilt, and their parents are required to sign a waiver of their legal rights.

Officers usually file written reports on incidents where children are taken into custody. Police reports can be used internally by the law enforcement agency, but they may be passed on to juvenile court intake personnel or to the local district attorney's office. Consequently, even children who are released shortly after arrest begin to accumulate criminal records. Most children who refuse to admit guilt are read their rights and are referred by the police to intake probation personnel for further categorizing and processing (Miller et al., 1976: 182). Most police departments attempt to keep complete records of all street-level police activity with children through contact cards filled out after each incident. In many jurisdictions, officers release children but file a report on their misbehavior with the police department or with juvenile court intake personnel. Thus, many problem children accumulate the beginnings of criminal records while being counseled and released.

Fourth, if law violation is serious and seems to forshadow future serious trouble, especially in the absence of immediate, effective parental control, if children are rebellious, if victims demand action, and if departmental policy favors such a decision, the police are empowered to take children into custody, meaning a form of arrest is executed.[1] In 1992, for example, a total of 1,939,456 American children were arrested (FBI, 1993: 236), as many as 10 to 25 percent because their parents either could not or

---

[1]More than half of the bodies of state law in the U.S. avoid using the term *arrest* in connection with the processing of juveniles, preferring instead the concept of 'taking them into custody'. Ten states specify that taking children into custody is not a form of arrest. In practice, however, arresting and taking a person into custody are the same acts, except that juveniles have opportunities to avoid permanent recording of the event (Inciardi, 1987: 688). There is also considerable confusion about when an arrest has been executed. Depending upon the police department handling a juvenile, arrest may mean having formal contact with a youth suspected of misbehavior, bringing a child to a police department, or filing charges (Kratkoski and Kratkoski, 1990: 221).

would not take them home (Miller et al., 1976: 188). If possible, street-level police officers pass arrested children on to juvenile specialists.

Law in most states requires that police officers immediately begin attempts to notify parents when a child is taken into custody. State law usually allows arresting officers to hold children in custody only for very short periods. If the police believe that a child should be kept in custody until a later resolution to his/her problem can be found, the child is notified of her/his legal rights, and a fifth option, called "detention," must be invoked. Detention is the short-term, nonpunitive incarceration of children in juvenile halls, detention centers, and adult jails. In 1987, there were 764 short-term juvenile custody facilities operating in the United States. Of the 764 juvenile custody facilities, 500 were administered by governmental units, and 264 were run by private organizations (U.S. Dept. of Justice, Bureau of Justice statistics, 1990: 565). On one day in 1989, 19,967 juveniles were incarcerated in government-operated short-term juvenile detention facilities. (U.S. Department of Justice, 1991: 5). When juvenile detention space is unavailable, problem children are locked up in one of America's approximately 3,316 adult jails (U.S. Dept. of Justice, Bureau of Justice Statistics, 1990: 569). In 1988, adult jails held 1,451 children on an average daily basis (575). In 1991, a one-day survey of U.S. jails found 2,350 juveniles locked up (U.S. Department of Justice, Bureau of Justice Statistics, 1993b: 590).

When a child is arrested and detained, the police are required to file a citation (a written report of the case) with intake personnel (usually probation officers) of the juvenile court or perhaps with the local district attorney. At this point in processing, the child becomes the responsibility of the juvenile court, attorneys and detention center, or jail employees, rather than the police. In other words, when a child is locked up and a citation is filed, the police are excused from the case. Attorneys, detention officers, and intake probation officers take over. Table 9.1 shows the numbers of American children who are taken into custody and what the police do with them. We see that, in 1964, approximately 47 percent of all children taken into custody were handled by the police and released. Another 47 percent were referred to juvenile courts. By 1992, only 30 percent of all children taken into custody were handled by the police and released, while 62.5 percent were re-

TABLE 9.1

Police Disposition of Juveniles Taken into Custody, 1964–1992

	1964	1974	1984	1992
Total number	819,075	1,709,564	1,052,233	1,330,455
Percent of total	100.0	100.0	100.0	100.0
Handled within department and released	388,898	759,137	331,740	399,856
	47.4	44.4	31.5	30.0
Referred to other police agency	21,618	40,788	13,843	14,323
	2.7	2.4	1.3	1.1
Referred to criminal or adult court	14,364	63,527	54,344	62,180
	1.8	3.7	5.2	4.7
Referred to juvenile court	381,337	803,330	630,937	831,696
	46.8	47.0	60.0	62.5
Referred to welfare agency	12,858	42,782	21,369	22,400
	1.6	2.5	2.0	1.7

Sources: U.S. Department of Justice, Bureau of Justice Statistics, 1993a: 590; 1986: 443; FBI, 1975: 177; 1964: 102.

ferred to juvenile courts. These data clearly indicate that American police officers are today handling a much larger percentage of problem children more formally than they had in the past.

Upon detention of a juvenile, the first responsibilities of an intake probation officer are to notify parents, inform parents of their rights, and schedule a timely hearing before a magistrate or judge of the juvenile court, in order to determine if ongoing incarceration is justified. Most children stay in detention a short while, ranging from a few hours to a few days. Problem children who warrant detention, especially in big cities, are processed by as many as four different types of law enforcement agents, namely, the patrol officer, a juvenile specialist, detention workers, and intake probation personnel. Short-term handling by a succession of officers leaves little time and opportunity for rehabilitative relationships to evolve. Thus, quick, mass-handling of problem children by the police can become a major obstacle to helping them.

Police Prevention Programs

There are hundreds of delinquency prevention programs operated by police departments throughout the United States. Police delinquency prevention programs range from individual acts of officers, such as lending an ear to a youth in trouble or helping a problem child find shelter, to organized recreation, social service, and counseling activities.

One of the most promising prevention programs, operating today in more than three hundred law enforcement agencies, is called "community policing" (Trojanowicz and Bucqueroux, 1990: 4). Community policing assigns community police officers (CPOs), with good communication skills and a deep concern for disadvantaged people, on a long-term basis in high-crime neighborhoods. Sometimes community policing is done through the public schools. For example, in Flint, Michigan, many of the original twenty-two CPOs established base stations in school buildings. Similarly, in Warren, Ohio, the police department initiated a Student Resource Officer Program. Student resource officers (CROs) engage in traditional investigative and arrest activities, but they also provide counseling, serve as guest lecturers in classes, and establish ties among students, teachers, and service agencies. The Los Angeles Police Department works with Los Angeles Unified School District personnel to operate Project DARE, a program that sends police officers into public school classrooms to encourage children to resist drugs (DeJong, 1986).

CPOs and CROs, although retaining their responsibilities to investigate crimes and make arrests, emphasize enlisting the cooperation of children, parents, and school personnel in designing grassroots programs that fight crime and other social problems. CPOs organize and operate health care clinics, fishing derbies, excursions, esteem clubs, rallies, teen pregnancy prevention programs, teen entrepreneur programs, prep clubs, and cable television shows. CPOs enlist the help of social service agencies to provide counseling and care for needy children and parents. CPOs act as role models for children and parents, teaching them to respect the law, work hard for positive change in their neighborhoods, and care for others. CPOs show residents of poor neighborhoods that the police can do more than show up after a crime has been committed and make arrests. In short, CPOs rely "on brains, not brawn," they "openly demonstrate care and concern" (237). Community policing teaches parents and children to take care of their own neighborhoods.

Many police departments sponsor recreational programs for children. For example, the Police Athletic League operates clubs where children are exposed to competitive boxing and participate in baseball, basketball, and other organized sports. The Police Athletic League, begun in Philadelphia in 1940, has been joined by police departments throughout the United States and today functions as a major tool in preventing delinquency (Kratcoski and Kratcoski, 1990: 228–29).

Law enforcement agencies also sponsor drug abuse prevention programs. For example, in 1984, the Drug Enforcement Administration created the Sports Drug Awareness Program. The Sports Drug Awareness Program works to prevent drug abuse in schools by educating coaches and athletes. The National Association of Broadcasters supports the Sports Drug Awareness Program by televising and broadcasting antidrug commercials, featuring famous professional athletes, on television and radio stations. Another successful program is run by the Boy Scouts of America. The Boy Scouts Law Enforcement Explorer Program fights drug use by creating peer pressure among members of its troops (Coffey, 1990: 360–61).

TABLE 9.2
Factors in Assessing Police Roles

Police History and Structure	Police Work Environment	Police Tools	Police Roles	Police Options with Juveniles
Military	Crime fighting and order maintenance emphasized	Communication skills	Peace keeper	Ignore them
Bureaucratic	Dangerous, stressful, hidden work involving violence and force	Force	Crime fighter	Refer to youth specialist
Run by corrupt governments	Strong temptation to violate procedural laws	Arrest		Counsel and release
Secretive	Work organized by biased, conservative conception of law violation; officers rejected by others in society; high citizen demand for police services	Court Referral; discretion	Servant	Take child into custody; detention

SUMMARY

In this chapter we examined important aspects of policing that help determine how problem children are categorized and processed. We paid special attention to the history and structure of community-level police organizations, gangs, and police options with juveniles. Table 9.2 summarizes factors that must be considered when assessing the police role in caring for problem children. As indicated by the left column of table 9.2, in terms of history and structure, police organizations are better mandated and organized to maintain public order and fight crime than they are to help children. Similarly, the next column to the right shows that police officers work in an environment that is hidden, dangerous, and stressful, where violence and force must be used. The working environment for most street-level officers is overdemanding, alienating, and full of opportunities to use authority, force, and violence. Thus, when the police do stop to offer care to a child, they are taking on a totally different, and somewhat alien, social worker role.

The middle column of table 9.2 lists the basic tools of police work, namely, communication skills, force, arrest, court referral, and discretion. Even though police tools are skewed toward violence and authoritarian, legalistic handling of situations, street-level officers manage to use communication and discretion to solve the vast majority of children's problems, without resorting to force, arrest and court referral. For example, one source estimates that for each juvenile arrest made, American police officers encounter children in approximately five hundred situations in which legal action would be warranted (Morris and Hawkins, 1969: 91).

The next column to the right lists three basic roles that police officers play: peacekeeper, crime fighter, servant. Local government officials want the police to be peacekeepers and crime fighters. Most police officers see themselves as crime fighters. Yet citizens usually want services or peacekeeping help from the police. In other words, there are considerable opportunities for the police to feel role conflict and role strain while, in the midst of their many other obligations, attempting to help problem children.

In the rightmost column of table 9.2 we see that the police have relatively few options when confronting problem children. Juveniles can be ignored or, where possible, referred to a youth specialist. Most situations, however, must be resolved on the street in relatively short periods of time. Consequently, the police counsel and release the vast majority of children they encounter, while reporting some to the juvenile court or district attorney. Sometimes the situation or offense warrants considerable attention; parents are unavailable, unable, or unwilling to help; victims demand action. In such cases, the police will take children into custody, counseling, and releasing some shortly thereafter, but referring most children on to adult or juvenile court. American police officers process millions of problem children each year without resorting to force, arrest, and court referral. Due to the many demands placed upon them, and to the varied nature of their work, whatever help the police can give to problem children must be rendered in a short time and, in most cases, without establishing lasting relationships.

CHAPTER 10

Courts and Delinquency

INTRODUCTION

Juvenile courts are "all courts having jurisdiction in children's cases, including . . . probate, domestic relations and family courts in which juvenile jurisdiction is placed" (Nimick et al., 1987: 5). All 3,091 counties in the United States operate juvenile courts. Juvenile courts exist in the midst of fifty independent state judicial systems and the powerful federal judiciary. While the basic structure of the American judiciary remains unchanged, the number of courts and judges has increased dramatically in the last twenty years. Even with expansion, however, American courts are "largely archaic, suited better to the horse-and-buggy past than to the contemporary space age" (Jacob, 1965: 131).

Figure 10.1 outlines the basic structure of the U.S. federal and state court systems. In theory, all American courts are hierarchically ordered, with each higher court holding review powers over the court(s) below, and with federal courts possessing review and corrective power over cases in state courts that involve federal law, or the U.S. Constitution (Hinsdale, 1891: 278–91). In practice, however, all courts have considerable freedom from legislative, administrative, and higher judicial controls (U.S. Department of Justice, Bureau of Justice Statistics, 1983: 64).

The lowest state courts are listed at the bottom of figure 10.1. Lower state courts process minor civil, criminal, and traffic cases. Before 1960, most state legislatures situated their juvenile court among lower tribunals (fig. 10.1, type 1), frequently as a branch of the district or county court. For example, Colorado's 1903 Act Concerning Children stipulates that "the county courts of the several counties in this state shall have jurisdiction in all of the cases coming within the terms and provisions of this Act. For convenience the court in the trial and disposition of such cases may be called 'The Juvenile Court'" (Colorado General Assembly, 1903).

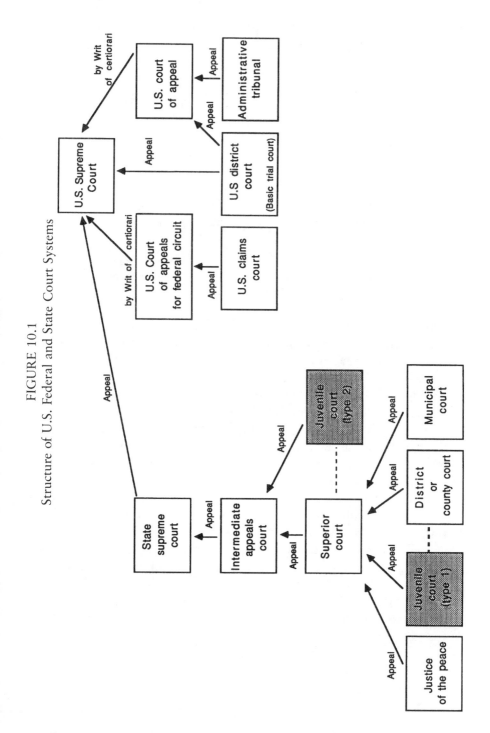

FIGURE 10.1
Structure of U.S. Federal and State Court Systems

More recently, many state legislatures elevated the status of their juvenile court so that it equates with the superior court (fig. 10.1, type 2). Superior Court is the state trial court that processes more important felony and civil cases.

All states have some form of appellate court that reviews appeals of cases coming from superior court. The highest appellate state court is usually called the "supreme court," although it has many other names and serves as the last state tribunal to which appeals of decisions made by lower courts can be taken. In recent years, state appellate courts have reviewed hundreds of appeals of juvenile cases and have, thus, become a major force in shaping juvenile law (Senna and Siegel, 1992).[1]

The upper-right section of figure 10.1 outlines the American federal court system. Federal courts have jurisdiction over cases involving federal law, the U.S. Constitution, or disputes between states. Cases that begin in state superior courts or involve federal law or the U.S. Constitution may be removed, before trial begins, to a U.S. district court. In 1981, 2,590 juvenile delinquency proceedings were filed in U.S. district courts. In 1991, 3,412 juvenile delinquency proceedings were filed in the U.S. district court system, down considerably from the peaks of 4,000–5,000 cases processed by U.S. district courts in the 1980s (U.S. Department of Justice, Bureau of Justice Statistics, 1993a: 494).

District court cases may be appealed either to a U.S. court of appeal or to the U.S. Supreme Court. Similarly, cases involving federal law or the U.S. Constitution that have been appealed through the state courts may be appealed to the U.S. Supreme Court. Many juvenile cases originating in state courts have been appealed to federal courts; recently, this has resulted in significant change in American juvenile law. My main purpose in outlining the structure of the American judiciary is to make the point that juvenile courts do not operate in a vacuum. Rather, juvenile courts are situated among other courts and are, thus, influenced by their decisions.

Table 10.1 provides an overview of state court caseflow for 1983. State courts handle more than 96 percent of all court cases in

---

[1]See Miller et al., 1976 and Senna and Siegel, 1992 for descriptions of hundreds of state-level juvenile court cases whose appeals have been heard by higher courts.

TABLE 10.1
State Court Judicial Caseflow, 1983

	Civil	Criminal	Delinquency	Dependency and Neglect	Total, Excluding Traffic	Traffic
Number of cases	12,839,400	10,511,116	1,275,600	196,200	24,822,316	57,287,920

Source: U.S. Dept. of Justice, Bureau of Justice Statistics, 1986: 454; Nimick et al., 1987: 10, 15.

the United States and are, thus, busy places (U.S. Senate, 1983: 105). Table 10.1 shows that delinquency, dependency, and neglect cases account for a relatively small part of total caseflow. The 1,275,000 delinquency cases and approximately 200,000 dependency and neglect cases are dwarfed by the flow of almost 13,000,000 civil, over 10,000,000 criminal, and 57,000,000 traffic matters through state courts. In other words, data in table 10.1 suggest that judges have much more on their minds than juvenile problems.

CHARACTERISTICS OF CASES HANDLED BY JUVENILE COURTS

Juvenile courts in the United States have broad jurisdiction over concerns of problem children including delinquents, status offenders, dependent, and neglected youth. Juvenile law encourages the courts to resolve children's problems through informal family- and community-based means. But juvenile law also vests in judges the authority to terminate family custody of children and to incarcerate or otherwise "correct" offenders.

There are many types of juvenile courts. In approximately half of the nation's 3,091 counties, one judge presides over all types of cases. In urban areas, where 80 percent of the population lives, specialized courts serve the needs of masses of people. For example, the New York State court system is one of the largest in the world, employing more than thirty-three hundred judges and almost ten thousand nonjudicial officials. Approximately one thousand New York judges hear cases in trial courts. New York State trial courts process more than two million actions, proceedings, and indictments each year (U.S. Senate, 1983: 105). New York City employs fifteen juvenile court judges, compared to Houston's seven.[2] New York City courts also carry a backlog of more than twenty thousand cases from one year to the next (108).

Table 10.2 displays caseload data for U.S. juvenile courts for selected years from 1940 through 1990. These data show that the numbers of delinquency cases brought before the courts increased considerably between 1964 and 1974 but leveled off in the 1980s.

---

[2]Estimates are based upon information provided by Richard Gable on September 1, 1987.

TABLE 10.2
Cases Handled by U.S. Juvenile Courts, 1940–1990

	1940	1950	1964	1974	1983	1990
Total	—	373,000	836,000	1,403,000	1,471,800	—
Delinquency cases	200,000	280,000	686,000	1,252,000	1,275,600	1,264,800
Dependency and neglect cases	—	93,000	150,000	151,000	196,200	—
U.S. population under 18 years of age	—	—	69,625,000	69,114,000	63,812,000	64,083,000

Sources: Total, delinquency cases, and dependency and neglect cases data for 1940, 1950, and 1964 are from U.S. Bureau of the Census, 1975a: 419; 1974 figures are from U.S. Bureau of the Census, 1979: 194; 1983 figures are from Nimick et al., 1987: 10, 15; and 1990 figures are from U.S. Dept. of Justice, Bureau of Justice Statistics, 1993a: 540. For population under 18: Nimick et al., 1987: 15 for 1964–83; U.S. Bureau of the Census, 1991: 12 for 1990.

Even with this leveling off, current court caseloads are high. Processing of more than one and one-quarter million delinquency cases each year is costly, and it severely strains the resources of judicial, social service, and corrective agencies. Dependency and neglect cases brought before the court increased significantly in the 1950s, leveled off in the 1960s, and increased again in the 1970s and 1980s. There is considerable evidence that most dependency and neglect goes untended by judges. According to the National Council of Juvenile and Family Court Judges: "National Statistics on children who have been abused or neglected show judges see only an average 3.4 percent of minor injury cases, 8.3 percent of major injury cases and 15.4 percent of sexual abuse cases . . . only about 18 percent of the total abuse and neglect caseloads" (1986: 6).

Table 10.3 breaks down the number of juvenile court cases processed in selected years between 1957 and 1990 by the gender of the child involved. Table 10.3 indicates that, where delinquency is concerned, eight out of each ten children referred to the courts are boys. For dependency and neglect, however, roughly equal proportions of boys and girls are referred to juvenile courts. Historically, juvenile courts have stringently enforced the laws exerting parental control over children, especially females. Juvenile courts have also been highly interested in regulating female sexuality. Thus, while far fewer girls than boys are processed by juvenile courts, females charged with status offenses are often treated more harshly by court officials than males charged with more serious crimes, creating a "double standard of juvenile justice" (Chesney-Lind and Shelden, 1992: 112–13).

Table 10.4 provides information about whether judges (petitioned cases) or probation officers (nonpetitioned cases) handle children's matters. In general, over the last thirty years, judges have seen approximately half of all delinquency cases that come to the attention of court personnel and 70 to 80 perent of the dependency and neglect cases that reach the court. In 1983, approximately 55 percent of the children referred for delinquency and 29 percent of the children referred for abuse and neglect were processed by intake probation personnel without petitioning a judge. In 1990, equal numbers of delinquency cases were processed by intake probation officers and judges.

TABLE 10.3

Estimated Number of Juvenile Court Cases, by Gender of Child, 1957–1990

	1957		1963		1973		1983		1990	
	Number	%	Number	%	Number	%	Number	%	Number	%
Delinquency cases										
Male	358,000	81	485,000	81	845,300	74	980,400	77	1,027,017	81
Female	82,000	19	116,000	19	298,400	26	295,200	23	237,782	19
Dependency cases										
Male	—	—	—	—	—	—	98,000	50	—	—
Female	—	—	—	—	—	—	98,200	50	—	—

Source: Nimick et al., 1987: 8–9, 15; U.S. Dept. of Justice, Bureau of Justice Statistics, 1993a: 540.

TABLE 10.4
Estimated Number of Juvenile Court Cases, by Method of Handling, 1957–1990

	1957		1963		1974		1983		1990	
	Number	%	Number	%	Number	%	Number	%	Number	%
Delinquency cases										
Nonpetitioned	201,000	46	303,000	50	585,000	47	703,900	55	632,400	50
Petitioned	239,000	54	298,000	50	667,700	53	571,700	45	632,400	50
Dependency and neglect cases										
Nonpetitioned					28,700	19	56,000	29		
Petitioned					122,600	81	140,200	71		

Source: Nimick et al., 1987: 14, 19; U.S. Dept. of Justice, Bureau of Justice Statistics, 1993a: 540.

Children in Adult Courts

All state legislatures make provisions whereby some children may be processed through adult criminal courts (Marcotte, 1990). In 1990, these provisions resulted in about 82,900 felony convictions in state-level criminal courts of persons between thirteen and nineteen years of age (U.S. Department of Justice, Bureau of Justice Statistics, 1993: 528). There are four basic ways to give criminal courts jurisdiction over children: by lowering the age of jurisdiction, by excluding offenses, through judicial waiver and via concurrent jurisdiction (Krisberg et al., 1986: 9; U.S. Dept. of Justice, Bureau of labor Statistics, 1983: 61; Bartollas, 1993: 433). Usually more than one provision is in operation in most states.

Lowering the age limit of jurisdiction is the most common way to route children into adult court. By 1978, approximately thirty-eight state legislatures had determined that persons are under juvenile court jurisdiction up to the age of eighteen and that adult criminal court jurisdiction begins at age eighteen, eight states had lowered juvenile court jurisdiction to the age of seventeen, and four states had set it at sixteen. In 1978, in the twelve states where juvenile court jurisdiction ends before the age of eighteen, approximately 250,000 sixteen- and seventeen-year-old juveniles were arrested. The exact number of these juveniles who were referred to adult criminal courts is not known, but there is reason to believe that a high proportion were referred to adult court (Hamparian et al., 1982: 95–99).

Another common means for routing some children into adult criminal court is through legislative action, which excludes some offenses, usually very minor or very serious infractions, from juvenile court jurisdiction. By 1978, thirty-one states had laws excluding some offenses from juvenile court jurisdiction: twenty states excluded traffic, hunting, fishing, and boating infractions; eleven states excluded extensive lists of serious crimes, and in all but four of those eleven states minimum age limits were attached to the offenses (63). In general, the trend is for state legislatures to exclude felonies committed by children over sixteen years of age from juvenile court jurisdiction, although there is tremendous variation in the configuration of such laws from state to state (Feld, 1987). In 1978, approximately 1,300 children were processed through adult criminal courts as a result of excluded offense provisions (Hamparian et al.: 99).

By 1978, thirteen state legislatures had given concurrent jurisdiction to prosecuting attorneys. Concurrent jurisdiction is the authority to charge youth, who are in most cases over minimum age limits and who are suspected of committing certain offenses (usually felonies), in either juvenile or adult criminal court (White, 1987; *Rocky Mountain News,* July 10, 1993: 16A). Five states allow concurrent jurisdiction only in cases involving traffic, boating, hunting, and fishing infractions. Eight states provide for concurrent jurisdiction in delinquency cases, but there is considerable variation in the lists of specific offenses covered and in the age cutoffs for offenders. For example, Florida allows concurrent jurisdiction in cases involving children of any age who are charged with offenses punishable by death or by life imprisonment, whereas Arkansas provides concurrent jurisdiction for children over fifteen years old who have committed any criminal offense (Hamparian et al., 1982: 61–62). In 1978, approximately two thousand juveniles were charged in adult criminal court as a result of concurrent jurisdiction provisions in state law (99).

Next to lowering the age of jurisdiction, judicial waiver is the most common mechanism through which juvenile cases are transferred into adult criminal court. All but four state legislatures provide for a process whereby juvenile court jurisdiction over a case can be waived and transferred to an adult criminal court. The same laws also provide a way for adult criminal court judges to transfer cases involving children to juvenile court (Szymanski, 1989). Usually prosecutors and juvenile court judges make decisions regarding waiver, but they do so under legislative restraint regarding age of offender, nature of the offense, and the child's prior record and suitability for treatment as a juvenile (White, 1987). In the 1970s and 1980s, almost half of America's state legislatures amended their juvenile waiver laws (Schwartz, 1989: 7) In 1990, 2.7 percent of all juvenile court cases in the United States were waived to adult criminal courts (U.S. Dept. of Justice, Bureau of Justice Statistics, 1993a: 541). Today, law regarding judicial waiver of juveniles is in flux and varies greatly from state to state (Osbun and Rode, 1991: 379). For example, in 1982, twenty states set sixteen as the minimum age of waiver; fourteen states allowed the transfer of persons as young as fourteen; eleven states allowed transfer at fifteen; and three permitted waiver at thirteen years of age (Hamparian et al., 1982: 47). As of 1993, sixteen states have no specific age set for waiver; seven states set the age at sixteen; seven states, at fifteen; fourteen states, at fourteen; three states, at thirteen; one state, at twelve; and one state, at ten (Siegel and Senna, 1994: 534). A few states permit waiver for any offense, but throughout most of the nation waiver is allowed only for cases involving children who have committed felonies or a series of minor infractions (535).

In *Kent v United States* (383 U.S. 541 [1966]), the Supreme Court established four federal requirements for state courts to follow when considering the waiver of juveniles. First, a separate hearing is held to consider the issue of waiver. This in most states is called a "waiver hearing." Second, children and parents are entitled to use attorneys at waiver hearings. Third, attorneys representing juveniles and their parents are entitled to examine most information assembled and held by court employees, at least one day prior to the waiver hearing. Fourth, if a child is transferred to an adult criminal court, the juvenile court executing the waiver must issue a detailed written explanation for its decision (Hamparian et al., 1982: 7; Senna and Siegel, 1992: 101).

In 1978, approximately nine thousand children were transferred into adult criminal court through waiver (Hamparian et al., 1982: 99). Approximately 30 percent of the cases involved offenses against persons; 44 percent of all waivers were for property offenses. More than 90 percent of the juveniles waived into adult court pled guilty or were convicted after trial and 1 percent were found not guilty; 8 percent of the cases were dismissed (106). In 1978, judicial waiver eventuated in conviction after trial in adult criminal court of approximately 2,769 juveniles. Of those convicted, 830 were sent to state adult correctional facilities, 717 were put on probation, 681 received fines, 317 went to jail, 63 were incarcerated in state juvenile corrections facilities, and 37 got some other disposition. One hundred twenty-four convictions resulted in unknown action (114).

In 1989, sixteen thousand juvenile cases were waived to adult criminal court, representing a 78 percent increase in eleven years. Currently, 49 percent of all juvenile waivers are for property offenses, 29 percent for violent offenses, 16 percent are for drug-related offenses, and 6 percent are for public order offenses (Snyder et al., 1992: 21). Most children tried in adult courts today plead guilty or are convicted. The majority are given probation. However, more than 45 percent of the children waived to adult courts end up serving time in adult incarceratories. Youth waived to adult court usually serve more time in incarceratories than they would have had they been tried in a juvenile court (Siegel and Senna, 1994: 538).

Judicial waiver is a highly subjective process. For example, a study of Minnesota's 1980 attempt to legislate a detailed criteria to govern its waiver process yielded the following conclusions: "The criteria single out many juveniles whose records do not appear to be very serious," and they "fail to identify many juveniles whose records are characterized by violent, frequent, and persistent delinquent activity." County prosecutors failed to ask for waiver in almost half of the cases that qualified (Osbun and Rode, 1991: 385–88). The issue of transferring juveniles to adult criminal courts is far from settled. Considerable litigation, especially at the appellate level, continues today (Senna and Siegel, 1994: 101–28).

JUVENILE COURT PROCESS

Juvenile court employees learn about problem children from three main sources: police, parents, and school officials. Some children referred to the courts by police officers were taken into custody and put into detention. All others are at large in the community when the court learns about them. Whatever the referral source, juvenile courts require that formal written complaints or "requests for services" be filed against children before investigation begins. Written complaints contain the following information: parent's name, address, and telephone number, alleged problem or offense(s); victim(s) name(s), address(es) and telephone number(s); and evidence available in support of allegations. If a child is arrested and placed in detention, police officers are usually required to file a separate additional report detailing the circumstances in the case that prompted arrest and incarceration.

As intake probation officers sift through complaints or "requests for services," they must be aware of the multiple purposes of the juvenile court, including doing what is "best" for the child, protecting minor offenders from adjudication, saving court resources for more serious cases, and investigating and formally processing unresolvable or serious cases. The many purposes of the juvenile court are highlighted in the following statement made by a former judge: Juvenile court "is law and it is social work; it is control and it is help . . . it is both formal and informal . . . concerned not only with the delinquent, but also with the battered child and many others" (Rubin, 1976: 66).

Figure 10.2 presents a flowchart of juvenile court process, which we will use throughout the remainder of this chapter to consider the many directions that a case may take. It is important to remember that about 50 percent of all children in the United States who are referred to juvenile courts for delinquency and 20 percent to 30 percent of the dependency and neglect cases are processed by intake probation officers without any judicial intervention. Today, only about 50 percent of all delinquency cases and 70 percent of the dependency and neglect cases that reach juvenile or family court are referred on by probation for formal judicial handling. Box A in figure 10.2 shows that juvenile court processing begins when complaints or requests for services are received and checked by intake probation personnel for accuracy and completeness. A decision is made regarding whether or not the court has jurisdiction over the child in question. Jurisdiction decisions will concern the child's age, where the alleged offense or problem occurred, and where the child lives. In general, juvenile or family courts have jurisdiction over cases involving children who allegedly committed offenses (or are having problems) within the geographical area served by the court, and over children whose problems or possible offenses occurred elsewhere but who live in the court's territory. For example, a child who lives in Utah but is arrested in Florida as a runaway will fall under the jurisdiction of both Utah and Florida juvenile courts. In such cases children are often transported back to their homes and are processed by local courts, thus resolving the problem of overlapping jurisdiction.

If an intake officer is satisfied that the court has jurisdiction, s/he will review information in the complaint in order to determine whether there appears to be sufficient evidence of an offense or problem to warrant further investigation. Referrals lacking sufficient evidence will be dismissed. If sufficient evidence exists, the officer reviewing complaints will check juvenile court records to determine whether the child is already under supervision by another officer. Children who are already under the supervision of an-

FIGURE 10.2
Flowchart of the Juvenile Court Process

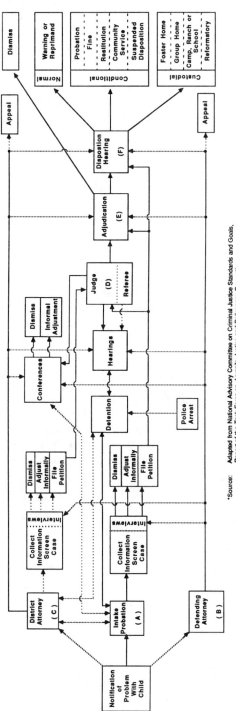

*Source: Adapted from National Advisory Committee on Criminal Justice Standards and Goals,
Report of the Task Force on Juvenile Justice and Delinquency Prevention
Washington, D.C.; Government printing office, 1976, P. 9

217

other probation officer will be referred to that officer to process the current offense or problem. Children new to the court will be assigned to an available intake officer.

Boxes B and C of figure 10.2 show that prosecuting and defending attorneys may also be notified of court cases involving problem children and that lawyers can participate at many stages of court process. Solid lines with arrows in figure 10.2 indicate the phases of juvenile court process in which important legal actors are most likely to participate. Broken lines with arrows show where intake officers, attorneys, and judges might be involved. Most juvenile or family court cases that are resolved in the early phases of processing do not involve attorneys. Currently, only around 15 percent of all juvenile court cases in the United States employ attorneys. However, in a few jurisdictions, lawyer participation may be seen in as many as 40 percent of all children's court cases (Thornton and Voight, 1992: 392). Every juvenile court case carries with it the potential for a formal legal contest.

Intake Interviews

If the court has jurisdiction over a child who is referred, and if there is sufficient evidence to warrant processing a case, the next step for intake probation is to set up an interview with the child and his/her parents. For children who are placed in detention this involves having a probation officer call the child's parents, inform them of their child's arrest, and invite them to come to the office for an interview. With children who are not incarcerated, the process is much the same. Parents are called by an intake probation officer and are invited to bring their child to the probation office for a voluntary scheduled interview. Where district attorneys have jurisdiction over juvenile cases, a similar procedure is followed by a deputy district attorney who sets up voluntary appointments with parents and their problem children. The arrows to the right of boxes A and C of figure 10.2 show movement into the voluntary interview phase of early juvenile court processing.

Intake probation officers and deputy district attorneys have little direct authority in juvenile cases during early court processing. Intake probation officers and deputy district attorneys with jurisdiction are authorized to file petitions requesting adjudication. Threat of adjudication usually induces parents and children to voluntarily cooperate with probation officers and prosecutors in finding ways to informally resolve cases before they reach a judge. Almost always, in order to avoid appearance before a judge, children and/or their parents are obliged to voluntarily sign a form admitting guilt. Parents and problem children must also sign a form that voluntarily waives their rights to due process. Defending attorneys are generally unwelcome participants in early court processing, since defense lawyers are prone to advise their clients not to admit guilt and not to sign waivers of procedural rights. Consequently, intake probation officers and deputy district attorneys tend to view all but the most cooperative defending attorneys as impediments to informally resolving juvenile court cases. Juvenile cases involving attorneys take hours and days to resolve, instead of minutes. Juvenile cases involving attorneys have created massive backlogs of unfinished litigation.

In many states, in cases where the court decides that children lack the capacity to represent their own best interests, judges are empowered to appoint a *guardian ad litem*—an attorney whose primary responsibility is to represent the interests of the child (Golden, 1992; Davidson, 1981). A guardian ad litem is most likely to be appointed in divorce, dependency, and neglect cases, where parental interests might diverge considerably from those of their children. However, a guardian ad litem can be appointed in delinquency cases, especially those involving termination of parental authority, hospitalization, or incarceration of a child when it is aggressively resisted by parents and their attorney.

At the intake interview, problem children, intake probation officers (or deputy district attorneys), and one or more parents are the principal participants. Sometimes defense attorneys and victims are included. An intake probation officer or deputy district attorney begins by explaining what the child has been charged with or what the nature of the complaint is. Parents and children are informed of their legal rights. During intake interviews it is not uncommon for the officer of the court to discover that one or more parents is emotionally disturbed or otherwise unable to care for a child, complicating the process considerably (Miller et al., 1976: 198). Intake officers ask children for information about the offense or problem. The vast majority of juveniles admit guilt during the interview, thus qualifying for informal adjustment (201). Parental behavior is observed by the court official in order to determine whether or not it is likely that a child can be controlled at home.

Children and parents are asked about how the suspect is doing at school and elsewhere in the community. Most juvenile cases are resolved quickly after a single intake interview. Some difficult cases require months to resolve, necessitating several voluntary intake interviews with parents, problem children, and others.

Intake Probation and District Attorney Options

A second set of arrows to the right of boxes A and C in figure 10.2 shows the options that are open to intake probation officers and deputy district attorneys as they process juvenile cases. Cases involving minor infractions or problems are often dismissed, with children and parents receiving a stern lecture from a court official and a warning that any future referral to the court will likely result in more severe treatment. Other children are diverted out of juvenile court by an officer's suggesting, for example, that the family seek counseling (or some other form of help) at their own expense as a condition of dismissal. Many cases are resolved during early court processing by a court official's telling children and parents that the offense or problem at hand is serious enough to warrant judicial attention and harsh punishment but that, with their voluntary consent, informal probation can be worked out, eliminating the need to formally involve a judge. Informal probation means that a child and his/her parent(s) sign a form agreeing to behavioral restrictions and treatment imposed by a court official, and promising that the child will attend regularly scheduled meetings with an officer. Informal probation usually lasts for six months. Violations of informal probation allow a court official to proceed with an application for adjudication.

Intake officers report that age and attitude are major considerations in selecting children for appearance before a juvenile court judge (201). Additionally, if a court intake officer believes that parents are unable or unwilling to control a child, if an officer believes the current offense or problem (or accumulation of offenses or problems) is serious, if parents or children refuse to admit guilt and will not waive their rights, if a defense attorney is uncooperative and contentious, or if state law requires that a child committing certain offenses be automatically referred to a judge, then intake probation officers and deputy district attorneys (with jurisdiction) are obligated to file a petition with the court asking that a case be adjudicated. Similarly, if court intake officials believe that a child should remain in detention, then a hearing must be scheduled before a judge, magistrate, or referee to consider the merits of the request. In 1984, the U.S. Supreme Court ruled in *Schall v. Martin* (104 U.S. 2403) that, if juvenile court judges perceive children to be dangerous to themselves or to the community and if acceptable due process procedures for detention hearings are followed, then pretrial detention is acceptable. As petitions are filed, or hearings are requested, the balance of authority and control over juvenile court cases shifts toward prosecuting attorneys and judges.

Pretrial Hearings and Conferences

By looking at box D of figure 10.2 and the area surrounding it, we see what happens to children who are put into detention and to youth for whom petitions are filed by court intake personnel. Children for whom petitions are filed are likely to attend one or more semiformal preadjudication hearings presided over by a judge, magistrate, or referee. For example, most children who are petitioned are required to attend a preliminary hearing (known variously as, e.g., "first hearing," "plea hearing," or "adjudication inquiry"). At the preliminary hearing intake probation officers, problem children, judges, magistrates, or referees are the most frequent participants. Prosecuting and defending attorneys, parents, victims, bailiffs, or sheriffs also regularly take part in proceedings. At a preliminary hearing a child is notified of the charges made against her/him. Children and their parents are told of their right to counsel and to other legal protections. If children and/or parents wish to be represented by an attorney but cannot afford to retain one, the court will usually appoint a public defender or private counsel paid for by state funds. In rare cases, judges will appoint a guardian ad litem. Judges, magistrates, or referees also determine whether or not sufficient evidence exists to warrant adjudication. Sometimes children are asked to enter a plea of guilty or not guilty. If, before the preliminary hearing but after a petition is filed, a plea bargain is worked out, a child might enter a guilty plea at the hearing in order to qualify for a predetermined form of punishment to be announced later at a disposition hearing. Especially in urban courts, many juvenile cases for which petitions have been filed will not reach adjudication, because they are resolved at preliminary hearings through plea bargaining.

Shortly after a child is placed in detention (locked up) or in a shelter situation (housed outside the home but not locked up), or if a legal official wishes to incarcerate or shelter a juvenile, a detention hearing must be held before a judge, magistrate, or referee. At the detention hearing the main goal of a judge, magistrate, or referee is to determine whether or not a child should be kept in detention or in shelter housing or should be released to his/her parents. Children whose parents are either unable or unwilling to provide them with housing are at high risk of being placed into detention or shelter. At the detention hearing a prosecutor, probation officer, or other legal official presents arguments in favor of detention or shelter. Prosecutors will almost always assert that problem children are either a threat or danger to themselves or that they pose a danger or threat to the community. Either type of threat or danger is defined by state law as grounds for detaining or sheltering a juvenile. Some children (or parents) will choose to represent themselves in preadjudicatory hearings. Parents who can afford to do so will often retain private counsel to speak on their behalf. Most poor children are represented at pretrial hearings by court-appointed lawyers who, in big cities, spend as little as five to fifteen minutes with juveniles they represent prior to appearing before a judge, magistrate, or referee (230). Counsel for a child, a prosecutor, and a judge, magistrate, or referee have opportunities to cross-examine the probation officer (or other legal official) who is advocating detention or shelter. Prosecutors are most likely to actively participate in hearings when older children are charged with relatively serious law violations. The child's attorney is allowed to present information and to make arguments in support of release or shelter as alternatives. Prosecutors, judges, magistrates, or referees and protagonist probation officers are given opportunities to cross-examine the defending attorney. Finally, after hearing all of the testimony, the judge, magistrate, or referee will decide to release a child to his/her parents or to place the juvenile in detention or into a shelter. If the detention or shelter decision is made by a magistrate or referee, it can be appealed to a juvenile court judge who has jurisdiction in the case. Children who are released go home with their parents shortly after the hearing ends, but they very likely spent from one to three days in detention before a hearing could be scheduled.

Youth ordered held in detention are returned by a sheriff or bailiff to juvenile hall, a detention center, or adult jail to await other hearings and adjudication. Females often face discrimination at the detention phase of juvenile court processing. Females are more likely than males to be held in detention for minor infractions, including status offenses (Chesney-Lind, 1988). Up to 75 percent of all female juveniles taken into custody may be locked up while awaiting further court processing. As few as 25 percent of all male juveniles arrested are held in detention (Mann, 1984: 148).

The 1974 Juvenile Justice and Delinquency Prevention Act requires that juveniles in adult jails be kept separate from adult offenders. The 1974 act makes illegal the confining of dependent, neglected, or status-offending children in adult jails. In 1980, when the Juvenile Justice Act was ammended, Congress stipulated that American adult jails should be rid of children by 1985. Later, Congress extended the deadline until 1988. Unfortunately, the jailing of children in adult facilities remains commonplace throughout the United States (Swanger, 1988: 211). Despite a twenty-year effort to remove children from adult jails, on June 30, 1988, America's 3,316 adult jails housed 1,451 juveniles (U.S. Dept. of Justice, 1991: 569, 575). On June 28, 1991, 2,350 children were locked up in adult jails throughout the United States (U.S. Department of Justice, Bureau of Justice Statistics, 1993a: 590). Experts estimate that about 250,000 juveniles are locked up each year in American adult jails (Polier, 1989: 32).

Children who are incarcerated after a detention hearing frequently spend one month or more in a lock-up. In many states, children who are incarcerated must be considered for bail. Where bail is allowed for juveniles, judges, magistrates, or referees usually rule on this possibility as a final item at the detention hearing. Children who are to be put in shelter housing are held in detention until a placement can be arranged and until a social services worker is able to transport each child to her/his new temporary home. If shelter space is unavailable, dependent and neglected children are often placed in detention on a temporary basis.

Judges, magistrates, or referees may also hold other hearings prior to adjudication. For example, waiver of a child to adult court, change of venue—transfer of jurisdiction over a case from one juvenile court to another—and petitions for dismissal are items of concern to the court that are frequently determined in hearings occurring prior to adjudication. Prosecuting and defending attorneys, intake probation officers, as well as parents and victims may participate in all pretrial hearings. Juvenile court hearings sometimes take only a few moments and are relatively cooperative in tenor. Other hearings evolve into formal, time-consuming, and costly battles between hostile legal contestants.

Some juvenile court judges use preliminary conferences as a means for disposing of cases. Conferences involve the same actors as do hearings, but they are often held in more informal settings like, for example, a judge's office. Rules of procedure are relaxed, and participants are encouraged to talk freely, off the record. At conferences, a judge may encourage plea bargaining between attorneys. A judge might go as far as to suggest a set of conditions for informally resolving a case. Judges can be either passive at conferences or more assertive, aggressively lobbying for informal resolution. Since judges make vital rulings about how juvenile court cases take form and about how trials proceed, they are in a strong position to induce participants to cooperate in finding a solution that makes trial unnecessary. Thus, much as at preadjudicatory hearings, judges eliminate a good many potential juvenile trials through agreements that are worked out at informal conferences. Judges may dismiss cases, informally adjust them, or determine that adjudication is necessary after attempting resolution via pretrial conference.

In big American cities, as many as 90 percent of the petitions filed are disposed of through dismissal or bargaining during the hearings and conferences stage of juvenile court process.[3] As few as 10 percent of juvenile court cases that merit the filing of a petition actually come to trial or adjudication (U.S. Dept. of Justice, 1991: 601). One line of thinking suggests that informal resolution, or dismissal, is the best way to handle the vast majority of juvenile court cases because it protects problem children from the embarrassment, punishment, and psychic depression that accompanies adjudication. Informal disposition of juvenile cases allows probation officers, lawyers, magistrates, referees, and judges the flexibility to tailor voluntary corrections programs to the needs of each child. In large metropolitan areas, however, where thousands of

---

[3]For example, investigators report that "ninety percent of the children named in petitions filed in the Denver Juvenile Court enter admissions of guilt" (in Miller et al., 1976: 604).

children must be processed through the court, there is a great risk that legal officials will fall into routines whereby most children are channeled into a handful of available, but often less than ideal, treatment options in order to manage a large flow of cases. Attorneys, referees, magistrates, judges, and probation officers in overloaded court systems are tempted to encourage children and parents to waive their rights to due process, even though doing so could be less in "the best interests of the child" than to the advantage of the court.

ADJUDICATION

Box E of Figure 10.2 shows movement of a few remaining juvenile court cases to the trial phase. Throughout the United States juvenile court trials are called by many names: Most common is "adjudication," but labels like "omnibus hearing" and "fact-finding hearing" are also used. The main purpose of adjudication in juvenile court is for a judge (or jury) to decide whether or not a child is delinquent or in need of services. Before the *Gault* decision in the late 1960s, and even today in theory, trials in juvenile court were not considered criminal in nature but were a form of civil litigation. *In re Gault* (387 U.S. 1 [1967]) affirmed the right of children on trial to many of the protections that are guaranteed by the Fourteenth Amendment to all adult criminal defendants, namely, adequate notice of charges, the right to a defense attorney, opportunity to confront and cross-examine witnesses, protection against self-incrimination, proof of guilt beyond a reasonable doubt,[4] and transcripts of court proceedings. Thus, some juvenile court trials are today still run in accordance with the historical prescriptions of state law as relatively informal hearings where legalism is kept to a minimum, a judge presides for the state in order to represent the "best interests" of a child, and legal officials cooperate with each other in order to determine what is "best for the child." At the same time, however, many other modern juvenile court trials are just like adult criminal court proceedings.

In the least formal type of juvenile adjudication, intake probation officers present the case against a child, and each trial usually

---

[4]In many states cases against children who are charged with status offense violations may be proven if a "preponderance of the evidence" indicates guilt.

consumes fewer than five minutes of court time. Witnesses and victims are sometimes questioned by a judge. Problem children are asked a series of questions by a judge, usually about their involvement in alleged offenses. Parents, when available, are frequently questioned by a judge. After considering testimony and examining available evidence, judges announce their findings and determine if a child is nondelinquent, delinquent, or in need of services. Cases are dismissed against nondelinquent children. Youth who are pronounced delinquent or in need of services are scheduled for a disposition hearing.

More legalistic juvenile court trials often last for several hours. Prosecutors are active in presenting the case against a problem child; witnesses and victims may be called and questioned; and defense attorneys have an opportunity to present the child's side of a case, call and question witnesses, and cross-examine prosecution witnesses. Judges oversee trials, make rulings in disputes over procedure. After each side has presented its case, judges (occasionally juries) determine that the youth on trial is either nondelinquent, delinquent, or in need of services. Cases are dismissed against children adjudicated nondelinquent; youth in need of services are scheduled for a disposition hearing.

DISPOSITION OPTIONS

If at adjudication children are determined to be delinquent or in need of services (in some states, labels like "miscreant," "wayward," and "truant" are used), a judge is obligated by federal law to schedule a separate and distinct dispositional hearing at which resolution to a case will be announced. Box F of figure 10.2 represents the dispositional phase of juvenile or family court processing. In some states (New York, for example) disposition hearings may follow immediately after adjudication. Most other states allow more time to pass since, before the disposition hearing is held, judges usually request a presentence report. Presentence reports contain the following types of information: description of circumstances relating to the present offense(s), child's prior legal record, school achievement and social data, description of child's home life and after-school associations, and psychological, psychiatric, and social evaluations. Presentence reports also include the probation officer's recommendation regarding a disposition alternative.

Some simple dispositional hearings involve only a judge, problem child, intake probation officer, and possibly parents and witnesses. In simple dispositional hearings, a judge reviews the presentence report, listens to witnesses, asks questions of participants, and, finally, announces a finding either that the child needs rehabilitation or that a disposition is required in order to protect the public. The judge then proceeds to announce the disposition. In a more complex dispositional hearing the judge must allow formal presentations by prosecutors and defending lawyers and cross-examination of witnesses. At the conclusion of a complex dispositional hearing, the judge considers the information available and declares either that the child needs rehabilitation or that a disposition is required in order to protect the public. The judge then announces the disposition. In all types of dispositional hearings, children and their parents are again advised of their rights and told of their right to appeal any decision made at the hearing.

At disposition, judges are obligated by modern state juvenile law to protect the child *and/*or the best interests of the community. In general, there are three correctional alternatives used by judges in order to meet the obligations listed above. Judges punish, isolate, and rehabilitate juvenile offenders. During the 1960s and 1970s, many legal officials throughout the Unites States, including juvenile court judges, emphasized rehabilitation for young offenders. However, since the mid-1970s, many legal officials have embraced a "just deserts" philosophy, which asserts that youthful law violators deserve to be punished for their criminal acts (Bartollas, 1990: 95–96). According to Schwartz, "the result was an avalanche of "get tough" policies and practices." Consequently, "the rates of youth confined on any given day in juvenile detention centers (pretrial holding facilities) increased by more than 50 percent between 1977 and 1985." Training school incarceration rates also increased by 16 percent (1989: 7).

Dispositional options available to juvenile or family court judges are listed to the far right of figure 10.2. At the top of the list, we see that some children are released to their parents with a stern lecture and with warnings of harsher treatment should they appear before the court in the future. Other youth are put on probation under the supervision of an outtake probation officer. Judges typically specify conditions that must be met by a child and her/his parents in order to successfully complete probation. In most cases, probation lasts from six months to one year and requires that children and their parents appear for regularly scheduled meetings at a probation office. Sometimes separately, but often as a supplement to probation, children are fined, made to repay their victims (restitution), or sentenced to perform community service.

Disposition is suspended for some juvenile offenders who are instead put on a form of informal probation: judges specify behavior that the offenders must exhibit in order to avoid facing a more severe disposition alternative. If children meet court expectations, usually for six months to one year, then disposition is permanently suspended. Juveniles who fail to meet court expectations can be resentenced. Written agreements formalize almost all forms of informal and formal probation and must be signed by children and their parents.

In theory, status offenders and dependent and neglected children are disposed of via nominal or conditional options, since they have committed no crimes. However, many minor offenders, especially those who have no family support, are deemed to need rehabilitation, or pose a danger to themselves or to the public, are nevertheless put into custodial care. State law usually requires that custodial jurisdiction for status offenders and dependent and neglected children be transferred to a state social service agency and that non-crime-committing youth be housed separate from delinquents in foster homes or group homes. State law, however, gives social service agencies nearly unlimited discretion to transfer dependent, neglected, and status-offending children back into a detention home or *any other facility,* should they choose to do so. Thus, in reality, many status offenders and dependent and neglected children end up incarcerated in the same facilities that are used for delinquents. Finally, some delinquents are sentenced by judges to confinement in camps, ranches, schools, or reformatories where isolation, control, and punishment compete with rehabilitation as institutional priorities. Camps, ranches, schools, and reformatories are usually located in rural settings far away from urban centers. Children are held in closed facilities, where behavior is supervised around the clock and punishment looms for every violation of the rules. In 1990, more than 57 percent of all adjudicated juvenile court cases in the United States were disposed of via probation. Almost 33 percent of all adjucated juvenile court cases resulted in out-of-home placements. Fewer than 4 percent of all adjudicated cases were dismissed (U.S. Department of Justice, Bureau of Justice Statistics, 1993a: 541).

The Death Penalty

There is considerable debate in American society about whether or not children should be executed for capital offenses, like murder. While execution of juveniles is uncommon, it has generally been allowed by law. The American colonies identified many crimes (including, in Massachusetts, incorrigibility) as capital offenses. Colonial children above the age of seven could be put to death for committing capital offenses (Binder, Geis, and Bruce, 1988: 205–06). To date, legal officials in the United States have executed 281 persons who were juveniles at the time of their offenses; 10 of those executed were girls. Twenty-seven states currently permit execution of offenders who were under eighteen years of age when they committed the crime (Bartollas, 1990: 17; Chesney-Lind and Shelden, 1992: 50; Seligson, 1986). On May 30, 1990, 33 prison inmates in fourteen states awaited execution for offenses they committed as juveniles. All were males (U.S. Department of Justice, Bureau of Justice Statistics, 1990: 621; Chesney-Lind and Shelden, 1992: 50).

There is no nationwide policy on executing children. In a 1982 case, the U.S. Supreme Court ruled that "great weight" should be given to a youth's age in capital cases. In 1988, the Court set aside the death penalty of a person who was fifteen when he committed a capital offense. However, in 1989, the U.S. Supreme court ruled in *Stanford v. Kentucky* (109 U.S. 2969) that executing juveniles who committed capital offenses while they were sixteen to eighteen years of age does not constitute cruel and unusual punishment and is, therefore, allowed by the U.S. Constitution.

SUMMARY

In the first section of this chapter we looked at U.S. court structure and caseflow and saw that delinquency, dependency, and neglect cases represent a small part of overall judicial activity. Children's court cases must compete with civil, criminal, and traffic litigation for resources and attention in highly overloaded state court systems. Thus the pattern of court structure and caseflow dictates that children are not likely to receive abundant judicial attention.

We learned that juvenile or family courts annually process nearly one and one-third million delinquency cases and almost two hundred thousand dependency and neglect cases. Data showed that most youth referred to the court for delinquency are boys.

However, almost equal numbers of boys and girls are referred to the court for investigation of dependency or neglect. Only about 50 percent of the children who are referred to juvenile or family court for delinquency get passed on by intake probation officers to referees or judges for formal processing. Approximately 70 percent of the dependency and neglect cases that are referred to juvenile or family courts receive the formal attention of a referee, magistrate, or judge. Thus, many court cases involving problem children never reach a judge.

Our examination of early juvenile court processing showed that many children's cases are settled by court intake workers through interviews and through use of informal probation that requires young suspects to voluntarily admit guilt. In order to qualify for informal adjustment, children and their parents must voluntarily sign a waiver of their rights to due process. While legally entitled to do so, defense lawyers are generally not welcome to participate in early court processing of juveniles.

Juvenile court judges use hearings and conferences to encourage actors in children's cases to find informal solutions to problems. Since judges possess great power to determine the outcome of cases that go to trial, lawyers, intake probation officers, children, parents, and others who participate pay considerable attention to suggestions made by the bench about how to achieve informal adjustment. Evidence suggests that as many as 90 percent of the cases petitioned to big-city juvenile and family court judges are resolved short of trial, through bargaining.

Only a few children's cases reach adjudication. Today, some juvenile trials are still informal and involve only a judge, intake probation officer, problem child, and parents. Many other juvenile court trials include attorneys and thus closely resemble adult criminal litigation. After trial, children who are declared delinquent or in need of services must appear before a judge for sentencing at a subsequent disposition hearing. Judges have discretion to respond to delinquency or a need for service in many ways. Some cases receive nominal disposition, while others warrant imposition of punishment or conditional rehabilitation. A few delinquent, dependant, and neglected children are put into custodial care. A small number of serious offenders are put to death.

PART 5

Prevention and Correction of Delinquency

CHAPTER 11

Community-Based Efforts to Prevent and Correct Delinquency

INTRODUCTION

In this chapter we focus on preventing and correcting delinquency. *Delinquency prevention* involves efforts of individuals, groups, and organizations to keep children from violating the law and from drawing the attention of legal authorities (Lundman, 1993: 17). Delinquency prevention functions "to preserve or retain youth in a relatively law-abiding status . . . to alter environments so as to preserve youth in a relatively law-abiding status" (Johnson, Bird, and Little, 1979: 1, 24). In contrast, *corrections*, revolves around government activities, in formal organizations, to punish or rehabilitate problem children after they are caught (Clear and Cole, 1994: 14–15). Thus, prevention focuses on eliminating problems for children, and on keeping young persons from violating the law in the first place, whereas corrections punishes, isolates, and rehabilitates youngsters after problems or misdeeds have occurred.

Delinquency prevention and correction are similar undertakings that cannot be totally disentangled. Prevention and correction are both based upon premeditated and organized activities to control childrens' behavior. As a result, both must rely upon primary and secondary forms of control.

Primary control, which involves establishing long-term bonds with children, is best achieved within the confines of strong family, neighborhood, and community structures. Secondary control, on the other hand, requires only temporary, indifferent human contact and operates where family, neighborhood, and community fail to constrain childhood behavior. Secondary control is the trademark of urban industrial life, and is administered through bureaucratic organizations.

Table 11.1 outlines social units that prevent and correct juve-

TABLE 11.1
Social Units Capable of Preventing and Correcting Delinquency

Primary Control			Secondary Control		
Family	Neighborhood	Community	Police	Courts	Corrections
Friends	Service agencies	Church		Attorneys	
		School			
				Social services	

nile delinquency. Units listed on the left side of table 11.1 are most effective at preventing delinquency, because primary relationships between problem children and adults are more likely within these types of social groupings. I stressed this point in several earlier chapters by highlighting the importance of family, neighborhood, community, friends, playmates, schools, and local service agencies in preventing delinquency. When family, neighborhood, and community break down, elements of secondary control invade some units on the left side of table 11.1, as, for example, churches, schools, and service agencies bureaucratize in order to process large numbers of clients. Units on the right side of table 11.1 were created by governments in order to impose secondary control over adults and children.

Punishment versus Rehabilitation of Problem Children

Legal *punishment* is defined as "payment for past misconduct . . . whereby pain is inflicted only to prevent future criminal behavior" (Springer, 1986: 25). Other scholars prefer to ignore the element of pain and, instead, define punishment more benignly as "any requirement that imposes costs, losses or other inconveniences" (Schneider, 1985: 9). Since courts decide what dispositions juvenile law violators receive, punishment, in practice, becomes "any sanction that the judge intends as punishment" (9; also see Clear and Cole, 1994: 72–73).

Punishment is an old and formidable means for achieving prevention and correction (Schmalleger, 1994: 272). Death, torture, and corporal punishment have been used for centuries as induce people to abide by the law and to encourage children to avoid legal attention. In the eighteenth century, English and American governments broadened the scope of legal punishment to include transportation of children away from their communities, incarceration in work shops, and indenture.

In the late eighteenth century and in the nineteenth century American local and state governments began to incarcerate adults and juveniles in jails, camps, farms, prisons, reformatories, and juvenile halls so that larger numbers could be efficiently isolated from society and punished. Until 1900, few Americans questioned the general belief that juvenile and adult offenders deserved punishment. Today, the punishment ethic is strongly supported by many scholars and legal officials. According to a veteran juvenile court judge, for instance, crime and delinquency are acts or omissions that should be held liable to punishment by society. In his words, "without punishment there is no criminal justice, and there is no juvenile justice" (Springer, 1986: 4, 26).

Punishment takes many forms when administered by employees of the legal system. For example, verbal, emotional, and physical abuse can be used on a child at all stages of legal handling. Children who are thrown out of school or who are adjudicated "delinquent" experience status degradation. Children who are incarcerated experience isolation from family and friends. Young persons who are locked up risk institutional violence and sexual abuse (Hewitt and Regoli, 1994: 395). Institutionalized problem children tend to suffer from heightened depression. In some states, solitary confinement, deprivation, and corporal punishment are used as "disciplinary measures" with incarcerated youth (Miller et al., 1976: 696; Lundman, 1993: 205–38).

Between 1900 and 1920, ideas about criminals and delinquents underwent some change. Reformers asserted that law violators should be rehabilitated (Rothman, 1979: 9). *Rehabilitation* is "productive work in connection with a program of education and counseling" (Miller et al., 1976: 696; Clear and Cole, 1994: 65–67; Schmalleger, 1994: 222–23). Rehabilitation involves "programs . . . providing educational opportunities and employment assistance" (Grizzle et al., 1982: 11). Rehabilitation has expanded in juvenile incarceratories in the form of counseling and educational and vocational programs. Throughout the twentieth century, probation also grew, and thus law violators could receive counseling, supervision, and employment assistance instead of, or in addition to, legal punishment. Classification systems were developed so that judges and correctional employees could determine whether offenders should receive punishment, rehabilitation, or both.

One popular classification system acknowledges four basic delinquent personality types. Neurotic-disturbed children feel inferior, are introverted, and, as a result of their delinquency, feel like failures. They feel inadequate and are riddled with guilt. Unsocialized-psychopathic delinquents, who are malicious and highly aggressive, do not regret their misdeeds. Subcultural-socialized children follow the prescriptions of members of a peer group, committing delinquency as a by-product of group membership and allegiance. Finally, inadequate-immature children lack direction, drifting into and out of delinquency as opportunities present themselves (Quay, 1965).

Another popular classification system was developed out of Interpersonal Maturity Levels (I-Levels) Theory (Warren, 1969 and 1976). The I-Levels classification system is used throughout the United States by juvenile corrections personnel to match problem children with different treatment modalities. The theory asserts that not all children reach the highest possible levels of maturity. Delinquents are stuck at maturity levels 2, 3, or 4. For various reasons, delinquents have not progressed to some higher level of maturity. The I-Levels classification system breaks delinquents down into nine subtypes within the three immaturity levels. At level 2, children are typed as either Asocial-Aggressive or Asocial-Passive. Level 3 children are typed as Immature-Conformists, Cultural-Conformists, or Manipulators. Level 4 youth are typed as Neurotic-Acting Out, Neurotic-Anxious, Situational-Emotional Reactors, or Cultural Identifiers (Gibbons and Krohn, 1991: 191–93).

Are punishment and rehabilitation compatible goals for prevention and corrections programs? Probably not. Where punishment and rehabilitation activities are allowed to coexist, the need to punish and control offenders tends to obviate effective rehabilitation. Almost any rehabilitation effort can be turned into a form of punishment (Miller et al., 1976: 696–97). Almost all programs to correct American problem children blend elements of punishment and rehabilitation together. Today, punishment and rehabilitation are often seen as essential parts of a correctional program for juvenile offenders. A veteran juvenile court judge asserts, for example, that "disapproval of, and punishment for, the wrongful act is probably the single most important rehabilitative measure available to the court" (Springer, 1986: 3).

Community-Based Treatment

Due to recent changes in federal and state delinquency laws, there has been a steady increase in the number of community-based treatment programs available in the U.S. for delinquents and for other problem children, although we do not know exactly how many (Best and Luckenbill, 1994: 205; Siegel and Senna, 1981: 547–48). We should also note, however, that the worsening U.S. economy and shrinking public expenditures for children's needs make it increasingly difficult for community-based prevention and corrections programs to survive (Bartollas, 1990: 426). Community-based programs for problem children were a basic part of the diversionary movement, which began in the 1960s. Proponents of diversion argued that community prevention and corrections programs should be developed for dependent and neglected children, and for minor offenders so that they could be kept separate from serious delinquents. Today, however, community-based treatment is used for predelinquents, minor and serious juvenile offenders, and dependent and neglected children (Lundman, 1993; Little, 1981a). Critics of diversion point out that community-based prevention and corrections programs expand considerably the jurisdiction of legal officials, increase costs, and raise the number of children who come under the control of the legal system (Bartollas, 1990: 362, 443; Gibbons and Krohn, 1991: 310; Seigel and Senna, 1981: 413, 471).

There are three general types of community-based treatment programs: nonresidential, short-term residential, and residential (Little, 1978b: 1–2). Community-based prevention and corrections philosophy assumes that children can be rehabilitated through counseling, education, job training, employment placement and provision of other essential services, for example, medical aide and housing. Community-based prevention and corrections usually emphasizes rehabilitation and downplays punishment. Community-based programs stress that rehabilitation is most likely to occur within the city, where problem children can be given help with family, job, and school concerns. Nevertheless, community-based corrections relies on secondary control techniques in order to implement programs with large numbers of youthful clients.

TYPES OF COMMUNITY-BASED PREVENTION
AND CORRECTIONS PROGRAMS

Effective and committed families provide the most successful means for preventing delinquency. Where families are not able to adequately instruct and control children, some nonlegal help may be available. For example, mental health clinics and other service agencies within cities offer individual and family counseling for problem children (Rothman, 1979: 65–67). Counseling involves "helping individuals understand and solve their adjustment problems" (Siegel and Senna, 1981: 497). Counseling is the most common form of secondary help available to problem children (497).

For example, in Helena, Montana, The Family Teaching Center runs a counseling program for parents of aggressive or out-of-control children. The center helps approximately 150 families each year and receives funding from federal, state, and local agencies. The Family Teaching Center employs professional and paraprofessional counselors and utilizes volunteer help in order to offer in-home counseling, evening classes, and school liaison services to parents of problem children. Family Teaching Center counselors assume that parents can learn to control their children. In counseling sessions and at weekly evening classes, parents are taught the following child management skills: identifying and specifying acceptable and unacceptable behavior, using rewards to shape desired behavior, applying punishment effectively and humanely, and evaluating their child management efforts (Wall et al., 1981: 48). After counseling sessions and classes end, Family Teaching Center workers periodically contact participants by telephone.

General youth development programs are another source of help. Programs such as Boy and Girl Scouts, Campfire Girls, Boys and Girls Clubs, organized athletics, and cultural offerings encourage all children in the community to participate in educational and recreational activities (*Rocky Mountain News*, Nov. 11, 1993: 30A). General youth development programs offer opportunities to get involved in fruitful and productive aspects of community life (Johnson, Bird, and Little, 1979: 22). Similarly, affirmitive action programs aimed at disadvantaged children in urban areas offer some help to problem children.

For example, the Jobs For Youth program in Boston and Cambridge, Massachusetts, offers counseling services, basic education, employment training, job placement, and job retention services to almost one thousand disadvantaged high school dropouts each year. Jobs for Youth enrolls 40 percent females and 60 percent males: 50 percent of the children served are African American, 42 percent are Anglo, and 6 percent are Hispanic. Vocational counselors employed at Jobs For Youth work with dropouts, coaching them on job selection, teaching them job interview skills, and helping them to appreciate the responsibilities of employment. Counselors place children in paying jobs and follow up with job-site visits and regular contact with employers. When problems arise, counselors try to help dropouts find ways to successfully resolve them, thus encouraging continued employment. Jobs For Youth makes a two-year commitment to dropouts, providing opportunities to continue basic and vocational education programs. The program employs full-time and part-time professionals, paraprofessionals, and youths. Funding comes from federal agencies, private foundations, and corporations (Wall et al., 1981: 68; Lundman, 1993: 192–200).

The Juvenile Delinquency Prevention Act of 1972, the Juvenile Justice and Delinquency Prevention Act of 1974, Juvenile Justice Amendments of 1977, and the 1992 reauthorization by Congress of the federal Office of Juvenile Justice and Delinquency Prevention have recognized the existence of large numbers of at-risk children in the United States. These laws have encouraged development of more programs that prevent delinquent acts *before* children come to the attention of legal authorities. As a result, over the last twenty years, hundreds of new delinquency prevention programs have been initiated, usually with a combination of federal and local funding. Prevention programs intervene in childrens' lives through one or more of the following social units: family, peers, school, work, and community. While prevention programs display considerable variation in structure and approach, most use a combination of strategies from the following list of possibilities: psychological/mental health counseling, social network development, criminal influence reduction, instruction in role development/role enhancement, education/skill development, activities/recreation, providing consistent social expectations, helping with economic resources, power enhancement and deterrence (Johnson, Bird, and Little, 1979: 3–4). Unfortunately, millions of American children fall through the net of support provided by families, youth development programs, and affirmative action efforts.

Grassroots prevention programs also offer good ways to combat delinquency (*Daily Times-Call*, June 15, 1993: 9A; *Rocky Mountain News*, Dec. 10, 1993: 39A). Prevention programs that operate for several consecutive years and allow children to establish primary relationships with capable and committed adults can give problem youth the support and supervision that is otherwise missing. Unfortunately, community-based prevention programs face many common roadblocks; for example, securing stable and adequate funding is a chronic problem (*Rocky Mountain News*, June 21, 1993: 10A). Many prevention programs encounter more needy children than they are able to accomodate. Successful programs tend to grow large, forcing adoption of bureaucratic organization and mandating delivery of services through secondary control techniques.

Schools

Schools provide another important way to prevent delinquency (Goldstein, 1991: 225–38). In the United States, mandatory attendance laws force schooling on children. Much delinquency is prevented because teachers, counselors, and administrators act as control agents to keep a collective eye on children, rewarding desired behavior, discovering misbehavior, and punishing infractions of the rules. School helps teach most children how to obey the law— and how to hide misdeeds. School equips most children with knowledge, skills, and credentials enabling them to survive without resorting to criminal means (Barlow and Ferdinand, 1992: 161–63; Chesney-Lind and Shelden, 1992: 187–89).

For example, a Boulder, Colorado, junior high school social studies class, taught by uniformed Deputy Sheriff Valerie Johnson, takes this goal to the extreme. Under the supervision of the school principal and social studies teachers, Officer Johnson and her students meet with officials from the Drug Enforcement Administration, the FBI, the Secret Service, a police gang unit, a child abuse agency, a police canine unit, a private investigator, and the local sheriff. The children also visit traffic court and witness a criminal sentencing. This class is part of Officer Johnson's duties as a community education specialist (Taylor, 1991: 1E).

For many American children, however, school means trouble and represents a place where failure is forced upon them (Barlow and Ferdinand, 1992: 161). Teachers, administrators, and legal officials tend to blame children for educational problems. Unsuccessful youth are labeled "learning disabled," "lazy," or "disinterested." Remedial education programs, counseling, and social casework are offered by schools as solutions. Remedial education is almost anything that teachers and administrators try to do with children who are having trouble at school; for example, learning disabled young persons and "slow learners" are often put into segregated classes, where course content and teaching style are presumably tailored to fit their special needs. Tutorial programs, which use volunteers to help problem youth with school assignments, can be effective.

In the 1980s, the federal government began supporting student initiated crime, violence, and disruption prevention programs in public schools throughout the United States. Student initiated and operated prevention programs are varied, and they include combinations of the following activities: school/community advisory council development; teacher corps staff training; training for parents, police officers, community agency representatives, and students, academic tutoring/counseling; and school curriculum development (Office of Juvenile Justice and Delinquency Prevention, 1980: 24–26).

Thornton, James, and Doerner believe that seven fundamental changes in schooling could result in more effective prevention of delinquency (1982: 468). They say that communities could

1. increase chances of academic success for marginal youth;
2. make school relevant;
3. create ways to get underachieving children more involved with, more committed to, schooling;
4. keep children with learning disabilities fully integrated into the normal school curriculum (in other words, give slow learners and learning disabled youngsters special help, but don't label and isolate them);
5. better integrate schools with other community agencies;
6. make special efforts to include underprivileged families in school activities;

7. encourage the best-educated, most capable and most caring persons to become teachers.

Alternative education, a last-ditch preventive measure, is often required of children who fail at school. Alternative education is almost anything that teachers and administrators try to do with children who are failing (Little, 1979a: 3; Goldstein, 1991: 232). For example, some schools provide tutorial services. Other schools set up time-out rooms where young persons with problems can go to receive counseling. In general, youth who fail are seen by teachers and administrators as deserving of punishment and legalistic treatment. When failing children are thought to be at fault, alternative education can involve behavioral contracts and punitive work assignments (Little, 1979a: 7–8). Some failing problem children are put on in-school suspension, segregated from other students and supervised closely by special personnel (5). In extreme cases, troublesome students who fail are suspended or expelled from school. Many suspended or expelled children are required to attend special schools where supervision is intense (5).

Probation

Probation, by far the most common form of juvenile corrections in the United States, is legal supervision of delinquents in the communities where they live (Senna and Siegel, 1992: 180). In terms of organization, probation varies greatly from state to state. In some states probation is run out of the same offices as parole (which we will get to later). Elsewhere, probation operates independently. Some probation officers supervise adult and juvenile cases; other probation operations specialize in either adult or childrens' services. In all, there are approximately four thousand probation and parole offices in the United States (Grizzle, et al., 1982: 21; Lundman, 1993: 115–22). Probation is often operated by state government, but there are many jurisdictions in the U.S. in which probation is run locally. Industrial states organize probation bureaucratically and employ thousands of probation officers. Rural states usually operate relatively small probation offices in large cities.

There are two types of probation. First, as we noted in earlier chapters, many police departments and most intake probation organizations employ *informal probation* as a corrective tool. If parents and children voluntarily agree to informal probation, many police and intake probation officers negotiate a set of conditions that must be met in order to avoid formal processing of a case. Second, *formal probation* is a juvenile court function. Formal probation is "the imediate post-conviction release of offenders into the community under some type of supervision" (Rothman, 1979: 8). Juvenile court judges frequently sentence offending children to a period of confinement but suspend incarceration while probation is tried (Springer, 1986: 32). Both informal and formal probationers can face heightened punishment if they violate the terms of their agreement. In this sense, probation almost always involves some degree of punishment or the threat of punishment.

Probation was introduced into American cities in the early twentieth century. In 1900, fewer than ten states had enacted laws providing for probation. By 1920, every state had begun a program of juvenile probation (Rothman, 1979: 8). Probation is thought of today as an alternative to placing offenders in a correctional institution (see, Grizzle, et al., 1982: 20). However, Rothman reports that early juvenile court judges saw probation as a means for extending their authority over children whose cases might otherwise be dismissed (13), rather than as an alternative to incarceration (57).

In large American cities, over the last ten years, due to budget cuts, the number of probation officers has declined by 20 to 30 percent (Walker, 1994: 217). Even without reductions in numbers, probation work is difficult, in part because it involves two conflicting functions (Lundman, 1993: 121; Miller et al., 1976: 657–58; Grizzle et al., 1982: 21; Walker, 1994: 215–21). First, probation officers are responsible for supervising children while they are on probation and for determining whether or not children are carrying out the probation plan that they committed themselves to. Thus, probation officers must do a great deal of surveillance and investigative work that can be perceived by children as threatening and punitive. Young persons who violate the conditions of probation and get caught must be reported by their probation officer to the court. Consequently, a large part of the juvenile probation officer's role involves policelike supervision and surveillance of problem children (Rothman, 1979: 17). Second, probation officers are also expected to fill a therapeutic role, in which emphasis is placed on counseling and on helping children gain access to services such as, for example, employment assistance, medical attention, substance abuse treatment, housing assistance, legal advice, and financial aid (23; Miller, et al., 1976: 657–58). Thus, probation officers are expected to be a combination of police officer, counselor, and servant, making probation both punitive and rehabilitative.

Today, the American Correctional Association prescribes an M.A. degree, in social work or another related discipline, with ample coursework in criminology, juvenile delinquency, and criminal justice, for persons planning to become probation officers (Pursley, 1991: 566). However, state-level requirements for entry-level probation officers are more in keeping with those suggested by the President's Commission on Law Enforcement and the Administration of Justice. This commission recommends the following set of minimum qualifications for probation officers: a B.A. degree in one of the social sciences; one year of graduate study in social work or in a related social science (or one year of full-time, paid experience under professional supervision in a recognized social agency), emotional and intellectual maturity, ability in interpersonal relations, positive value systems and dedication to the service of others (in Miller et al., 1976: 658; Pursley, 1991: 566). Because of their educational background and personal characteristics, many probation officers favor the therapeutic side of their work and feel somewhat uncomfortable with the mandate to provide policelike supervision for clients.

In theory, in order to make possible effective supervision, probation officers would carry no more than 50 supervision cases each. It is assumed that a new case requires five times as much investigation and supervision as an ongoing case. Consequently, probation officers should carry fewer than 50 cases, if some are new. In reality, this standard is seldom met. In the 1970s, big-city probation officers often handled 70 or more cases, in addition to meeting many other responsibilities (Miller et al., 1976: 663). If probation officers spent all of their working time supervising clients, and if each officer had a stable caseload of 50, each client would receive an average of three hours of supervision per month. Unfortunately, probation officers spend only approximately one-quarter of their time supervising clients (Grizzle et al., 1982: 21). In the 1990s, big-city caseloads average as many as 130–300 offenders per probation officer, making effective supervision impossible (Walker, 1994: 217).

Probation is actually a three-part process involving presentence investigation, supervision, and termination of the sentence. First, before judicial disposition, a probation officer prepares a presentence report for each juvenile case, including a combination of the following: legal data, prior record of defendant, biographical data, educational history, family history, medical/drug history, official report of the offense(s), the juvenile's version of the offense(s), evaluation/diagnosis of the child, and a disposition recommendation. If at disposition a child is placed on probation, then the second phase of the process begins. Probation officers supervise problem children and conduct surveillance aimed at determining whether or not they are meeting the terms of their agreement with the court. Third, if a child meets the terms of probation throughout the period of supervision, then probation officers recommend to the court that whatever sentence was held in suspension while probation was tried be terminated. If children do not meet the terms of their agreement with the court, probation officers are empowered to recommend to the court that probation be revoked and that the original suspended sentence be imposed (22–24). Thus, threat of revocation can be used by probation officers in order to induce young persons to abide by the rules. Problem children are likely to perceive threat of revocation as a punitive measure. Sometimes all phases of a child's probation are overseen by a single officer. In large cities, several successive probation officers might supervise a child. Probation usually lasts for a few months, but it can go on for more than a year.

A probation program that is gaining in popularity involves intensive supervision of 20 to 30 offenders by a single officer and monitoring of delinquents at home. Such programs usually require house arrest—or home confinement, for juveniles—combined with electronic monitoring. House arrest can be adapted to include attending school, working at a job, competing in athletics, and attending counseling sessions. House arrest can be monitored through telephone calls made by a probation officer. However, house arrest is far more efficient when children are required to wear nonremovable electronic monitoring devices that alert, by telephone, a probation department computer if the probationer leaves the site of confinement. House arrest combined with electronic monitoring costs less than confinement, reduces overcrowding in incarceratories, and allows children who might otherwise be held in detention to remain at home (Ball and Lilly, 1986; Charles, 1989; Petersilia, 1986; Schmidt, 1986). In a survey of eight probation programs using house arrest and electronic monitoring, Vaughn reported that the programs had reduced overcrowding in incarceratories, and that the number of days children spent in detention was reduced. Vaughn (1989) also noted that children under house arrest benefitted from increased access to counseling, school, and vocational opportunities.

However, there is considerable debate about the legality, and desirability, of house arrest and electronic monitoring (Walker, 1994: 221–23; Hewitt and Regoli, 1994: 399; Pursley, 1991: 564). Intensive supervision and electronic monitoring costs far more than traditional probation (Walker, 1994: 223). California probation officers report that many juveniles remove and destroy electronic monitoring devices—which cost about two hundred dollars each. In Houston, a sixteen-year-old boy recently removed his electronic bracelet, left home undetected and shot another boy at a nearby fast-food outlet. At least eighteen of forty-three juveniles recently fitted in Houston with electronic monitors removed or tampered with them (Daily Times-Call, Dec. 9, 1993: 6A). Consequently, many legal agencies are decreasing the use of electronic monitoring devices, because they are often ineffective and because they are too expensive to replace when broken or tampered with.

Traditional probation costs the state one-sixth to one-half as much as incarceration (Walker, 1994: 216). Consequently, in 1991, more than 57 percent of all adjudicated juveniles were given probation (U.S. Dept. of Justice, Bureau of Justice Statistics, 1993a: 541). Additionally, some unknown, but large, number of American problem children are put on informal probation each year. In urban areas, probation caseloads are so large that efforts at legal investigation, supervision, and counseling are often defeated (Gibbons and Krohn, 1991: 279; Walker, 1994: 217). In order to supplement budgeted labor, approximately 60 percent of the juvenile courts in the United States use some type of volunteer program. Volunteers work with problem youth in more than twenty job categories and offer troubled youngsters much-needed support, supervision, acceptance, and affection (Little, 1978a: 1). The following are common types of volunteer programs: volunteer probation officer, friendship/companion, tutorial, counseling, youth transportation, medical and dental services, religious support and counseling, art enrichment and volunteer homes (10–12).

The Volunteer Probation Counselor Program in Lincoln, Nebraska, offers a good example of this kind of program. Volunteers are selected and trained to work with probation officers in counseling and supervising youthful misdemeanant offenders. Volunteers and offenders are matched in terms of mutual interests, volunteer's abilities, and offender's specific personal needs. Volunteers provide friendship, role modeling, counseling, and supervision, hoping to discourage a return to crime (Ku, 1980). Unfortunately, there are far more problem children in America's cities than there are volunteers (Little, 1981b: 10; Lundman, 1993: 121–22).

Restitution and Community Service

Restitution is one of the oldest forms of corrections. Some type of restitution program can be used at every stage of the legal handling of juveniles (Waldron and Lynch, 1978: 10–15). Restitution is repayment of a victim by the offender for losses suffered as a result of a crime (Schneider, 1985: 1; Hewitt and Regoli, 1994: 399–400). Repayment through the exchange of money is the most popular type of restitution. When offenders are unable to pay for their crimes with money, they are sometimes allowed by a court to work for the victim or to do community service work for a public or nonprofit agency. Most victims do not want prolonged contact with persons who have criminally violated them. As a result, most work restitution undertaken by juveniles involves community service (Schneider, 1985: 1). A majority of children put on restitution are Anglo and come from middle- or working-class families (Nelson, Omart, and Harlow, 1978: 29). More innovative restitution programs help disadvantaged children find paid employment so that a portion of their income can go to victims (Beville and Cioffi, 1979: 1; Nelson, Omart, and Harlow, 1978: 3).

There are two types of restitution, informal and formal. If children and their parents volunteer to participate, then some youngsters are put on informal restitution. Informal restitution is frequently used, often along with other correctional techniques, by police officers and intake probation officers. Formal restitution is a court function, and it is often combined by judges with other disposition options (Springer, 1986: 31–32).

Restitution can be rehabilitative if it offers problem children opportunities for supervision by, and bonding with, responsible adults (Croan, Bird, and Beville, 1979: 13). Restitution becomes punishment when offenders are forced into dangerous or oppressive work situations, or when children are coerced into making unreasonable monetary payments (Schneider, 1985: 9). Almost all forms of juvenile restitution involve some punishment. Most courts use both informal and formal restitution programs (14). Most American restitution programs have monetary and service components (3).

There are three basic ways to organize juvenile restitution (12–13). First, restitution can be run as part of probation. Some probation programs require that each officer supervise a few children who are on restitution as part of their overall caseload. Other probation departments operate separate restitution units. Second, restitution can be run on a contract basis by a religious, charitable, or private nonprofit organization. In Rapid City, South Dakota, for instance, the Girls Club operates a restitution program for female juvenile offenders. With county and private funding, girls are referred by the Probation Department to the Girls Club, where they receive counseling and do service work. The Rapid City Work Restitution Program is one of several services offered to troubled youth and their families by the Girls Club. Other services are temporary foster homes, family therapy, individual and group counseling, employment training, and job search help (Little, 1981b: 9–10). Third, a few juvenile restitution programs in the United States are operated by the court but are kept separate from, and equal to, probation.

Other Nonresidential Programs

Nonresidential programs, which are usually clusters or sets of programs, provide counseling, supervision, and services but allow problem children to live at home or to reside in a temporary home or shelter (Goldstein, 1991: 148–62). The degree of emphasis on counseling, supervision, or services varies greatly from program to program (Pappenfort and Young, 1980: 59). Many nonresidential programs have residential components, like group or foster homes. Nonresidential programs mix types of problem children together by taking juvenile court and school referrals as well as self-referrals

(Little, 1981b: 1). Some programs are administered by juvenile probation departments, while others are run by private organizations. Many children who are placed in non-residential programs come from detention. Court-referred children who fail to meet program requirements can be put back into detention (Pappenfort and Young, 1908: 59). Nonresidential programs blend full-time and part-time employees with large numbers of volunteers. Most employees in nonresidential programs are called "counselors" or "outreach workers" (Goldstein, 1991: 207–42).

New Directions for Young Women, in Tucson, Arizona, is a good example of a nonresidential program. New Directions serves approximately sixteen hundred young women each year who are at risk of delinquency, and it provides an alternative to detention for young women in trouble. Clients served by New Directions average sixteen years of age. Ninety percent are pregnant, have experienced sexual abuse or incest, have severe family problems leading to a runaway, or are considering running away from home. Forty-two percent of all clients are Anglo, 31 percent are Mexican-American, 20 percent are Native-American, and 7 percent are African American. Counselors and volunteers offer individual, group, and family counseling; education; and a summer retreat program in the mountains. Although New Directions offers services only on a short-term basis, it commits approximately fourteen hours per week to each client. New Directions provides services not only at its center but also through local schools, service agencies, and in children's homes. Funding came originally from a federal agency, and has since been provided by local public sources, a federal grant and private donations (Little, 1981b: 5–6).

Nonresidential programs tend to serve fewer problem children per counselor than do probation programs (Pappenfort and Young, 1980: 59). Counselors or outreach workers try to have one in-person contact every day with children on their caseload. They maintain close ties with family members, school officials, friends, and legal officials who are involved in problem children's lives.

Most nonresidential programs require participants to regularly attend school; abide by a curfew; notify parents or outreach worker of their whereabouts when not in school, at home, or on the job; eschew drug and alcohol use; and avoid companions or places that could lead to trouble. Programs impose additional restrictions on children on a case-by-case basis. Children who are accepted into such a program usually negotiate a behavioral contract with their counselor and parents. Terms of the contract are put into writing, and all parties sign the agreement. If a child has been referred by a court, the contract might take the form of a judicial order. Children who fail to meet the terms of their contracts are expelled from the program and are often incarcerated.

There are four basic types of nonresidential programs for problem children: diversion, home detention, independent living and education (Little, Inc., 1978b: 1).

1. Diversion programs serve as alternatives to detention and court referral for juvenile offenders and for dependent and neglected children. Along with the usual fare of individual, family, and group counseling, these programs often offer education, crisis intervention counseling, and referral to other community services (Goldstein, 1991: 142–44; Chesney-Lind and Shelden, 1992: 193–95). New Directions for Young Women, described above, is a diversion program.

2. Home detention, which provides close supervision of children in trouble, allows youth who might otherwise be locked up to live at home. Children are required to abide by a set of behavioral expectations that include curtailment of much freedom of movement (Symposium Planning Committee, 1980: 43–44; Walker, 1994: 222–23). Most home detention programs are administered by juvenile probation departments, and the actual supervision is performed by paid or volunteer staff with small caseloads on an intensive basis, but it usually lasts only for a few days. Home detention is based upon a behavioral contract and almost always includes the rules of nonresidential programs that were listed above.

3. Independent living programs provide supervision, counseling and services for problem children who are not incarcerated and who no longer live with their families. Independent living means that children have taken up residence in an apartment, a "Y," or a residence that is operated by a community agency. Independent living counselors tailor programs to the individual needs of each child. In addition to offering counseling, independent living programs tend to provide vocational and educational training (Little, 1978b: 8). For example, Children's Service, Incorporated, places and supervises older at-risk Philadelphia youth in a variety of independent living facilities. Children's Service, Incorporated, workers

directly supervise youth placed in independent living facilities, but Department of Public Welfare social workers also maintain contact. The program provides placement, supervision, education, and vocational training (Little, 1978b: 7–8).

4. Some nonresidential programs emphasize intensive remedial education as a core component of their work with children. For example, in the St. Louis, Missouri, area the Providence Educational Center uses teams of counselors, teachers, and social workers to provide an individualized and concentrated program of education for each child who is referred by the local juvenile court (8). The program appears to be especially effective in helping adjudicated children who have histories of truancy and poor school performance. The Providence Educational Center offers education, social services, and aftercare.

Residential Programs

Residential programs provide housing as well as counseling, supervision and services for problem children (*Denver Post,* Dec. 15, 1993: 12B). Residential programs were traditionally used to house dependant and neglected children but today serve as host to increasing numbers of delinquents. Residential programs are especially popular preventive or corrective alternatives for runaways (Pappenfort and Young, 1980: 70). Residential programs can involve primary or secondary control. Residential programs tend to include elements of rehabilitation and punishment in their offerings.

Children are put into residential programs by legal authority for two reasons. First, judicial officials believe that home life for some children is so destructive and unsettling that it overcomes all efforts to find solutions to their problems. Second, legal officials believe that there are some children who need more supervision than nonresidential programs provide but should not be incarcerated. Both types of children are mixed together in most residential programs. There are three basic kinds of residential facilities for problem children in the United States: foster homes, shelter or group homes, and halfway houses.

Foster homes are "real families" that have volunteered (or are paid) to take problem children in and provide housing, food, and supervision (Miller et al., 1976: 664; Little, 1980: 3). Access to most foster homes is controlled by social service agencies rather than by probation. Foster homes put adults into a substitute parent role with problem youth. Foster homes force problem children to establish relationships with surrogate parents and with other youngsters in the household. Thus, foster homes can add beneficial primary relationships to a troubled child's life. However, evidence suggests that many problem children react negatively to the intense relationships imposed by foster homes (Pappenfort and Young, 1980: 81; Chesney-Lind and Shelden, 1992: 195–96).

The Florida Youth Services Division operates a 750-bed state-wide short-term volunteer foster home program for children who might otherwise be held in detention. The program provides food, shelter, and supervision to over thirty-five hundred problem children each year. Volunteer foster families receive no payment for their services and open their homes to children for up to two weeks. The average length of stay is less than seven days. Only about 6 percent of the children placed in Florida foster homes run away. Funding for the Florida foster home program comes from federal and state agencies (Little, 1978b: 13).

In Massachusetts, foster care has been used as a way to impose intensive home-based detention on troublesome youth (Pappenfort and Young, 1980: 83). In general, the number of available foster homes is relatively small. In fact, today there is a critical shortage of foster homes in most U.S. cities. Consequently, many problem children cannot be given foster care (Schwartz, 1989: 13).

Shelter or group homes are community-based facilities that employ residential staff in semiparental/counselor roles to temporarily house, supervise, and care for children in need (Little, 1978b: 16; 1979b: ix; Chesney-Lind and Shelden, 1992: 196–97). In addition to providing parentlike care, shelter or group homes offer counseling, job training, employment search services, educational opportunities, medical help, financial assistance, and a host of other services to youngsters. Most group or shelter homes, either intentionally or through misdiagnosis, mix dependant, neglected, and delinquent children under the same roof. Some shelter and group homes are operated by government agencies. An increasing number of shelter and group homes are privately run, either on a nonprofit or for-profit basis. Shelter or group homes can emphasize rehabilitation, punishment, or both, although in most cases the predominant focus is on helping children. Punitive qualities are almost always present, however, because most shelter or group homes provide a form of "soft detention" for problem children whereby their movement is highly restricted and supervised (Miller et al., 1976: 664; Pappenfort and Young, 1980: 81). Shelter or group homes seem to make fewer emotional demands on young persons than do foster homes and, in that respect, can provide a haven for a troubled child. However, many youth run away from shelter and group homes. The normal length of stay in a shelter or group home is a few weeks to several months. Children who are under juvenile or family court jurisdiction, and who fail to fit into a shelter or group home, can be locked up.

Job Corps, which is federally funded through CETA–Title IV, is the largest group home program in the United States. It serves youths sixteen to twenty-one years old who are economically disadvantaged and out of school. Job Corps provides employment training and basic education at seventy-four residential facilities, where participants can live for up to two years. Thie program enrolls approximately fifty thousand youth per year, and has enrolled more than six hundred thousand disadvantaged children since its inception. Participants are 68 percent African American, 26 percent Anglo, 12 percent Hispanic, and 2 percent Native-American. (U.S. Department of Justice, 1980: 81–82).

Halfway houses are residential facilities that employ custodial staff and counselors to provide housing, partial incarceration, close supervision, and services for problem children (Allen et al., 1978: 1). Imposing strict rules and regulations on problem children, they exert more secure control over children than do foster, shelter, or group homes. Dependent and neglected children are often kept in the same halfway house with children who are on probation and who are returning from an incarceratory. Most halfway houses offer problem children counseling, job services, educational opportunities, financial help, and medical attention. Troubled youth are generally allowed to leave halfway houses during the day to attend school and to work. Halfway house counselors often have the authority to allow children to go unsupervised into the city as an incentive to abide by the rules and regulations. Most children who are put into halfway houses are one step away from judicial placement in a locked facility. Dependent and neglected youngsters are placed in such houses because no other residential options are available to the state at the time of their processing (Chesney-Lind and Shelden, 1992: 197).

SUMMARY

In this chapter we explored children's prevention and corrections programs. Prevention of delinquency is most effective when done in the family, neighborhood, and community, where primary relationships can control children. Unfortunately, much primary control has broken down in many American cities. When primary relationships no longer constrain children, government and private agencies introduce elements of secondary control.

Today, community-based delinquency prevention and corrections programs are common in the United States, even though most government resources are still spent on police, courts, and incarceratories. Corrections has grown into a large industry, encompassing community-based and institutional alternatives. While almost all modern corrections programs blend punishment with rehabilitation, in general, community-based corrections emphasizes rehabilitation, while incarceratories favor punishment.

We must recognize the dual reality of community-based delinquency prevention and corrections programs. On the one hand, community-based programs help thousands of problem children avoid incarceration, providing critical supervision and aid. On the other hand, community-based juvenile prevention and corrections programs in the United States are chronically underfunded and overcrowded. Consequently, many American problem children go without any help at all. Tragically, critical shortages of foster homes and other safe shelters compel judges to incarcerate children who do not need to be locked up.

Nowhere is government ignorance about problem children better demonstrated than in the areas of community-based prevention and corrections. Most children in trouble are blamed by government officials for their condition and are punished rather than helped. By underestimating the magnitude of children's problems, officials leave prevention and corrections programs starved for resources. Moreover, volunteers of all kinds are in short supply. As a result, many American children who need help are either ignored altogether, processed superficially, or punished. To the extent that civilizations are measured by their efforts to help children in trouble, the United States is falling far short of its potential when it comes to community-based delinquency prevention and corrections.

CHAPTER 12

Incarceration and Parole of Juveniles

INTRODUCTION

Incarcerate means "confine" or "imprison." In western democracies only a few government agents have the authority to take juveniles into custody and to incarcerate them. In the United States, for example, police officers, intake probation officers, parole officers, some social workers, and a few school officials are authorized to take problem children into custody and to temporarily incarcerate them. Incarceration is a court function, however, in the sense that juvenile court judges, magistrates, and referees are empowered by law to decide whether or not incarceration should continue for a child who has been taken into custody.

There are two types of confinement, informal and formal. Informal confinement can begin for a problem child when s/he is locked up in a patrol car or seated on a chair for a few hours in a legal official's office. Informal confinement is short-term incarceration of a child without the execution of an arrest and without notification of others. This practice offers teachers, police, probation officers, and social workers a way to punish problem children without consulting judges, magistrates, and referees. Most modern state juvenile codes prohibit using informal confinement as a punitive measure, and the practice has diminished somewhat.

There are three categories of formal confinement, called "adjudication statuses." *Detained children* are locked up before adjudication, or after disposition while awaiting transfer to some other form of treatment. *Committed children* have been declared delinquent, guilty, dependent, or neglected by a court and have been incarcerated as part of their disposition. A few children are *voluntarily admitted,* either by themselves or their parents, to incarceration (U.S. Dept. of Justice, Bureau of Justice Statistics, 1987: 391).

Incarceratories are places where humans are locked up by legal officials. Incarceratories are either for short-term (a few days) or

255

long-term (a few months to years) confinement of individuals. Local, state, regional, and national government agencies, and private organizations own and operate children's incarceratories in the United States. In addition to law violators, persons suffering from, for example, dependency, neglect, abuse, mental illness, and physical disability are put into incarceratories.

Incarceratories, or sections of incarceratories, are ranked according to the level of security they force on inmates (Clear and Cole, 1994: 246–48; Goldstein, 1991: 195–96). Maximum security incarceratories make escape unlikely by employing extreme measures to deny privileges and freedom of movement to inmates. For example, in maximum security settings, inmates are held behind thick concrete walls, barred doorways, and electrified and razored fences. Almost all physical movement in a maximum security facility is restricted and requires prior permission. Inmates are intensely supervised by guards who employ rigid rules and harsh means of discipline. Body counts of inmates occur frequently, as often as every two hours (Allen and Simonsen, 1986: 366). Security and punishment concerns tend to dominate rehabilitation efforts in most maximum security situations.

Medium security incarceratories also stress preventing escape and knowing where inmates are at all times. But, at least in theory, medium security incarceratories practice control and surveillance techniques that are somewhat less noticeable to inmates. Daily inmate routines are a bit less regimented, but rules are nevertheless rigid, and discipline is harsh: Punishment and escape prevention concerns remain paramount.

Minimum security incarceratories are also regimented and dedicated to achieving behavioral control over inmates. However, minimum security incarceratories tend to allow a great deal of movement of inmates within the facilities so that education, employment, and counseling activities can go on. Many minimum security incarceratories are open, rather than institutional, meaning that they allow inmates to leave for short periods of time (Goldstein, 1991: 195–96).

In theory, psychological and correctional diagnostics have evolved to a point that allows legal officials to divide problem children into four distinct categories, those who (1) do not require incarceration, (2) require only a minimum of confinement, (3) must be confined, but with only moderate loss of freedom and privileges, and (4) are so dangerous to themselves and the community that rigid rules, harsh discipline, and maximum security are necessary when dealing with them. In reality, legal diagnostics are far from error proof. Today, all types of problem children are confined in all kinds of incarceratories.

Punishment and Control versus Rehabilitation

There is considerable debate over whether incarceratories punish and control or rehabilitate problem children (Senna and Siegel, 1992: 201–24). Many legal officials believe that confinement is an effective form of rehabilitation that allows for the care of children in physically restricting facilities. Persons who believe that confinement and rehabilitation can be effectively combined point out that denial of freedom and privileges does not preclude offering inmates counseling, education, and employment (Clear and Cole, 1994: 352–62). On the other hand, incarceration of children can be dangerous and destructive (Schmalleger, 1994: 298–99). In fact, some experts warn that fear of disorder and escape may dominate the organization and operation of all types of incarceratories, making rehabilitation difficult, perhaps impossible (Rothman, 1979: 61).

Punishment and control are the oldest purposes of incarceratories. Until recently, incarceration almost always included physical punishment and the possibility of torture. Today, if considered necessary by legal officials in order to maintain discipline and control, the following types of punishment can be used on incarcerated children: denial of privileges, corporal punishment, hand constraints, tranquilizers, strip cells, isolation/solitary confinement, censorship of personal mail, and denial of counseling, educational, and employment opportunities. Punishment of incarcerated children also comes from inmate social systems, which commonly feature exploitation of the weak and irrational violence. In the early 1900s, rehabilitation programs were introduced into American incarceratories. But, especially in maximum and medium security settings, rehabilitation has lagged behind punishment and control as a purpose of legal confinement. In fact, not until the 1970s did U.S. courts see a need to guarantee inmates a right to treatment (Senna and Siegel, 1992: 201–24).

Overcrowding in incarceratories, defined as holding the number of inmates in a facility from at least 90 and to more than 100 percent of bed capacity, is another factor that encourages punishment. U.S. juvenile incarceratories are notoriously overcrowded, and overcrowding almost always defeats rehabilitation efforts. According to Pappenfort and Young, overcrowded juvenile facilities lead to the following: a strained, nervous custodial/counseling staff, a tension-ridden atmosphere, frequent escapes or escape attempts, homosexuality, assaults on staff, physical abuse of children, suicide, and homicide (1980: 34).

Preventive Detention

Throughout 1984, more than 521,000 children were admitted to all types of public juvenile incarceratories in the United States, and hundreds of thousands of others were held in private incarceratories (U.S. Dept. of Justice, Bureau of Justice Statistics, 1986: 390). On a single day in 1985, 49,322 problem children were being held in public juvenile facilities, and 34,080 others were confined in private settings. Of the children held on February 1, 1985, in public incarceratories, 86 percent were male, and 14 percent female. 47 percent were Anglo, 37 percent African American, and 13 percent Hispanic. 82 percent were between the ages of fourteen and seventeen, 11 percent between the ages of eighteen and twenty, and 6 percent between the ages of ten and thirteen (390). On a single day in 1987, 53,503 problem children were being held in public juvenile incarceratories, and another 38,103 were confined in private facilities (U.S. Dept. of Justice, Bureau of Justice Statistics, 1990: 560). In 1989, 619,181 children were admitted to U.S. public juvenile incarceratories throughout the year, and another 141, 463 young persons were admitted to private juvenile incarceratories (U.S. Dept. of Justice, Bureau of Justice Statistics, 1993a: 580). These data show a steady recent climb in the number of American problem children who are incarcerated.

Part of this increase in incarceration comes from the common use of preventive detention with children. Preventive detention is incarcerating a person before trial, in order to protect the community or the person incarcerated. Advocates of preventive detention point out that this tactic prevents children from committing additional crimes while awaiting trial. Critics of preventive detention argue that it is unfair to punish children by denying them freedom before they are given a trial, especially children who, after trial, will be released from custody. Every state allows preventive detention of juveniles.

In 1984, the U.S. Supreme Court upheld a New York preventive detention law. The Court found no proof that the law had resulted in punishment of problem children and concluded that it was not unreasonable to put young persons in preventive detention for their own protection. In *Schall v. Martin* (104 U.S. 2403 [1984]) the Supreme Court concluded "that preventive detention . . . serves a legitimate state objective, and that the procedural protections afforded pretrial detainees by the New York statute satisfy the Due Process Clause of the Fourteenth Ammendment to the United States Constitution." The Court also proclaimed that "if parental control falters, the state must play its part as parens patriae." According to data for fourteen states, juvenile courts securely detained more than 25 percent of the delinquents they processed (U.S. Department of Justice, Bureau of Justice Statistics, 1990: 543). *Schall v. Martin* is likely to contribute to increasing use of detention with problem children. Below, we examine common types of juvenile incarceratories.

TYPES OF JUVENILE INCARCERATORIES

Currently, there are approximately thirty-two hundred public and private juvenile incarceratories operating nationwide. On a daily basis, U.S. juvenile incarceratories house more than ninty-two thousand children. In public juvenile incarceratories alone, more that 1,228,000 admissions and discharges occur each year. State governments operate 70 percent of all public long-term juvenile incarceratories, with local governments controlling the other 30 percent. County and city agencies operate 79 percent of all public short-term juvenile incarceratories in the United States; state agencies are responsible for the remaining 21 percent. American taxpayers spend about $1.67 billion each year for public juvenile incarceratories, where fifty-nine thousand persons are employed. In 1988, the annual average per resident cost of public juvenile incarceratories was $29,600. African Americans, Hispanics, and other minority children account for 60 percent of all persons locked up in public juvenile incarceratories in the United States (U.S. Dept. of Justice, Office of Juvenile Justice and Delinquency Prevention, 1991: 1–7).

Juvenile Halls and Detention Centers

Juvenile halls and detention centers are used to incarcerate children on a short-term basis. Today, there are about 550 short-term juvenile incarceratories in the United States. Each year they admit approximately five hundred thousand problem children (Cahalan and Parsons, 1986: 138; Allen and Simonsen, 1986: 301; U.S. Dept. of Justice, Office of Juvenile Justice and Delinquency Prevention, 1991: 7). Several types of problem children, including youth awaiting adjudication, adjudicated delinquents who have not yet been transferred to long-term institutions, and dependent and neglected youth, are incarcerated in juvenile halls and detention centers. The physical appearance of U.S. juvenile halls and detention centers varies tremendously: some short-term incarceratories are located in old jail-like buildings, while other juvenile halls and detention centers are in newer buildings that resemble offices and schools.

Almost all juvenile halls and detention centers keep children behind locked doors. Almost all juvenile halls and detention centers stress security and minimize rehabilitation activities. Detained children are held an average of twelve days each in short-term facilities. Committed children stay an average of thirty days each in short-term facilities. Voluntarily admitted youngsters average eighteen days (U.S. Department of Justice, Bureau of Justice Statistics, 1987: 391). Some juvenile halls and detention centers have counseling and educational offerings and thus are able to hold children on both a short-term and long-term basis. An increasing number of short-term incarceratories in the United States are operated by private organizations. In 1991, 44 juvenile detention centers and 1,496 halfway houses for children were run by private organizations (U.S. Department of Justice, Bureau of Justice Statistics, 1993: 579). Currently, about 500 short-term juvenile incarceratories are run by state and local governmental agencies throughout the United States (U.S. Dept. of Justice, Office of Juvenile Justice and Delinquency Prevention, 1991: 7).

Industrial Schools and Training Schools

In the 1820s, most facilities in the United States that confined children on a long-term basis were called "prisons" or "houses of refuge." In the 1850s, the name for long-term childrens' incarceratories was changed to reformatories. Regardless of name, early American long-term incarceratories for children were usually constructed in rural areas and were operated as punitive, work-oriented prisons. Children, encircled by thick concrete walls, housed in cell blocks behind locked doors, were subjected to constant violence, rigid rules of conduct, and harsh discipline. Corporal punishment and inmate violence extinguished all but the most determined efforts at rehabilitation of inmates. In the 1850s, a few progressive juvenile incarceratories moved children out of cell blocks and put them into sets of cottages dispersed throughout the prison grounds.

As probation and parole became more common in the early 1900s, more and more juvenile prisons moved to the cottage system and introduced elements of rehabilitation into their programs. Consequently, today most long-term incarceratories in the U.S. house children in cottages and, in recognition of their recent commitment to rehabilitation, many are called "industrial" or "training" schools. In the 1940s, camps, farms, and ranches began to receive some problem children on a long-term basis. Such facilities are usually located in forested or rural areas, where children are put to work under minimum security conditions. Today, almost all long-term incarceratories for children in the United States combine some elements of punishment with rehabilitative goals. In other words, incarceration, denial of privileges, and corporal punishment operate alongside medical, counseling, educational, vocational, and recreational programs.

Table 12.1 gives some indication of the number and character of U.S. facilities that house delinquents and status offenders. Before 1923, there were relatively few places to hold delinquents and status offenders. Most were government run. By 1966, however, confinement of children had blossomed into an industry with hundreds of facilities. Private enterprise had begun to acquire significant ownership of juvenile incarceratories. Today, problem children are housed at more than three thousand locations, and private organizations operate approximately 60 percent of all children's incarceratories (U.S. Department of Justice, Bureau of Justice Statistics, 1993a: 584). Table 12.1 also shows that most facilities house delinquents and status offenders on a long-term basis.

Currently, there are approximately twenty-five hundred long-term juvenile incarceratories in the United States (U.S. Department of Justice, Bureau of Justice Statistics, 1990: 565). Long-term juve-

TABLE 12.1
Estimates of number of U.S. Juvenile Facilities Housing Delinquents
and Status Offenders, 1880–1991

	1880	1923	1966	1982	1987	1991
Total number	53	145	656	2,900	3,299	3,130
Public control	—	123	507	1,023	1,107	1,098
Private control	—	22	149	*1,877*	*2,194*	*2,032*
Short-term	—	—	209	623	763	—
Longer term	—	—	454	2,277	2,536	—

Source: Calahan and Parsons, 1986, 138; U.S. Dept. of Justice, Bureau of Justice Statistics, 1990: 565; U.S. Dept. of Justice, Bureau of Justice Statistics, 1993a: 579.

nile incarceratories are administered and operated by a wide variety of local, state, federal, and private agencies. In rural states, a single long-term juvenile incarceratory typically receives all types of adjudicated children and separates them into minimum, medium, and maximum security housing groups. Industrial states operate systems of children's prisons. Diagnostic centers separate children by types (e.g., male/female, minor offender/major offender, passive/aggressive, violent/nonviolent, drug user/nonuser) and funnel youth into training or industrial schools that function as maximum, medium, or minimum security facilities.

Many older training and industrial schools look just like prisons, recently constructed training and industrial schools tend to resemble private boarding schools. Cottage-style housing is common in both settings; it is hard to tell from architecture whether punishment or rehabilitation is emphasized within. However, some aspects of punishment seem to prevail almost everywhere in juvenile corrections. For example, children are locked up in all medium and maximum security incarceratories. Violence is commonplace in all long-term incarceratories. Corporal punishment is still legal in most states. Almost all long-term juvenile incarceratories employ an arbitrary and inclusive style of discipline. Arbitrary and inclusive discipline gives corrections workers control over all (or most) inmate activities and can result in abuses of authority (Rothman, 1979: 42).

Table 12.2 shows the average daily population of long-term

TABLE 12.2

Gender, Ethnicity, and Median Age of Children in Long-Term Juvenile Correctional Facilities, 1880–1980

	1880	*1923*	*1960*	*1980*
Number Present	11,468	27,238	57,883	59,414
Gender (%)				
Male	81	72	73	81
Female	19	28	27	19
Ethnicity (%)				
Anglo	89	83	68	57
Non-Anglo	11	17	32	—
African American				31
Hispanic				11
Median Age (years)	13.1	—	15.1	16.6

Source: Calahan and Parsons, 1986: 130.

juvenile correctional facilities in the United States for selected years between 1880 and 1980. Data in the top row of Table 12.2 indicate that the number of American children incarcerated on a long-term basis increased throughout the first half of this century and recently leveled off at around sixty thousand on a given day, of whom approximately 80 percent are male. About 57 percent of the children confined on a long-term basis are Anglo, 31 percent are African American, and 11 percent are of Hispanic origin. The median age of long-term juvenile incarcerates has increased throughout the century, and in 1980 it stood at 16.6 years. It is important to note that private organizations operate a significant number of long-term juvenile incarceratories. In 1991, eighty-one training schools, eighty ranches or camps, and twenty-two juvenile reception centers were run by private organizations throughout the United States (U.S. Department of Justice, Bureau of Justice Statistics, 1993a: 579).

Table 12.3 presents information about children incarcerated in long-term U.S. juvenile correctional facilities in 1989 and 1991. In 1989, 36,156 children were locked up in long-term public facilities. In long-term public incarceratories, 14,527 of the children were Anglo, 15,105 were African American, and 5,586 were Hispanic. In other words, both in proportionate and absolute terms,

TABLE 12.3
Gender and Ethnicity of Children in Long-Term
Juvenile Correctional Facilities, 1989 and 1991

	1989 Public Facility	1991 Private Facility
Number committed	36,156	10,811
Gender		
Male	—	9,205
Female	—	1,606
Ethnicity		
Anglo	14,527	5,072
African American	15,105	4,602
Hispanic	5,586	977
Other	938	160

Source: U.S. Dept. of Justice, Bureau of Justice Statistics, 1993: 576, 579; U.S. Dept. of Justice, Office of Juvenile Justice and Delinquency Prevention: 1991: 6.

more minority children than Anglos were held in American public long-term incarceratories. In 1991, 10,811 juveniles were held in privately-run long-term facilities. Of them, 9,205 were male, and 1,606 were female; they included 5,072 Anglos, 4,602 African Americans, and 977 Hispanics. We should also note that, in 1989, 2,180 *adults* were incarcerated on a daily basis in public long-term juvenile facilities throughout the United States (U.S. Department of Justice, Bureau of Justice Statistics, 1993a: 578).

Table 12.4 shows why children were locked up for long terms in 1880. According to table 12.4, in the 1880s, almost 50 percent of the total were sent to prison for relatively minor criminal offenses. Twenty percent did time because of status offenses.

Table 12.5 presents partial information about why children were confined on a long-term basis in public and private incarceratories in 1989. There is a considerable difference between public facilities and private incarceratories. Ninty-five percent of the children confined in long-term public facilities were adjudicated delinquent; 4 percent were status offenders; and only 1 percent were incarcerated because of dependency, neglect, or abuse. In private facilities, however, 47 percent of the incarcerates were dependent,

TABLE 12.4
Juveniles in Correctional Facilities,
by Reason for Incarceration, 1880

Reason	Percent
Larceny	24.2
Vagrancy	24.0
Disobedience, incorrigibility runaway, etc.	21.4
All other offenses	17.7
Offense not known, unclassified, etc.	12.7
Total	100

Source: Calahan and Parsons, 1986: 122.

neglected, or abused; 18 percent committed status offenses; and 35 percent were adjudicated delinquent. These data clearly demonstrate the potential that exists for mixing a wide variety of problem children together in long-term incarceratories.

Table 12.6 displays 1989 data about the reasons for which juveniles were held in public incarceratories. The top row of table 12.6 shows that most children were held in public incarceratories

TABLE 12.5
Juveniles in Public and Private Correctional Facilities,
by Reason for Incarceration, 1989

Reason	Public Facilities		Private Facilities		Total
	Number	Percent	Number	Percent	
Delinquency	53,037	95	13,095	35	66,132
Status offense	2,245	4	6,853	18	9,098
Dependency, neglect, abuse, etc.	841	1	17,874	47	18,715
Totals	56,123	100	37,822	100	93,945

Source: U.S. Dept. of Justice, Bureau of Justice Statistics, 1993a: 581.

TABLE 12.6
Female and Male Juveniles Held in Public Facilities,
by Reason for Incarceration, 1989

Reason	Total	Male	Female
Delinquency	**53,037**	**47,843**	**5,194**
Serious violence	8,566	7,976	590
Other violence	5,761	5,234	527
Serious property offenses	15,181	14,112	1,069
Other property offenses	7,599	6,737	862
Alcohol/drug offenses	6,586	6,067	519
Public order offenses	2,788	2,406	382
Probation violations	4,920	3,942	978
Other delinquent offenses	1,636	1,369	267
Nondelinquent offenses	**3,086**	**1,600**	**1,486**
Status offenses	2,245	1,128	1,117
Abuse/neglect	426	205	221
Other	113	78	35
Voluntarily admitted	302	189	113

Source: U.S. Department of Justice, Office of Juvenile Justice and Delinquency Prevention, 1991: 4.

for delinquency offenses. Roughly 90 percent of the children held for delinquency offenses were male. If we look at children incarcerated for nondelinquent offenses, however, the pattern changes considerably: *almost 50 percent* of the children incarcerated for nondelinquent offenses were females.

Table 12.7 provides information, for selected years from 1868 to 1982, about the average length of stay for a juvenile in a long-term incarceratory. One hundred years ago, children sentenced to prison were confined for an average of almost two years, but as the twentieth century progressed the average length of sentence for a child dropped. In 1982, problem children spent an average of six months confined in public incarceratories and about nine months locked up in private facilities.

Females in Long-Term Juvenile Incarceratories

On the average, girls are held in long-term incarceratories for less serious offenses than boys (Chesney-Lind and Shelden, 1992: 144).

TABLE 12.7
Estimates of Average Length of Stay in U.S. Juvenile Incarceratories,
1868, 1923, 1964, and 1982*

				1982	
Source of Estimate	*1868*	*1923*	*1964*	*Public*	*Private*
U.S. Bureau of Education	22.2				
U.S. Bureau of the Census		16.8			
U.S. Children's Bureau			9.3		
U.S. Department of Justice Office of Juvenile Justice and Delinquency Prevention				6	9

* in months
Source: Calahan and Parsons, 1986: 127–28.

During the first half of the century, females were often held in long-term U.S. juvenile incarceratories "for their own good," often for status offenses, rather than for serious delinquency (162). In 1988, 50 percent of the females in U.S. correctional facilities were Anglo, 32 percent were African American, 6 percent were Hispanic, and 8 percent were Native American. Most incarcerated females were between sixteen and seventeen years of age. Many incarcerated juvenile females are mothers themselves (147). A majority of incarcerated juvenile females in the United States have been victims of extensive physical and sexual abuse, which began when they were quite young. Eight out of ten incarcerated juvenile females had run away from home, and many were chronic runaways. More than 50 percent of all incarcerated juvenile females in the United States have attempted suicide at least once (147).

Adult Jails and Prisons

Problem children are incarcerated in every possible type of adult jail, lock-up, and prison that operates in the United States. In 1991, 4,552 persons seventeen or younger were confined in state prisons for adults throughout the United States (U.S. Department of Justice, Bureau of Justice Statistics, 1993b: 31). In 1992, 50 persons under eighteen years of age were serving time in adult U.S.

federal prisons (U.S. Dept. of Justice, Bureau of Justice Statistics, 1993a: 635).

No one knows exactly how many community-level U.S. jails and lock-ups there are. Some put the total near sixteen thousand (Rademacher, 1980: 7). The Bureau of Justice Statistics, however, estimates that there are only four thousand local jails in the United States (1986: 1). In 1980, government figures showed an average daily population of almost 6,000 American children incarcerated in adult jails (Cahalan and Parsons: 113). In 1984, more than 95,000 children were held throughout the year, but the average daily population of children in U.S. adult jails was only 1,482 (U.S. Department of Justice, Bureau of Justice Statistics, 1986: 2). In 1991, an average daily population of 2,350 juveniles were held in U.S. adult jails (U.S. Dept. of Justice, Bureau of Justice Statistics, 1993a: 590).

Some states have made excellent progress in moving children from adult jails. For example, in 1978, California jailed 131 children on an average day. By 1983, this number was down to 66, and in 1988, it was 35 (U.S. Dept. of Justice, Bureau of Justice Statistics, 1990: 575). However, many other states have made far less progress.

In many respects jail provides a poor environment for children. Jails, which are short-term incarceratories with scant rehabilitation programs, house all conceivable types of adult offenders. They are busy, dangerous places where children can be overlooked and undersupervised by custodial personnel. In the 1980s, there were more than fifteen million admissions into and releases from U.S. adult jails each year. American jails operated, on the average, at 90 percent of bed capacity and had an average daily population of approximately 400,000 inmates (U.S. Dept. of Justice, Bureau of Justice Statistics, 1993a: 590). 51 percent of the persons in adult jails had not yet gone to trial, but 49 percent of the jail population had already been convicted: adults outnumber children by ninty-nine to one (U.S. Dept. of Justice, Bureau of Justice Statistics, 1990: 1–2).

All types of problem children are held in jail. One study of more than 449 jails and lock-ups in nine states revealed that children were held for the following variety of reasons: 27.8 percent for property crime, 17.9 percent for status offenses, 12.3 percent for behavior acts, 11.7 percent for serious crimes against persons, 6.8 percent for minor property offenses, and 3.7 percent for minor assaults (Rademacher: 8). In 1984, 49 percent of the juveniles in adult jails in the United States had not yet been tried; only 20 percent had already been adjudicated or convicted; and approximately 30 percent were runaways, or youth awaiting transfer to other facilities (U.S. Dept. of Justice, Bureau of Justice Statistics, 1990: 2). Since the early 1970s, increasing numbers of gang members have been locked up in American jails and prisons (Clear and Cole, 1994: 273–75; Goldstein, 1991: 148–49; and *Rocky Mountain News*, Jan. 16, 1994: 4A, 26A). Gang members are major contributors to violence and other forms of disruption in incarceratories.

PAROLE

American children who are incarcerated on a long-term basis frequently return to their home cities via parole. Parole is a legal program that conditionally releases committed offenders, after they have served part of a sentence in a long-term incarceratory, back into their home cities under the supervision of a parole officer (Clear and Cole, 1994: 404–24; Lundman, 1974; Grizzle et al., 1982: 20; Schmalleger, 1994: 239–44). Probation and parole are similar. I noted earlier that many states and local governments combine probation and parole supervision into the same office, where both types of cases are handled by the same agents.

Forty-five states and the District of Columbia are indeterminate sentencing jurisdictions. Almost 75 percent of the indeterminate sentencing jurisdictions empower juvenile correctional agencies to make parole decisions. Other states allow juvenile court judges, or parole boards, to make release decisions (Forst, Fisher, and Croates, 1985). In many states juvenile parole is similar to the adult parole process. In fact, some juvenile parole releasing authorities use guidelines that were originally developed for adult parolees (Siegel and Senna, 1981: 592–93).

Parole extends the authority of legislatures, judges, and corrections agencies into the cities where children live. Parole relieves some of the pressure of overcrowding that plagues children's incarceratories. Parole costs much less than incarceration and expands the capability of corrections organizations to process large numbers of children. Parole was first tried at the Elmira Reformatory in New York in the 1880s. By the 1920s, many judges in the United

States were combining parole with indeterminate sentences. Rather than setting a fixed term of imprisonment, judges gave adjudicated children sentences of one to five years and kept open the possibility that, if offenders behaved themselves while locked up, part of the sentence could be served back home on parole.

The philosophy of parole recognizes that almost all incarcerated children return to freedom. Parole assumes that children who should be released early from incarceration can be distinguished from children who should be imprisoned for the maximum allowable time. Today, most children are given indeterminate sentences and are released on parole after serving part of the prescribed sentence. Parole systems for adults and juveniles vary widely and currently operate in every state. In order to be eligible for parole in most states, children must serve a minimum amount of their sentences, or reach a certain age, make progress toward rehabilitation, and show potential for successfully returning to the community. Juvenile parole releasing authorities also look at employment and education prospects, the potential parolee's community living environment, attitudes of family members and friends, and attitudes of the parole candidate (Binder, Geis, and Bruce, 1988: 364–65).

Arnold studied juvenile parole in Pennsylvania and concluded that parole officers vary widely in the ways that they approach their work. Some are friendly and helpful, while others are mean and cynical (1970: 70). Like their counterparts in probation, juvenile parole officers have surveillance and counseling duties. However, the most startling finding Arnold made was that parole officers averaged forty-nine minutes per month in personal contact with each juvenile under their supervision (39). In general, juvenile parole caseloads are too large to allow parole officers to do an adequate job of supervision and counseling (Siegel and Senna, 1981: 593; Walker, 1994: 226). Consequently, parole has not proven to be an effective form of aftercare for many institutionalized children.

In order to overcome some of the limitations of traditional parole, a few states operate programs of intensive parole for juvenile offenders (U.S. Dept. of Justice, Bureau of Justice Statistics, 1993a: 571–72). Much like intensive probation, intensive parole allows officers to carry smaller caseloads and to monitor some parolees electronically (Walker, 1994: 227). This kind of parole allows authorities to release small numbers of juveniles from incarceratories earlier than would be the case if only traditional parole was available (Lundman, 1993: 126–27). Intensive parole is more costly than traditional parole. Electronic monitoring devices are expensive and are frequently destroyed by parolees. At best, intensive parole has proven to be only partly successful (Walker, 1994: 227).

SUMMARY

In this chapter we examined minimum, medium, and maximum security incarceratories where American problem children are held. We saw that the number of children's incarceratories in the United States and the number of youth detained therein increased significantly throughout the 1980s. Today, there are more than three thousand lock-ups for children in the United States.

In 1978, 568,802 children were admitted to public juvenile incarceratories in the United States. By 1988, the number of juvenile admissions into public facilities had increased to 619,181 per year. In 1978, 69,507 juveniles were admitted to private incarceratories in the United States. By 1988, this number had increased to 141,463 admissions per year (U.S. Dept. of Justice, Bureau of Justice Statistics, 1993a: 583). Thus, today most problem children are still held in public incarceratories. However, admissions of children into private incarceratories are growing at a faster rate than are admissions into public facilities. At an average annual per child cost of over $29,000, these figures are alarming. Today, in most states, taxpayers spend more money to lock children up than it would cost to send them to high schools and colleges.

Many states are expanding their juvenile corrections systems in order to accomodate increasing numbers of children. Colorado, for example, is creating a new Youth Offender System, which will be part of the state's adult corrections system. The new Youth Offender System is for children whom legislators, judges and corrections officials do not wish to place "in the more lenient juvenile corrections system" (*Denver Post*, Dec. 31, 1993: 2B).

Building incarceratories for children is an industry that can eat up alarming amounts of tax money. California, for example, admits more than 150,000 children each year into its 113 public juvenile incarceratories, where more than 5,000 persons are employed (U.S. Dept. of Justice, Bureau of Justice Statistics, 1993a:

574, 585). On an average day, California has more than 17,000 children incarcerated in public facilities. This means that, at a current cost of more than $23,000 per child each year, Californians pay in excess of $400 million annually to lock children up (U.S. Dept. of Justice, Office of Juvenile Justice and Delinquency Prevention, 1991: 9).

Correctional diagnostics are primitive, and juvenile incarceratories are overcrowded. Thus, dependent and neglected children are often placed in the same incarceratories with major and minor law violators. In fact, all types of problem children are mixed together in all types of incarceratories. Similarly, all incarceratories blend rehabilitation programs with punishment. Unfortunately, where punishment and rehabilitation coexist, evidence indicates that punishment prevails.

Most problem children are currently incarcerated for indeterminate periods of time. Most children end up spending part of their sentences back home under the supervision of a parole officer. Parole helps corrections authorities to relieve institutional overcrowding, and it costs far less than incarceration. Parole provides supervision and guidance for problem children as they attempt to reenter their communities. However, parole officers handle large caseloads and must function as "double agents," making them relatively ineffective as advocates of rehabilitation.

CHAPTER 13

Epilogue

An epilogue is a concluding section that rounds out the design of a work, a place for retrospect and prospect. In the following pages, I review the major lessons we learned about delinquency. I suggest applications for these lessons in the present and future.

First, we learned that juvenile delinquency in contemporary American society has its roots firmly imbedded in the dark history of problem children. American delinquents are but one type of problem child. Others include abandoned youth; suicidal, disabled, dependent, or neglected youngsters; and status offenders. Second, we learned that behind most problem children stand unwilling or incapable parents of one type or another. Thus, absent or ineffective parenting becomes the backbone of delinquency. Parenting styles like infanticide, abandonment, ambivalence, intrusion, socialization, and even helping can produce children with severe problems.

What do these two basic lessons suggest about delinquency today and tomorrow? That there are more delinquents and potential delinquents in American society than most of us, including policy makers, realize. Consequently, our only hope for minimizing delinquency, today and in the future, is to recognize this fact, to radically expand support and prevention programs for American youth and their parents. Education, food support, housing subsidies, medical attention, child care, recreation, job training, job procurement, and creation must be expanded to sufficiently accomodate the basic needs of dispossessed and working-class Americans.

Critics will protest that American taxpayers cannot afford such measures. I believe that we already spend the money, just on the wrong mix of programs. Americans spend thirty to forty billion dollars each year fighting crime, busting gangs, and extinguishing drug use, in spite of a mounting body of evidence that these tactics do not work. Every arrest of a problem child costs taxpayers a few hundred dollars. Each time a problem child is handled by probation and court officials, taxpayers shell out a few hundred more dollars, or possibly several thousand dollars, depending upon the length, involvement of attorneys, and seriousness of the case. The cost of incarcerating children hovers at twenty-nine thousand dollars per year.

Experts estimate that every dollar invested in delinquency prevention saves six dollars that would eventually be spent on legally processing and correcting problem children. In sum, American taxpayers are already spending much of the money that is needed to save at risk children, but the emphasis is currently on gangbusting, drug denial, and punitive corrective measures rather than on education, empowerment, and humane, loving treatment.

Recurring urban uprisings like the 1992 Los Angeles riots also demonstrate that large sums of public tax money will be spent, one way or another, on the poor person's problems. More than fifty deaths, thousands of injuries and arrests, thousands of charred buildings, and millions of riot-damaged psyches attest to the lunacy of *not* investing in the health, happiness, and safety of poor youth and their parents. How many times must we watch a major city burn before this lesson is learned?

A third lesson involves children's law and juvenile courts in the United States. Beginning with the Stubborn Child Law, but continuing through early and more recent state-level juvenile enacting codes, we see a theme of harshness in legal dealings with problem children. All too often, children's law requires incarceration or some other form of punishment in reaction to delinquency, even though many problem children most need love, acceptance, and support. In recent years, state legislatures focused delinquency law on older, repeat, serious offenders and transferred jurisdiction over minor offenders and dependent and neglected children to already overloaded social welfare agencies. Thus, increasingly, children's law and juvenile courts resemble adult criminal law and trial courts, rather than agencies representing the best interests of troubled children.

In my opinion, American children's law and juvenile courts are due for a major overhaul. Older, serious, repeat delinquents should be automatically transferred to adult criminal courts. Juvenile courts should return to their original function of representing the needs of problem children. It is possible that we are making a mistake by allowing juvenile courts to exist alongside adult criminal courts. We might be better advised to remove juvenile courts physically from other types of courts and to appoint or elect local ministers and successful grandmothers as juvenile court judges, instead of criminal lawyers.

Probation officers should also be given reduced juvenile caseloads and should be freed from their obligations as double agents. Some probation officers could be assigned to do the policelike work, while others were deployed as counselors, able to focus fully on helping children with their problems.

Fourth, we learned that juvenile delinquency has many causes and that, in any individual case, a minimum of twelve or more factors can be involved. The meaning of this lesson differs depending upon your connection to delinquency.

For social scientists, the present and future involves developing simpler, more measurable, and testable explanations of delinquency. There are currently so many potential causes of delinquency that I believe general theories are unworkable. Instead, I recommend that social scientists first develop cumulative delinquency theories at micro, midrange, and macro levels and that such theories have a balance of conflict and consensus components. After measurable, testable micro, midrange and macro delinquency theories are produced, more general theory building will be appropriate.

Professionals who work with problem children—police officers, probation and parole officers, teachers, counselors, social workers, referees, magistrates and judges—should use the ideas they find in delinquency theories to develop conceptual models of problem children that make sense in their line of work. For example, problem children can be categorized according to energy level, stress level, anger level, intelligence level, family dynamics, friendship patterns, behavioral tendencies, employability, social class level, maturity, and so forth. By developing their diagnostic capabilities through application of ideas from delinquency theories, those who work with problem children will be better able to determine which skills and treatment alternatives are most likely to benefit children with specific clusters of background factors. In this sense, delinquency theory can become a useful tool for professionals.

For parents, other relatives, and friends of problem children, delinquency theory helps to systematize the many factors that could be operating in any particular case. Delinquency theory serves as a shopping list of things that might have gone wrong. It sometimes helps to remember that delinquency is a complex phenomenon but that its many potential causes can be unraveled and examined. One can identify and work toward possible solutions, and delinquency theory can help to get the process of understanding moving forward.

A fifth lesson is that schools occupy a special place in causing *and* preventing delinquency. Many American public schools, especially in the big cities, have grown so large, bureaucratized, and dangerous that they alienate and stultify a sizable number of children. Schools, on the other hand, also provide supervision and direction for millions of children whose families need the help. In this sense, schools prevent delinquency.

I believe that Americans must rededicate themselves to providing meaningful, high-quality education for all children and adults. This calls for obvious changes in education: smaller school districts, schools, and class sizes; better pay, improved working conditions, increased authority, and heightened respect for school teachers; and a deeper resolve on the part of parents to help their children maximize educational opportunities. Children of all types, parents, and teachers must be made to feel like important parts of their school community. In other words, legislators and educators must learn to practice the art of inclusion and empowerment. High-quality education is one of the best investments that advanced societies make in children and adults. Well-educated citizens pay large sums of taxes throughout their lives and contribute heavily in many other ways to their communities.

Sixth, police organizations are busy public service agencies that handle a wide variety of matters. Local police departments, especially those in large cities, are heavily bureaucratized, militaristic, and secretive. It is possible that legislators have made a serious mistake by allowing local police organizations to become the primary street-level agencies responsible for problem children. Many police officers are too busy or lack sufficient interest to effectively handle children's problems. Children's divisions are disappearing from police departments. Juvenile specialists are often made fun of by other police officers who value adult crime-fighting more highly.

I suggest that communities experiment with separate children's police departments, managed and staffed by local ministers, capable parents, and successful grandmothers. Children's police department employees would be dispached to respond to all juvenile problems, except those involving older, serious, repeat offenders, whose misbehavior would remain under the jurisdiction of conventional local police departments. Juvenile specialists, in children's police departments, which are administratively and physically separate from conventional local police departments, would be much more effectively positioned to help children with their problems, while minimizing costly legal processing and unnecessary punishment.

A seventh and final lesson is that delinquency control is a growing national industry in which private ownership of facilities is expanding rapidly. Delinquency control is moving beyond traditional incarceratories into the heart of American communities, often in the form of halfway houses and nonresidential programs. Unfortunately, most delinquency control organizations in American society emphasize punishment and offer problem children only secondary relationships with employees. In other words, problem children are handled by control officials who barely know them as human beings; who will only be around for a few hours, weeks, or, at most, months; and who fail to bond emotionally with their charges. Punishment and secondary relationships rarely produce significant positive change in troubled children.

We might try to reduce the size of correctional organizations and correctional employee caseloads in order to promote primary relationships with problem children. We must reconfigure corrections organizations to insure that employees work with problem children on a long-term basis, so that trust, commitment, and friendship can develop: corrections organizations must also be required to specialize in either rehabilitation or punishment. Corrections programs that blend punishment with rehabilitation almost always allow the harsh features of their programs to dominate.

Children's problems is a subject of immense importance that must be studied on a lifelong basis. In this sense, no single book can provide much beyond a series of starting points for a serious student. I hope that this book helps you see more clearly the conceptual and historical basis of juvenile delinquency and that it motivates you to delve deeper into the lives of America's troubled youth.

REFERENCES

AND BIBLIOGRAPHY

Abrahamsen, D. "Family Tension, Basic Cause of Criminal Behavior." in *Journal of Criminal Law and Criminology* 40 (Sept.–Oct., 1949): 330–43.

Advisory Committee on Child Development. National Research Council. *Toward a National Policy for Children and Families,* Washington, DC: National Academy of Sciences, 1976.

Ageton, S., and D. Elliott. *The Incidence of Delinquent Behavior in a National Probability Sample of Adolescents.* Boulder, CO: Behavioral Research Institute. 1978.

Aichhorn, A. *Wayward Youth.* New York: Viking, 1935. Trans. E. Bryant, J. Deming, M. O'Neil Hawkins, G. J. Mohr, E. J. Mohr, H. Ross, and H. Thun. (Note: The Vienese edition was published in 1925.)

Akers, R. *Deviant Behavior: A Social Learning Approach.* Belmont, CA: Wadsworth, 1973.

Allen, H., E. Carlson, E. Parks, and R. Seiter. *Halfway Houses,* Washington, DC: Government Printing Office, 1978.

Allen, H., and C. Simonsen. *Corrections in America: An Introduction.* 4th ed. New York: Macmillan, 1986.

———. *Corrections in America: An Introduction.* 6th ed. New York: Macmillan, 1992.

Allen-Hagen, B. "Public Juvenile Facilities: Children in Custody 1989." *Juvenile Justice Bulletin* US Department of Justice, Office of Juvenile Justice and Delinquency Prevention. Washington, DC: Government Printing Office, 1991: 1–10.

American Bar Association. Institute of Judicial Administration, Juvenile Justice Standards Project, *Standards Relating to Abuse and Neglect.* Cambridge, MA: Ballinger, 1977.

American Humane Association. *National Analysis of Official Child Neglect and Abuse Reporting-1978.* Washington, DC: Government Printing Office, 1980.

"Americans Show Less Tolerance for Those on Welfare." *Rocky Mountain News,* Dec. 27, 1993, 34A.

Anderson, E., and G. Spanier. "Treatment of Delinquent Youth: The Influence of the Juvenile Probation Officer's Perceptions of Self and Work." *Criminology* 17 (1980): 505–14.

Anti-Defamation League of B'nai B'rith. *Fact-Finding Report.* New York: Civil Rights Division, Anti-Defamation League of B'nai B'rith, 1988.

Aries, Philippe. *Centuries of Childhood: A Social History of Family Life.* New York: Knopf, 1962.

Ariessohn, R. M. "Offense vs. Offender in Juvenile Court." *Juvenile Justice,* 23 (1972): 17–22.

Arnold, W. R. *Juveniles on Parole.* New York: Random House, 1970.

Aron, Raymond. *Main Currents in Sociological Thought.* Vol. 1, Garden City, NY: Anchor, 1970a.

———. *Main Currents in Sociological Thought.* Vol. 2, Garden City, NY: Anchor Books, 1970b.

Asbury, H. *The Gangs of New York.* New York: Knopf, 1927.

"Babylonian Law." In *Encyclopaedia Britannica,* 11th ed., vol. 3, 115–21. Cambridge, England: University Press, 1910.

Bachman, J., L. Johnston, and P. O'Malley. "Monitoring the Future: Questionnaire Responses From the Nation's High School Seniors, 1988." Ann Arbor, MI: Institute for Social Research, 1989.

"Bad Child or Bad Diet?" *Prevention,* July 1979, 65–71.

Balkan, S., R. J. Berger, and J. Schmidt. *Crime and Deviance in America: A Critical Approach.* Belmont, CA: Wadsworth, 1980.

Ball, R., and J. R. Lilly. "A Theoretical Examination of Home Incarceration." *Federal Probation* 50 (1986): 17–25.

Banay, R. S. "Physical Disfigurement as a Factor in Delinquency and Crime." *Federal Probation* 7, (1943): 20–24.

Barancik, S. *1989 Poverty Tables.* Washington, DC: Center on Budget and Policy Priorities, 1989.

Barlow, H. and T. Ferdinand. *Understanding Delinquency.* New York: HarperCollins, 1992.

Barnes, H. E., and N. K. Teeters. *New Horizons in Criminology.* 3d ed. Englewood Cliffs, NJ: Prentice-Hall, 1959.

Bartollas, C. *Juvenile Delinquency.* New York: Wiley, 1985.

———. *Juvenile Delinquency.* 2d ed. New York: Macmillan, 1990.

———. *Juvenile Delinquency.* 3d ed. New York: Macmillan, 1993.

Bassett, J. S. *A Short History of the United States: 1492–1920.* New York: Macmillan, 1921.

Bayles, Fred. "Teen Homicide Takes Heavy Toll." *Longmont Daily Times-Call,* Aug. 1, 1993, final ed.

Beccaria, C. *An Essay on Crimes and Punishments.* London: Almon, 1767. Trans. H. Paolucci. Indianapolis: Bobbs-Merrill 1963.

Bell, D. *Race, Racism and American Law.* 3d ed. Boston: Little, Brown, 1992.

Bell, R. R. "Parent-Child Conflict in Sexual Values." *Journal of Social Issues* 22, no. 2 (1966): 34–44.

Bennett, I. *Delinquent and Neurotic Children.* New York: Basic Books, 1960.

Bennett, W. J. *The Index of Leading Cultural Indicators.* Washington, DC: Heritage Foundation, 1993.

Berg, I. *Education and Jobs: The Great Training Robbery.* Boston: Beacon Press, 1971.

Berger, R. J. "Organizing the Community for Delinquency Prevention." in R. J. Berger, ed., *The Sociology of Juvenile Delinquency,* 220–39. Chicago: Nelson-Hall, 1991.

Bergsmann, I. R. "The Forgotten Few: Juvenile Female Offenders." *Federal Probation* 53 (1989): 73–78.

Berman, L. *New Creations in Human Beings.* New York: Doubleday, 1938.

Best, J., and D. Luckenbill. *Organizing Deviance.* 2d ed. Englewood Cliffs, NJ: Prentice-Hall, 1994.

Beville, S., and C. Cioffi. *A Guide for Delinquency Prevention Programs Based in Work and Community Service Activities.* Washington, DC: Government Printing Office, 1979.

Binder, A., G. Geis, and D. Bruce. *Juvenile Delinquency.* New York: Macmillan, 1988.

Bingham, Janet. "Colorado Dropout Rate Grows." *Denver Post,* Dec. 15, 1993, final ed.

Birman, B., and G. Natriello. "Perspectives on Absenteeism in High School: Multiple Explanations for an Epidemic." In K. Baker and R. Rubel, eds., *Violence and Crime in the Schools* 167–78. Lexington, MA: Lexington Books, 1980.

Bittner, S., and E. H. Newberger. "Child Abuse: Current Issues of Etiology, Diagnosis, and Treatment." in J. S. Henning, ed., *The Rights of Children: Legal and Psychological Perspectives,* 64–98. Springfield, IL: Charles C. Thomas, 1982.

Black, D. J., and A. J. Reiss, Jr. "Police Control of Juveniles." *American Sociological Review* 35 (1979): 63–77.

Black, M., ed. *The Social Theories of Talcott Parsons: A Critical Examination.* Englewood Cliffs, NJ: Prentice-Hall, 1961.

Blalock, H. M., Jr. *Theory Construction: From Verbal to Mathematical Formulations.* Englewood Cliffs, NJ: Prentice Hall, 1969.

Blumer, H. *Symbolic Interactionism: Perspective and Method.* Englewood Cliffs, NJ: Prentice-Hall, 1969.

Board of Governors of the Federal Reserve System. *Survey of Financial*

Characteristics of Consumers. Washington, DC: Government Printing Office, 1962.

Boocock, S. *An Introduction to the Sociology of Learning*. New York: Houghton Mifflin, 1972.

Bouhdiba, A. *Exploitation of Child Labor: A Final Report*. New York: United Nations Subcommission on Prevention of Discrimination and Protection of Minorities, 1982.

Brammer, L., and E. Shostrom. *Therapeutic Psychology*. 2d ed. Englewood Cliffs, NJ: Prentice-Hall, 1968.

Braudel, F. *Civilization and Capitalism, 15th–18th Century*. Trans. S. Reynolds. Vol. 1. New York: Harper and Row, 1981.

Breckinridge, S., and E. Abbott. *The Delinquent Child and the Home*. New York: Russell Sage Foundation, 1912.

Brookover, W., and E. Erickson. *Sociology of Education*. Homewood, IL: Dorsey, 1975.

Burt, C. *The Young Delinquent*. London: University of London Press, 1925. (Note: Published by Appleton in New York, 1929.)

————. *The Subnormal Mind*. London: Oxford University Press, 1935.

Burt, R. A. "Children as Victims." In P. A. Vardin and I. N. Brophy, eds., *Children's Rights: Contemporary Perspectives*, 37–52. New York: Teachers College Press, Columbia University, 1979.

Bush, W. J., and K. W. Waugh. *Diagnosing Learning Disabilities*. 2d ed. Columbus: Charles E. Merrill, 1971.

Byrne, S. "Nobody Home: The Erosion of the American Family." *Psychology Today*, May 1977, 41–47.

Cahalan, M., and L. Parsons. *Historical Corrections Statistics in the United States, 1850–1984*. NCJ–102529. Washington, DC: Government Printing Office, 1986.

Caldwell, R. G. "The Juvenile Court: Its Development and Some Major Problems." In R. D. Knudten, and S. Schafer, eds., *Juvenile Delinquency*, 281–310. New York: Random House, 1970.

Carnahan, Anne. "Violent Crime Arrests of Kids Rise 80%." *Rocky Mountain News*, Dec. 23, 1993, final ed.

Carstens, C. C. "Dependent Children." In *Encyclopedia of the Social Sciences*, E. R. A. Seligman, ed. 403–6. New York: Macmillan 1930.

Chambliss, W. J. *Crime and the Legal Process*. New York: McGraw-Hill, 1969.

————. "Functional and Conflict Theories of Crime: The Heritage of Emile Durkheim and Karl Marx." In W. J. Chambliss and M. Mankoff, eds., *Whose Law? What Order?* 1–28. New York: Wiley, 1976.

————. ed. *Criminal Law in Action*. New York: Wiley, 1984.

Chambliss, W. J., and M. Mankoff. *Whose Law? What Order? A Conflict Approach to Criminology.* New York: Wiley, 1976.

Channing, Dierdre S. "Philanthropist Makes a Gift." *Longmont Daily Times-Call,* Dec. 26, 1993, final ed.

Charles, M. "The Development of A Juvenile Electronic Monitoring Program." *Federal Probation* 53 (1989): 3–12.

Chesler, P. *About Men.* New York: Simon and Schuster, 1978.

Chesney-Lind, M. "Young Women in the Arms of the Law." In L. H. Bowker, ed., *Women, Crime and the Criminal Justice System.* 171–96. Lexington, MA: Lexington Books, 1978.

———. "Girls in Jail." *Crime and Delinquency* 34 (1988): 150–68.

Chesney-Lind, M., and R. Shelden. *Girls, Delinquency and Juvenile Justice.* Belmont, CA: Wadsworth, 1992.

Chicago Police Department. Special Functions Group. *Collecting, Organizing, and Reporting Street Gang Crime.* Chicago: Chicago Police Department. 1988.

"Children's Courts." In *Encyclopaedia Britannica,* 11th ed., vol. 6, 140. Cambridge, England: University Press, 1910.

Children's Defense Fund. *Annual Report.* Washington, DC: Children's Defense Fund, 1987.

Chorey, Carol. "Poverty Hits More State Kids." *Boulder Daily Camera,* Dec. 4, 1993, final ed.

Clear, T., and G. Cole. *American Corrections.* 3d ed. Belmont, CA: Wadsworth, 1994.

Cloward, R. A., and L. E. Ohlin. *Delinquency and Opportunity: A Theory of Delinquent Gangs.* New York: Free Press, 1960.

Coffey, A. *Law Enforcement: A Human Relations Approach.* Englewood Cliffs, NJ: Prentice-Hall, 1990.

Cohen, A. K. *Delinquent Boys: The Culture of the Gang.* New York: Free Press, 1955.

———. Foreward and Overview to *Gangs in America,* 7-21. ed. C. R. Huff. Newbury Park, CA: Sage, 1990.

Cohen, S. *Visions of Social Control: Crime, Punishment and Classification.* Cambridge, England: Policy Press, 1985.

Cole, G. F. *The American System of Criminal Justice.* 3d ed. Monterey, CA: Brooks/Cole, 1983.

Collins, R. *Sociological Insight: An Introduction to Non-Obvious Sociology.* New York: Oxford University Press, 1982.

Colorado General Assembly. *S.B. 18—An Act Concerning Delinquent Children.* Denver: Smith-Brooks Printing Co., 1903.

———. *H. B. 1482—The Child Protection Act of 1975.* Denver: Colorado General Assembly, 1975.

———. *Colorado Children's Code.* Denver: LG Printing Co. 1981.

Colvin, M., and J. Pauly. "A Critique of Criminology: Toward An Integrated Structural Marxist Theory of Delinquency Production." *American Journal of Sociology* 89 (1983): 513–51.

Community Youth Gang Services. *Gang Information Guide: What You Should Know About Gangs in Your Community.* Los Angeles, CA: Community Youth Gang Services, 1993.

Condry, S. M., and I. Lazar. "American Values and Social Policy for Children." *The Annals of the American Academy of Political Social Science* 461 (May 1982): 21–31.

Connel, R. "Disruptions: Improper Masculinities and Schooling." In L. Weis and M. Fine, eds., *Beyond Silenced Voices: Class, Race and Gender in United States Schools,* 191–208. Albany: SUNY Press, 1993.

Cooley, C. H. *Social Organization.* New York: Scribner's, 1909.

Coughlin, B. J. "The Rights of Children." In A. E. Wilkerson, ed., *The Rights of Children,* 7–23. Philadelphia: Temple University Press, 1973.

Cox, S., and J. Fitzgerald. *Police in Community Relations: Critical Issues.* Dubuque, IA: Wm. C. Brown, 1983.

Cravens, H. "Child Saving in Modern America 1870s–1990s." In R. Wollons, ed., *Children At Risk in America,* 3–31. Albany: SUNY Press, 1993.

Croan, G., T. Bird, and S. Beville. *State Options for Supporting Delinquency Prevention.* Washington, DC: Government Printing Office, 1979.

Cummings, S., and D. J. Monti, eds. *Gangs: The Origins and Impact of Contemporary Youth Gangs in the United States.* Albany: SUNY Press, 1993.

Cummins, J. "Empowering Minority Students: A Framework for Intervention." In L. Weis and M. Fine, eds., *Beyond Silenced Voices: Class, Race and Gender in United States Schools,* 101–17. Albany: SUNY Press, 1993.

Dalton, E. G. "Menstruation and Crime." In *British Medical Journal* 2 (1961), 1752–53.

———. *The Premenstrual Syndrome.* Springfield, IL: Charles C. Thomas, 1964.

Damico, S., and J. Roth. "A Different Kind of Responsibility: Social and Academic Engagement of General-Track High School Students." In R. Donmoyer and R. Kos, eds., *At-Risk Students,* 229–45. Albany: SUNY Press, 1993.

Davidson, H. "The Guardian ad litem: An Important Approach to the Protection of Children." In *Children Today* 10 (1981), 23.

Davis, Joyce. "School Board, Legislatures Close Gap." *Longmont Daily Times-Call,* Jan. 5, 1994, final ed.

Deardorff, N. R. "Child Welfare." In *Encyclopedia of the Social Sciences,* E. R. A. Seligman, ed. 373–80. New York: MacMillan, 1930.

DeFrancis, V. *Protecting the Child Victims of Sex Crimes Committed By Adults.* Denver: American Humane Association, 1979.

DeJong, W. "Project DARE: Teaching Kids to Say "No" to Drugs and Alcohol." *Nij Reports* 196 (Mar. 1986): 2–5.

DeMause, L., ed. *The History of Childhood.* New York: Psychohistory Press, 1974a.

———. "The Evolution of Childhood." *History of Childhood Quarterly* 1, no. 4 (spring 1974b): 503–75.

Denver Police Department. *Gangs, Not My Kid!* Denver: Denver Police Department, 1992.

Devereux, E. C., Jr. "Parsons' Sociological Theory." In M. Black, ed., *The Social Theories of Talcott Parsons: A Critical Examination,* 1–63. Englewood Cliffs, NJ: Prentice-Hall, 1961.

Donmoyer, R. "Structuring for Idiosyncracy: Rethinking Policies, Programs and Practices for At-Risk Students." In R. Donmoyer and R. Kos, eds., *At-Risk Students,* 191–217. Albany: SUNY Press, 1993.

R. Donmoyer and R. Kos, eds. *At-Risk Students: Portraits, Policies, Programs and Practices.* Albany: SUNY Press, 1993a.

———. "At-Risk Students: Insights from/about Research." In R. Donmoyer and R. Kos, eds., *At-Risk Students,* 7–35. Albany: SUNY Press, 1993b.

Dryfoos, J. *Adolescents At Risk: Prevalence and Prevention.* New York: Oxford University Press, 1990.

Duke, D. "How Administrators View the Crisis in School Discipline." *Phi Delta Kappa* 59 (Jan. 1978): 325–30.

Duncan, G., and W. Rogers. "Has Children's Poverty Become More Persistent?" *American Sociological Review* 56 (1991): 538–50.

Duncan, Joyce. "Gramps and Champs." *Longmont Daily Times-Call,* June 15, 1993, final ed.

Dunn, P. P. "That Enemy is the Baby: Childhood in Imperial Russia." In L. DeMause, ed., *The History of Childhood,* 383–405. New York: Psychohistory Press, 1974.

Durant, Will. *The Life of Greece.* New York: Simon and Schuster, 1939.

———. *Caesar and Christ: A History of Roman Civilization and of Christianity from Their Beginnings to A.D. 325.* New York: Simon and Schuster, 1944.

———. *The Renaissance: A History of Civilization in Italy from 1304–1576 A.D.* New York: Simon and Schuster, 1953.

———. *Our Oriental Heritage.* New York: Simon and Schuster, 1954.

Durant, Will, and Ariel Durant. *Rousseau and the Revolution.* New York: Simon and Schuster, 1967.

Durkheim, Emile. *The Rules of Sociological Method.* 8th ed. Trans. S. A. Solovay and J. H. Mueller. Ed. G. E. G. Catlin. New York: Free Press, 1964. (Note: first French ed. published in 1895.)

———. *The Division of Labor in Society.* Trans. G. Simpson. New York: Free Press, 1965. (Note: first French ed. published in 1893.)

———. *On the Learning of Discipline.* Trans. Jesse Pitts. In T. Parsons, E. Shils, K. D. Naegele, and J. R. Pitts, *Theories of Society,* 860–65. New York: Free Press, 1961. (Note: first French ed. published in Paris by Felix Alcan in 1925.)

Elliott, D., S. Ageton, and R. Canter. "An Integrated Theoretical Perspective on Delinquent Behavior." In *Journal of Research in Crime and Delinquency* Jan. 1979: 3–29.

Elliott, D., D. Huizinga, and S. Ageton, *Explaining Delinquency and Drug Use.* Beverly Hills: Sage, 1985.

Elliott, D., and H. Voss. *Delinquency and the Dropout.* Lexington, MA: Lexington Books, 1974.

Elmer, E. "A Social Worker's Assessment of Medico-Social Stress in Child Abuse Cases." In *Fourth National Symposium on Child Abuse,* 88–90. Denver: American Humane Association, 1975.

Empey, L. T. *American Delinquency.* Homewood, IL: Dorsey, 1982.

Empey, L. T., and S. Lubeck. *Explaining Delinquency.* Lexington, MA: D.C. Heath, 1971.

Empey, L., and M. Stafford. *American Delinquency.* 3d ed. Belmont, CA: Wadsworth, 1991.

Ende, A. "Children in History: A Personal Review of the Past Decade's Published Research." *Journal of Psychohistory* 2, no. 1 (summer 1983): 65–68.

Eshleman, J. *The Family.* 6th ed. Boston: Allyn and Bacon, 1991.

"Experts Offer Advice on Leaving Children Home Alone." *Rocky Mountain News,* Jan. 12, 1993, 4A.

Fagan, J. "The Social Organization of Drug Use and Drug Dealing among Urban Gangs." *Criminology* 27 (1989): 633–69.

———. "Social Processes of Delinquency and Drug Use among Urban Gangs." In C. R. Huff, ed., *Gangs in America,* 183–219. Newbury Park, CA: Sage, 1990.

Faris, R. E. L. *Social Disorganization.* New York: Ronald Press, 1948.

Faris, R. E. L., and H. W. Dunham. *Mental Disorders in Urban Areas: An Ecological Study of Schizophrenia and other Psychoses.* Chicago: University of Chicago Press, 1939.

Federal Bureau of Investigation. *Crime in the United States.* Washington, DC: Government Printing Office, 1940–41.

_____. *Crime in the United States*. Washington, DC: Government Printing Office, 1950–51.

_____. *Crime in the United States*. Washington, DC: Government Printing Office, 1964.

_____. *Crime in the United States*. Washington, DC: Government Printing Office, 1965.

_____. *Crime in the United States*. Washington, DC: Government Printing Office, 1975.

_____. *Crime in the United States*. Washington, DC: Government Printing Office, 1982.

_____. *Crime in the United States*. Washington, DC: Government Printing Office, 1983.

_____. *Crime in the United States*. Washington, DC: Government Printing Office, 1985.

_____. *Crime in the United States*. Washington, DC: Government Printing Office, 1986.

_____. *Crime in the United States*. Washington, DC: Government Printing Office, 1987.

_____. *Crime in the United States*. Washington, DC: Government Printing Office, 1989.

_____. *Crime in the United States*. Washington, DC: Government Printing Office, 1991.

_____. *Crime in the United States*. Washington, DC: Government Printing Office, 1993a.

_____. *Crime in the United States*. Washington, DC: Government Printing Office, 1993b.

Feld, B. "The Juvenile Court Meets the Principle of the Offense: Legislative Changes in Juvenile Waiver Statutes." *Journal of Criminal Law and Criminology* 78 (1987): 512–14.

Ferdinand, T, and E. G. Luchterhand. "Inner-City youth, the Police, The Juvenile Court and Justice." *Social Problems* 17 (1970): 519–27.

Ferguson, T. *The Young Delinquent in His Social Setting*. London: Oxford University Press, 1952.

Feuer, L. S., ed. *Marx and Engels: Basic Writings on Politics and Philosophy*. Garden City, NY: Anchor, 1959.

Fine, M. "Sexuality, Schooling and Adolescent Females: The Missing Discourse of Desire." In L. Weis and M. Fine, eds., *Beyond Silenced Voices: Class, Race and Gender in United States Schools*, 75–99. Albany: SUNY Press, 1993.

Finkelhor, D., R. J. Gelles, G. T. Hotaling and M. A. Straws, eds. *The Dark Side of Families: Current Family Violence Research*. Beverly Hills: Sage, 1983.

Fischer, C. *The Urban Experience.* 2d ed. New York: Harcourt Brace Jovanovich, 1984.

Flanagan,T., and M. McLeod. *Sourcebook of Criminal Justice Statistics, 1982.* Washington, DC: Government Printing Office, 1983.

Fontana, V. *Somewhere a Child Is Crying.* New York: New American Library, 1976.

Forst, M. L., B. A. Fisher, and R. B. Coates. "Indeterminate and Determinate Sentencing of Juvenile Delinquents: A National Survey of Approaches to Commitment and Release Decision-Making." *Juvenile and Family Court Journal* 36 (1985): 1–12.

Foster, David. "Is Child Neglect a Neglected Issue." *Rocky Mountain News,* Jan. 12, 1993, final ed.

Foster, M. "Resisting Racism: Personal Testimonies of African American Teachers." In L. Weis and M. Fine, eds., *Beyond Silenced Voices: Class, Race and Gender in United States Schools,* 273–88. Albany: SUNY Press, 1993.

Fox, V. "Is Adolescence a Phenomenon of Modern Times?" *Journal of psychohistory* 5, no. 2 (fall 1977): 271–90.

Freud, Sigmund. *A General Introduction to Psychoanalysis.* New York: Boni and Liveright, 1920.

Freudenthal, K. "Problems of the One-Parent Family." *Social Work* 4 (Jan. 1959): 44–48.

Friedenberg, E. Z. *Coming of Age in America: Growth and Acquiescence.* New York: Vintage Books, 1963.

Friedlander, K. *The Psycho-Analytical Approach to Juvenile Delinquency.* London: Routledge and Kegan Paul. 1947.

Fuch, R. G. *Abandoned Children: Foundlings and Child Welfare in 19th Century France.* Albany: SUNY Press, 1984.

Fuller, R. G. "Child Labor." In *Encyclopedia of the Social Sciences,* E. R. A. Seligman, ed. 412–24. New York: MacMillan, 1930.

Fusfeld, D. R. "The Rise of the Corporate State in America." *Journal of Economic Issues* 6 (Mar. 1972): 1–23.

Gaines, D. *Teenage Wasteland: Suburbia's Dead End Kids.* New York: HarperCollins, 1991.

Galbraith, J. K. *Economics in Perspective: A Critical History.* Boston: Houghton Mifflin, 1987.

Gandara, P. "Language and Ethnicity as Factors in School Failure." In R. Wollons, ed., *Children At-Risk in America,* 183–201. Albany: SUNY Press, 1993.

Garbarino, J., and G. Gilliam. *Understanding Abusive Families.* Lexington, MA: D.C. Heath, 1980.

"Garvin Gives 10 Teachers $1,000 Each." *Denver Post,* Dec. 18, 1993, 20A.

Gavin, Jennifer. "Groff May Leave Senate to Take Corrections Post." *Denver Post,* Dec. 31, 1993, final ed.

Gelles, R. J. "Violence Towards Children in the United States." Paper presented at the American Association for the Advancement of Science, Denver, Feb. 1977.

Gibbons, D. "Differential Treatment of Delinquents and Interpersonal Maturity Levels Theory: A Critique." *Social Service Review* 44, (Mar. 1970): 22–33.

––––––. *Delinquent Behavior.* 3d ed. Englewood Cliffs, NJ: Prentice-Hall, 1981.

––––––. *Talking about Crime and Criminals: Problems and Issues in Theory Development in Criminology.* Englewood Cliffs, NJ: Prentice-Hall, 1994.

Gibbons, D., and M. Krohn. *Delinquent Behavior.* 5th ed. Englewood Cliffs, NJ: Prentice-Hall, 1991.

Gil, D. "Violence Against Children." In D. Gil, ed., *Child Abuse and Violence,* 182–83. New York: AMS Press, 1979.

Glasser, W. *Reality Therapy.* New York: Harper and Row, 1965.

––––––. *Schools without Failure.* New York: Harper and Row, 1969.

Glueck, S., and E. Glueck. *Unraveling Juvenile Delinquency,* Cambridge, MA: Harvard University Press, 1950. (Note: for the Commonwealth Fund.)

Goddard, H. H. *Feeblemindedness: Its Causes and Consequences.* New York: Macmillan, 1914.

––––––. *The Criminal Imbecile.* New York: Macmillan, 1915.

––––––. "Feeblemindedness and Delinquency." *Journal of Psycho-Asthenics* 25 (1921): 168–76.

Gold, M. *Delinquent Behavior in an American City.* Belmont, CA: Brooks/Cole, 1970.

Gold, M., and D. Mann. "Delinquency as Defense." *American Journal of Orthopsychiatry* 42 (1972): 463–77.

Golden, D. "Who Guards the Children?" *Boston Globe Magazine,* Dec. 27, 1992, 12.

Goldman, N. "The Differential Selection of Juvenile Offenders for Court Appearance." In W. Chambliss, ed., *Crime and the Legal Process,* New York: McGraw-Hill, 1969: 264–290.

Goldstein, A. P. *Delinquent Gangs: A Psychological Approach.* Champaign, IL: Research Press, 1991.

Goldstein, H. *Policing a Free Society.* Cambridge, MA: Ballinger, 1976.

Goldstein, M. S., and D. P. Drotman. "Psychiatry and the Children's Movement." *Journal of Psychohistory* 5, no. 1 (summer 1977): 107–19.

Goldstein, S. "The Scope and Sources of School Board Authority to

Regulate Student Conduct and Status: a Nonconstitutional Analysis." *University of Pennsylvania Law Review* 117 (1969): 373.

Goode, E. *Deviant Behavior.* 4th ed. Englewood Cliffs, NJ: Prentice-Hall, 1994.

Goodman, P. *Growing up Absurd.* New York: Vintage Books, 1960.

Goring, C. *The English Convict: A Statistical Study.* London: His Majesty's Stationery Office, 1913.

Goslin, D. *The School in Contemporary Society.* Glenview, IL: Scott, Foresman, 1965.

Grant, W. and T. Snyder. *Digest of Education Statistics, 1985–86.* Washington, DC: Government Printing Office, 1986.

Greenwood, P. *Juvenile Offenders.* NCJ-97235. Washington, DC: National Institute of Justice, 1988.

Grizzle, G., J. Bass, J. T. McEwen, D. Galvin, A. Jones, H. Mowitt, and A. Witte. *Basic Issues in Corrections Performance.* Washington, DC: Government Printing Ofice, 1982.

Grossberg, M. "Children's Legal Rights? A Historical Look At a Legal Paradox." In R. Wollons, ed., *Children At-Risk in America,* 111–40. Albany: SUNY Press, 1993.

Hackett, J., H. Hatry, R. Levinson, J. Allen, K. Chi, and E. Feigenbaum. *Contracting for the Operation of Prisons and Jails.* Washington, DC: U.S. Department of Justice, 1987.

Hagan, F. *Introduction to Criminology.* Chicago: Nelson-Hall, 1986.

Hagan, J. *Modern Criminology: Crime, Criminal Behavior and Its Control.* New York: McGraw-Hill, 1985.

Hakeem, M. "A Critique of the Psychiatric Approach." In J. S. Roucek, ed., *Juvenile Delinquency,* 79–112. New York: Philosophical Library, 1958.

Hall, C. S. *A Primer of Freudian Psychology.* New York: New American Library, 1954.

Hamparian, D., L. Estep, S. Muntean, R. Priestino, R. Swisher, P. Wallace, and J. White. *Major Issues in Juvenile Justice Information and Training—Youth in Adult Courts: Between Two Worlds.* Columbus: Academy for Contemporary Problems, 1982.

Haney, W. "Testing and Minorities." In L. Weis and M. Fine, eds., *Beyond Silenced Voices: Class, Race and Gender in United States Schools,* 45–73. Albany: SUNY Press, 1993.

Hargreaves, D. *Social Relations in a Secondary School.* New York: Humanities Press, 1967.

Haskell, M. R., and L. Yablonski. *Juvenile Delinquency.* 2d ed. Chicago: Rand McNally, 1978.

Hawke, D. F. *Everyday Life in Early America.* New York: Harper and Row, 1988.

Healy, W. *The Individual Delinquent.* Boston: Little, Brown, 1915.

Healy, W., and A. Bronner. *Delinquents and Criminals: Their Making and Unmaking.* New York: Macmillan, 1925.

———. *New Light on Delinquency and its Treatment.* New Haven: Yale University Press, 1936.

"Hearing Loss May Lead to Crime, Studies Find." *Rocky Mountain News,* Aug. 13, 1988, 66.

Helfer, R. E., and C. H. Kempe, eds. *Child Abuse and Neglect: The Family and the Community.* Cambridge, MA: Ballinger, 1976.

Hennesey, M., P. J. Richards, and R. A. Berk. "Broken Homes and Middle-Class Delinquency." *Criminology* 15 (1978): 505–28.

Hepburn, J. R. "Testing Alternative Models of Delinquency Causation." *Journal of Criminal Law and Criminology* 67 (1977): 450–60.

Herrington, L. H. "The Unspeakable Must Be Spoken." In T. F. Wilson, ed., *Data Quality Policies and Procedures,* 7–10. NCJ-101849. Washington, DC: Government Printing Office, 1986.

Hester, T. *Correctional Populations in the United States, 1985.* NCJ-103957. Washington, DC: Government Printing Office, 1987.

Hetherington, E. *Review of Child Development Research.* Beverly Hills: Sage, 1977.

Hewitt, J. D., and R. M. Regoli. *Delinquency in Society.* New York: McGraw Hill, Inc., 1994.

Hindelang, M. "Causes of Delinquency: A Partial Replication." *Social Forces* 21 (1973): 471–87.

Hindelang, M., T. Hirschi, and J. Weis. *Measuring Delinquency.* Beverly Hills: Sage, 1981.

Hinsdale, B. A. *The American Government.* Ann Arbor: Inland Press, 1891.

Hippchen, L., ed. *Ecologic-Biochemical Approaches to Treatment of Delinquents and Criminals.* New York: Van Nostrand, 1978.

Hirschi, T. *Causes of Delinquency.* Berkeley and Los Angeles: University of California Press, 1969.

Hobbs, N. *Issues in the Classification of Children.* Vol. 1. San Francisco: Jossey-Bass, 1975.

Hoffer, A. "The Relation of Crime to Nutrition." *Humanist in Canada* 8 (1975): 3–9.

Hohenstein, W. F. "Factors Influencing the Police Disposition of Juvenile Offenders." In T. Sellin and M. Wolfgang, eds., *Delinquency: Selected Studies.* New York: Wiley, 1969.

Holt, J. *The Under-Achieving School.* New York: Dell Publishing Co., 1969.

"Honor Students Planned Double Suicide." *Longmont Daily Times-Call,* Dec. 4, 1993, 10A.

Hooton, E. A. *The American Criminal: An Anthropological Study.* Cambridge, MA: Harvard University Press, 1939.

Horowitz, R. "Sociological Perspectives on Gangs: Conflicting Definitions and Concepts." In C. R. Huff, ed., *Gangs in America,* 37–54. Newbury Park, CA: Sage, 1990.

Hubbard, Burt. "Gang Ranks Soar in Colorado Prison Systems." *Rocky Mountain News,* Jan 16, 1994, final ed.

Huey, J. "War on Poverty." *Fortune,* Apr. 10, 1989, 124–36.

Huff, C. R., ed. *Gangs in America.* Newbury Park, CA: Sage, 1990.

Huizinga, D., and D. Elliott. *Juvenile Offenders Prevalence: Offender Incidence and Arrest Rates By Race.* Boulder: Institute of Behavioral Science, 1985.

Hulse, J., and K. Bailey. "War On Child Abuse Escalates into Hysteria." *Denver Rocky Mountain News,* Oct. 16, 1986, 6–7, 60–61.

Hunner, R. J., and Y. E. Walker, eds. *Exploring the Relationship between Child Abuse and Delinquency.* Montclair, NJ: Allanheld, Osmun, 1981.

Illich, I. "Why We Must Disestablish Schools." In M. Carnoy, ed., *Schooling in a Corporate Society,* 2d ed., 340–61. New York: David McKay Co., 1975.

Illick, J. E. "Child-Rearing in 17th Century England and America." In L. DeMause, ed., *The History of Childhood,* 303–50. New York: Psychohistory Press, 1974.

Inciardi, J. A. *Criminal Justice.* 2d ed. New York: Harcourt Brace Jovanovich, 1987.

Inciardi, J. A., R. Horowitz, and A. E. Pottieger. *Street Kids, Street Drugs, Street Crime: An Examination of Drug Use in Miami.* Belmont, CA: Wadsworth, 1993.

"Indiana Girl Gets Her Wish, Plus a Barbie." *Boulder Daily Camera,* Dec. 22, 1993, 9A.

Jackson, Robert. "Two New Organizations Join Effort to Help At-Risk Kids." *Rocky Mountain News,* Dec. 10, 1993, final ed.

Jacob, P. *Justice in America.* Boston: Little, Brown, 1965.

Jacobs, M. *Screwing the System and Making it Work: Juvenile Justice in the No-Fault Society.* Chicago: University of Chicago Press, 1990.

Jacobs, P., M. Brunton, and M. M. Melville. "Aggressive Behavior, Mental Subnormality, and the XYY Male." *Nature,* 208 (Dec. 1965), 1351–52.

Jaffe, E. D. "Family Anomie and Delinquency: Development of the Concept and Some Empirical Findings." *British Journal of Criminology* 9 (1969): 376–88.

Jensen, G. F. "Parents, Peers, and Delinquent Action: A Test of the Differential Association Perspective." *American Journal of Sociology* 78 (1972): 562–75.

Jensen, G. F., and R. Eve. "Sex Differences in Delinquency: An Examination of Popular Sociological Explanations." *Criminology* 13 (1976): 427–48.

Johnson, G., T. Bird, and J. Little. *Delinquency Prevention: Theories and Strategies.* Washington, DC: Government Printing Office, 1979.

Justice, B., and R. Justice. *The Abusing Family.* New York: Human Sciences Press, 1976.

Karacki, L., and J. Toby. "The Uncommitted Adolescent: Candidate for Gang Socialization." *Sociological Inquiry* 32 (1962): 203–15.

Katz, Margaret. "Urban Peak Takes Young Men Off Streets." *Denver Post*, Dec. 15, 1993, final ed.

Keller, F. S., and W. N. Schoenfeld. *Principles of Psychology.* New York: Appleton-Century-Crofts, 1950.

Kellum, B. A. "Infanticide in England in the Later Middle Ages." *The History of Childhood Quarterly* 1, no. 3 (winter 1974): 367–88.

Kelly, D., and R. Balch. "Social Origins and School Failure: A Re-Examination of Cohen's Theory of Working Class Delinquency." *Pacific Sociological Review* 14 (1971): 413–30.

Kelly, D., and W. Pink. "School Crime and Individual Responsibility: The Perpetuation of a Myth." *The Urban Review* 14 (1982): 47–63.

Kempe, C. H. "The Battered Child Syndrome." *Journal of the American Medical Association* 181, no. 1 (July 1962): 17–24.

Kempe, R. S., and C. H. Kempe. *Child Abuse.* Cambridge, MA: Harvard University Press, 1978.

_____. *The Common Secret: Sexual Abuse of Children and Adolescents.* New York: W. H. Freeman and Co., 1984.

Kihm, R. *Prohibiting Secure Juvenile Detention: Assessing the Effectiveness of National Standards Detention Criteria.* Washington, DC: Government Printing Office, 1980.

King, J. L. *A Comparative Analysis of Juvenile Codes.* Washington, DC: Government Printing Office, 1980.

Klein, H. A. "Behavior Modification as Therapeutic Paradox." *American Journal of Orthopsychiatry* 44 (1974): 353–61.

_____. "Towards More Effective Behavioral Programs for Juvenile Offenders." *Federal Probation* 41 (1977): 45–50.

Klein, M., and C. Maxson. "Street Gang Violence." In N. A. Weiner and M. E. Wolfgang, eds., *Violent Crime, Violent Criminals.* Newbury Park, CA: Sage, 1989: 198–234.

Klein, M., S. Rosensweig, and R. Bates. "The Ambiguous Juvenile Arrest." *Criminology* 13 (1975): 78–89.

Klein, P. "Delinquent Children." In *Encyclopedia of the Social Sciences*, 406–9. New York: Macmillan, 1930.

Knudten, R. D., and S. Schafer, eds. *Juvenile Delinquency.* New York: Random House, 1970.

Kobetz, R. W., and B. B. Bosarge. *Juvenile Justice Administration*. Gaithersburg, MD: International Association of Chiefs of Police, 1973.

Kolko, G. *Main Currents in Modern American History*. New York: Pantheon, 1984.

Kozol, Jonathan. *Death at an Early Age*. Boston: Houghton Mifflin, 1967.

———. *Rachel and Her Children: Homeless Families in America*. New York: Ballantine Books, 1988.

Kratcoski, P., and L. Kratcoski. *Juvenile Delinquency*. 3d ed. Englewood Cliffs, NJ: Prentice-Hall, 1990.

Krisberg, B., I. M. Schwartz, P. Litsky, and J. Austin. "The Watershed of Juvenile Justice Reform." *Crime and Delinquency* 32 (1986): 5–38.

Krohn, M. "The Web of Conformity: A Network Approach to the Explanation of Delinquent Behavior." *Social Problems* 33 (1986): 81–93.

Ku, R. *The Volunteer Probation Counselor Program, Lincoln, Nebraska*. Catalogue no. 027-000-00360-5. Washington, DC: Government Printing Office, 1980.

Kvaraceus, W. *Juvenile Delinquency and the School*. New York: World Book, 1945.

Laing, R. D. *Self and Others*. London: Tavistock Publications, 1961. (Note: published in New York by Pantheon in 1969.)

Langer, W. L. "Infanticide: A Historical Survey." *History of Childhood Quarterly* 1, no. 3 (winter 1974): 353–65.

La Piere, R. "Attitudes vs. Actions." *Social Forces* 13 (1934): 230–37.

"Law Relating to Children." In *Encyclopaedia Britannica* 11th ed., vol. 6, 138–40. Cambridge, England: University Press, 1910.

Lee, Patricia R. "Black Dialect Still School's Nemesis." *Denver Post,* Jan. 16, 1994, final ed.

Lemert, E. *Social Pathology*. New York: McGraw-Hill, 1951.

Lerman, R. "Reversing the Poverty Cycle with Job-Based Education." In R. Wollons, ed., *Children At Risk in America*, 230–58. Albany: SUNY Press, 1993.

Lewis, D., et al. *Delinquency and Psycho-Pathology*. New York: Grune and Stratton, 1976.

Liazos, A. "Schools, Alienation and Delinquency." *Crime and Delinquency* 24 (1978): 355–61.

Linden, E., and J. C. Hackler. "Affective Ties and Delinquency." *Pacific Sociological Review* 16 (1973): 27–46.

Lipson, K. "Cops and Tops: A Program for Police and Teens That Works." *Police Chief* 49 (1982): 45–46.

Little, A. D., Inc. *Volunteer Services*. Washington, DC: Government Printing Office, 1978a.

———. *Community Alternatives*. Washington, DC: Government Printing Office, 1978b.

———. *Alternative Education Options*. Washington, DC: Government Printing Office, 1979a.

———. *Group Home Management*. Washington, DC: Government Printing Office, 1979b.

———. *Volunteer Shelter Bed Programs*. Washington, DC: Government Printing Office, 1980.

———. *Programs for the Serious and Violent Juvenile Offender*. Washington, DC: Government Printing Office, 1981a.

———. *Programs for Young Women in Trouble*. Washington, DC: Government Printing Office, 1981b.

Lombroso, C. *L'uomo Delinquente* (The criminal man). Milan: Hoepli, 1876.

———. *L'uomo Delinquente*. 5th ed., Turin: Bocca, 1896–97.

———. *Crime: Its Causes and Remedies*. Trans. H. P. Horton. Boston: Little, Brown, 1911.

Lowry, M. "When the Family Breaks Down: Massive and Misapplied Intervention by the State." In P. A. Vardin and I. N. Brophy, eds., *Children's Rights: Contemporary Perspectives*, 53–66. New York: Teachers College Press, Columbia University, 1979.

Lundman, R. J. "Routine Arrest Practices: A Commonwealth Perspective." *Social Problems* 22 (1974): 127–41.

———. *Prevention and Control of Juvenile Delinquency*. 2d ed. New York: Oxford University Press, 1993.

Lundman, R. J., R. E. Sykes, and J. P. Clark. "Police Control of Juveniles: A Replication." in R. J. Lundman, ed., *Police Behavior: A Sociological Perspective*. New York: Oxford University Press, 1980: 130–51.

Lyman, Jr., R. B. "Barbarism and Religion: Late Roman and Early Medieval Childhood." In L. DeMause, ed., *The History of Childhood*, 75–100. New York: Psychohistory Press, 1974.

Maestro, M. T. *Voltaire and Beccaria as Reformers of the Criminal Law*. New York: Columbia University Press, 1942.

Magid, K., and C. A. McKelvey. *High Risk: Children without a Conscience*. New York: Bantam Books, 1989.

Malmquist, C. P. *Handbook of Adolescence*. New York: Jason Aronson, 1978.

Manis, J. *Serious Social Problems*. Boston: Allyn and Bacon, 1984.

Mann, C. *Female Crime and Delinquency*. University, AL: University of Alabama Press, 1984.

Marcotte, P. "Criminal Kids." *American Bar Association Journal* 76 (1990): 60–66.

Marvick, E. W. "Nature versus Nurture: Patterns and Trends in 17th Century French Child-Rearing." In L. DeMause, ed., *The History of Childhood*, 259–301. New York: The Psychohistory Press, 1974.

Marx, Karl. *The Communist Manifesto*. Trans. Samuel Moore. Baltimore, MD: Penguin Books, 1967. (Note: German first edition published in 1848.)

Matza, D. *Delinquency and Drift*. Englewood Cliffs, NJ: Prentice-Hall, 1964.

Maxson, C., and M. Klein. "Street Gang Violence: Twice as Great or Half as Great?" In C. R. Huff, ed., *Gangs in America*, 71–100. Newbury Park, CA: Sage, 1990.

McCord, W., and J. McCord. *Psychopathy and Delinquency*. New York: Grune and Stratton, 1956.

———. "The Effects of Parental Role Model on Criminality." *Journal of Social Issues* 14 no. 3 (1958): 66–75.

McCord, J., W. McCord, and E. Thurber. "Some Effects of Paternal Absence on Male Children." *Journal of Abnormal and Social Psychology* 64 (1962): 361–69.

McCord, W., J. McCord, and I. Zola. *Origins of Crime*. New York: Columbia University Press, 1959.

McCullough, B., B. Zaremba, and W. Rich. "The Role of the Juvenile Justice System in the Link between Learning Disabilities and Delinquency." *State Court Journal* 3 (spring 1979).

McDermott, J. "Crime in the School and in the Community: Offenders, Victims and Fearful Youth." *Crime and Delinquency* 29 (1983): 270–83.

McEachern, A. W., and R. Bauzer. "Factors Related to Disposition in Juvenile Police Contacts." In M. Klein, ed., *Juvenile Gangs in Context: Theory, Research and Action*. Englewood Cliffs, NJ: Prentice-Hall, 1967: 148–60.

McLaughlin, M. M. "Survivors and Surrogates: Children and Parents from the 9th to the 13th Centuries." In L. DeMause, ed., *The History of Childhood*. 101–81. New York: Psychohistory Press, 1974.

Mead, G. H. *Mind, Self, and Society*. Ed. C. W. Morris. Chicago: University of Chicago Press, 1934.

Meckel, R. A. "Childhood and the Historians: A Review Essay." *Journal of Family History*, 9 winter 1984: 415–24.

Meier, R. F., ed. *Theoretical Methods in Criminology*. Beverly Hills: Sage, 1985.

Merton, R. K. "Social Structure and Anomie." *American Sociological Review* 3 (Oct. 1939): 672–82.

———. *Social Theory and Social Structure*. enl. ed. New York: Free Press, 1968. (Note: first published in 1947.)

Messner, S., S. Krohn, and A. Liska. *Theoretical Integration in the Study of Deviance and Crime*. Albany: SUNY Press, 1989.

Mezzacappa, Dale. "Administration Mulls School Violence." *Boulder Daily Camera*, June 12, 1993, final ed.

Miller, F. W., R. O. Dawson, G. E. Dix, and R. I. Parnas. *The Juvenile Justice Process.* 2d ed. Mineola, NY: Foundation Press, 1976.

Miller, W. "Lower-Class Culture as a Generating Milieu of Gang Delinquency" *Journal of Social Issues,* 14, no. 3 1958a: 5–19.

———. "Inter-Institutional Conflict as a Major Impediment to Delinquency Prevention." *Human Organization* 17 (fall 1958b): 20–23.

Mitchell, B. "A Policy Perspective: Overcoming Gridlock Beyond Schools." In R. Donmoyer and R. Kos, eds., *At-Risk Students,* 395–400. Albany: SUNY Press, 1993.

Monahan, T. P. "Family Status and the Delinquent Child: A Reappraisal and Some New Findings." *Social Forces* 35 (1957): 250–58.

———. "Broken Homes by Age of Delinquent Children." *Journal of Social Psychology* 51 (1960): 387–97.

Morris, N., and G. Hawkins. *The Honest Politician's Guide to Crime Control.* Chicago: University of Chicago Press, 1969.

Morris, R. "Female Delinquency and Relation Problems." *Social Forces* 43 (1964): 82–89.

Morton, J. H., R. G. Additon, L. Addison, L. Hunt, and J. J. Sullivan. "A Clinical Study of Premenstrual Tension." *American Journal of Obstetrics and Gynecology* 65 (1953): 1182–91.

Murray, C. A. *The Link Between Learning Disabilities and Juvenile Delinquency.* Washington, DC: Government Printing Office, 1976.

Nanda, S. *Cultural Anthropology.* 3d ed. Belmont, CA: Wadsworth, 1987.

National Advisory Commission on Criminal Justice Standards and Goals. *Report on Police.* Washington, DC: Government Printing Office, 1973.

National Advisory Commission on Juvenile Justice Standards and Goals. *Juvenile Justice and Delinquency Prevention.* Washington, DC: Government Printing Office, 1976.

National Advisory Committee for Juvenile Justice and Delinquency Prevention. *Serious Juvenile Crime: A Redirected Effort.* Washington, DC: Government Printing Office, March, 1984.

National Advisory Committee on Criminal Justice Standards and Goals. *Report of the Task Force on Juvenile Justice and Delinquency Prevention.* Washington, DC: Government Printing Office, 1976.

National Advisory Committee on Handicapped Children. *Special Education for Handicapped Children, First Annual Report.* Washington, DC: Government Printing Office, 1968.

National Advisory Council on Supplementary Centers and Services. *Dropout Prevention.* Washington, DC: U.S. Government Printing Office, 1975.

National Conference on Prevention and Control of Juvenile Delinquency.

Report on Home Responsibility. Washington, DC: Government Printing Office, 1974.

National Council of Juvenile and Family Court Judges. *Deprived Children: A Judicial Response.* Reno, NV: National Council of Juvenile and Family Court Judges, 1986.

National Education Association. *Nationwide Teacher Opinion Poll, 1981.* Washington, DC: National Education Association, 1982.

National Research Council. Assembly of Behavioral and Social Sciences. Advisory Committee on Child Development. *Toward a National Policy for Children and Families.* Washington, DC: National Academy of Sciences, 1976.

Nelson, E., H. Ohmart, and N. Harlow. *Promising Strategies in Probation and Parole.* Washington, DC: Government Printing Office, 1978.

Newberger, E., Newberger, C. M., and R. Hampton. "Child Abuse: The Current Theory Base and Future Research Needs." *Journal of Child Psychiatry* 22 (1983): 262–68.

Newbolt, H. L., W. Philpot, and M. Mandell. "Psychiatric Syndromes Produced by Alergies: Ecologic Mental Illness." Paper presented at the Orthomolecular Psychiatry Association, Dallas, TX, 1972.

Newcomer, Kris. "Denverite Touts Big Brothers at Summit." *Rocky Mountain News,* Nov. 11, 1993, final ed.

Nimick, E., H. Snyder, D. Sullivan and N. Tierney. *Juvenile Court Statistics—1983.* Pittsburgh: National Center for Juvenile Justice, National Council of Juvenile and Family Court Judges, 1987.

Nisbet, R. A. *Emile Durkheim.* Englewood Cliffs, NJ: Prentice-Hall, 1965.

———. *The Social Bond: An Introduction to the Study of Society.* New York: Knopf, 1970.

———. *Twilight of Authority.* New York: Oxford University Press, 1975.

Norland, S., and N. Shover. "Gender Roles and Female Criminality: Some Critical Comments." *Criminology* 15 (1977): 87–104.

Norland, S., Shover, N., W. Thornton, and J. James. "Intrafamily Conflict and Delinquency." *Pacific Sociological Review* 2 (1979): 223–40.

Norman, S. *The Youth Service Bureau—A Key to Delinquency Prevention.* Hackensack, NJ: National Council on Crime and Delinquency, 1972.

Nye, F. I. *Family Relationships and Delinquent Behavior.* New York: Wiley, 1938.

———. "Child Adjustment in Broken and Unhappy Unbroken Homes." *Marriage and Family* 19 (1957): 356–61.

Nye, F. I., and J. Short. "Scaling Delinquent Behavior." *American Sociological Review* 22 (1957): 326–31.

———. "Extent of Unrecorded Delinquency, Tentative Conclusions."

Journal of Criminal Law, Criminology, and Police Science 49 (1958): 296–302.

O'Connor, R., N. Albrecht, B. Cohen, and L. Newquist-Carroll. *New Directions in Youth Services: Experience With State-Level Coordination.* Washington, DC: Government Printing Office, 1984.

Office of Juvenile Justice and Delinquency Prevention. *Federal Juvenile Delinquency Programs: Third Analysis and Evaluation.* Washington, DC: Government Printing Office, 1980.

Osbun, L. A., and P. A. Rode. "Prosecuting Juveniles as Adults: The Quest for Objective Decisions." In R. J. Berger, ed., *The Sociology of Juvenile Delinquency,* 379–91. Chicago: Nelson-Hall, 1991.

Osgood, D., O'Malley, P., Bachman, J., and L. Johnston. "Time Trends and Age Trends in Arrests and Self-Reported Illegal Behavior." *Criminology* 27 (1989): 389–417.

Park, R. E. "Human Migration and the Marginal Man." *American Journal of Sociology* 33 (1928): 881–93.

———. "Social Change and Social Disorganization." In R. E. Park, E. W. Burgess, and R. D. McKenzie, *The City,* 105–10. Chicago: University of Chicago Press, 1967.

Park, R. E., and E. W. Burgess. *Introduction to the Science of Sociology.* Chicago: University of Chicago Press, 1924.

———. *The City.* Chicago: University of Chicago Press, 1925.

Park, R. E., E. W. Burgess, and R. D. McKenzie. *The City.* Chicago: University of Chicago Press, 1967. (Note: first published with three authors in 1928.)

Parsons, T. *The Structure of Social Action.* New York: McGraw-Hill, 1937.

———. *The Social System.* New York: Free Press, 1951.

———. "The School Class as a Social System." In R. Bell and H. Strub, *The Sociology of Education: A Sourcebook,* 199–218. Homewood, IL: Dorsey, 1968.

Pappenfort, D., and T. Young. *Use of Secure Detention for Juveniles and Alternatives to Its Use.* Washington, DC: Government Printing Office, 1980.

Patty, Mike. "Adams DA Cracks Down on Kids, Guns." *Rocky Mountain News,* July 10, 1993, final ed.

Paulson, M. J., L. Strause, and A. Chaleff. "Intra-Familial Incest and Sexual Molestation of Children." In J. S. Henning, ed., *The Rights of Children: Legal and Psychological Perspectives,* pp. 39–63. Springfield, IL: Charles C. Thomas, 1982.

Paulson, Stephen K. "More States Toughening Gun Laws." *Boulder Daily Camera,* Oct. 21, 1993, final ed.

Pavlov, I. P. *Conditioned Reflexes: An Investigation of the Physiological*

Activity of the Cerebral Cortex. Trans. G. V. Anrep. London: Oxford University Press, 1927.

Pawlak, V. *Megavitamin Therapy and the Drug Wipeout Syndrome.* Phoenix: Do It Now Foundation, 1972.

Pepinsky, H. "Police Patrolmen's Offense Reporting Behavior." *Journal of Research in Crime and Delinquency* 13 (Jan. 1976): 33–47.

Perry, D. C. *Police in the Metropolis.* Columbus: Charles E. Merrill, 1975.

Petersilia, J. "Exploring the Option of House Arrest." *Federal Probation* 50 (1986): 50–56.

Peterson, D. R., and W. C. Becker. "Family Interaction and Delinquency." In H. C. Quay, ed., *Juvenile Delinquency: Research and Theory.* 63–99. Princeton: Van Nostrand, 1965.

Peterson, D. R., H. C. Quay, and G. Cumeron. "Personality and Background Factors in Juvenile Delinquency." *Journal of Consulting Psychology* 23 (1959): 392–99.

Peterson, D. R., H. C. Quay, and T. Tiffany. "Personality Factors Related to Juvenile Delinquency." *Child Development* 32 (1961): 355–72.

Phillips, E. L. "Achievement Place: Token Reinforcement Procedures in a Home-Style Rehabilitation Setting for Predelinquent Boys." *Journal of Applied Behavior Analysis* 1 (1968): 213–23.

Phillips, K. *The Politics of Rich and Poor: Wealth and the American Electorate in the Reagan Aftermath.* New York: Random House, 1990.

Piliavin, I., and S. Briar. "Police Encounters With Juveniles." *American Journal of Sociology* 70 (1964): 206–14.

Platt, A. M. *The Child Savers: The Invention of Delinquency.* Chicago: University of Chicago Press, 1969.

Pleck, E. *Domestic Tyranny: The Making of American Social Policy against Family Violence from Colonial Times to the Present.* New York: Oxford University Press, 1987.

Podboy, J., and W. Mallory. "The Diagnosis of Specific Learning Disabilities in a Juvenile Delinquent Population." *Federal Probation* 42 (1978): 26–33.

Polier, J. *Juvenile Justice in Double Jeopardy: The Distanced Community and Vengeful Retribution.* Hillsdale, NJ: Lawrence Erlbaum, 1989.

Polk, K., D. Frease and F. Richmond. "Social Class, School Experience and Delinquency." *Criminology* 12 (1974): 84–85.

Polk, K., and D. Halferty. "School Cultures, Adolescent Commitments and Delinquency." In K. Polk and W. Schafer, eds., *Schools and Delinquency,* 71–90. Englewood Cliffs, NJ: Prentice-Hall, 1972.

Polk, K., and F. Richmond. "Those Who Fail." In K. Polk and W. Schafer, eds., *Schools and Delinquency,* 56–69. Englewood Cliffs, NJ: Prentice-Hall, 1972.

Polk, K., and W. Schafer. "Schools and Delinquency." In K. Polk and W. Schafer, eds. *Schools and Delinquency* 4–8. Englewood Cliffs, NJ: Prentice-Hall, 1972.

Polk, K., and W. Schafer. "Some Perspectives on Delinquency." In K. Polk and W. Schafer, eds. *Schools and Delinquency* 17–29. Englewood Cliffs, NJ: Prentice-Hall, 1972.

Polk, K., and W. Schafer, eds. *Schools and Delinquency.* Englewood Cliffs, NJ: Prentice-Hall, 1972.

Popper, K. R. *Conjectures and Refutations: The Growth of Scientific Knowledge.* New York: Basic Books, 1962.

Post, C. H. "The Link between Learning Disabilities and Juvenile Delinquency." *Juvenile Family Court Journal* 32 (1981): 61.

Powell, D. R. "From Child To Parent: Changing Conceptions of Early Childhood Intervention." *The Annals of the American Academy of Political Social Science* 461 (May 1982): 135–44.

President's Commission on Law Enforcement and the Administration of Justice. *Task Force Report: Juvenile Delinquency and Youth Crime.* Washington, DC: Government Printing Office, 1967.

Price, W., P. Whatmore, and W. Mclement. "Criminal Patients with XYY Sex-Chromosome Complements." *The Lancet* 1 (1966): 565–66.

Pursley, R. *Introduction to Criminal Justice.* 5th ed. New York: Macmillan, 1991.

Pursuit, D. G., J. D. Gerletti, R. M. Brown and S. M. Ward. *Police Programs for Preventing Crime and Delinquency.* Springfield, IL: Charles C. Thomas, 1972.

Quay, H. C. "Dimensions of Personality in Delinquent Boys." *Child Development* 35 (1964a): 479–84.

———. "Personality Dimensions in Delinquent Males." *Journal of Research on Crime and Delinquency* 1 (Mar. 1964): 33–37.

———. "Personality and Delinquency." In H. C. Quay, *Juvenile Delinquency,* 139–69. New York: Liton, 1965.

———. "Personality Patterns in Preadolescent Delinquent Boys." *Educational and Psychological Measurement* 26 (1966): 99–110.

———. "Classification in the Treatment of Delinquency and Antisocial Behavior." In N. Hobbs, ed., *Issues on the Classification of Children,* vol. 1, 377–92. San Francisco: Jossey-Bass, 1975.

Quinney, R. *The Social Reality of Crime.* Boston: Little, Brown, 1970.

Rademacher, D. "The Problem of Children in Jails." In Symposium Planning Committee, *National Symposium on Children in Jail,* 7–9. Washington: Government Printing Office, 1980.

Rahav, G. "Birth Order and Delinquency." *British Journal of Criminology* 20 (1980): 385–95.

Reckless, W. C. "A New Theory of Delinquency and Crime." *Federal Probation* 24 (Dec. 1961): 42–46.

Reckless, W. C., and S. Dinitz. *The Prevention of Juvenile Delinquency.* Columbus: Ohio State University Press, 1972.

Reckless, W. C., S. Dinitz, and E. Murray. "Self-Concept as an Insulator against Delinquency." *American Sociological Review* 21 (1956): 744–46.

Reiman, J. *The Rich Get Richer and the Poor Get Prison.* 3d ed. New York: Macmillan, 1990.

Reiss, A., and A. Rhodes. "The Distribution of Juvenile Delinquency in the Social Class Structure." *American Sociological Review* 26 (1961): 720–32.

Reutter, E. E., Jr. *Legal Aspects of Control of Student Activities by Public School Authorities.* Topeka: National Organization on Legal Problems of Education, 1970.

Reynolds, G. S. *A Primer of Operant Conditioning.* Glenview, IL: Scott, Foresman, 1968.

Reynolds, P. D. *A Primer in Theory Construction.* New York: Bobbs-Merrill, 1971.

Robertson, P. "Home as a Nest: Middle-Class Childhood in 19th Century Europe." In L. DeMause, ed., *The History of Childhood,* pp. 407–31. New York: Psychohistory Press, 1974.

Robinson, B. *Teenage Fathers.* Lexington, MA: D. C. Heath, 1988.

Rodham, H. "Children's Rights: A Legal Perspective." In P. A. Vardin and I. N. Brody, eds., *Children's Rights.* 21–36. New York: Teachers College Press, Columbia University, 1979.

Rodman, H., and P. Grams. "Juvenile Delinquency and the Family." In President's Commission on Law Enforcement and the Administration of Justice," *Task Force Report: Juvenile Delinquency and Youth Crime,* Washington, DC: Government Printing Office, 1967.

"Roman Law." In *Encyclopaedia Britannica* 11th ed., vol. 23, 529–30. Cambridge, England: University Press, 1911.

Ross, J. B. "The Middle-Class Child in Urban Italy, 14th to Early 16th Century." In L. DeMause, ed., *The History of Childhood,* 183–228. New York: Psychohistory Press, 1974.

Rothman, D. *Incarceration and its Alternatives in 20th Century America.* Washington, DC: Government Printing Office, 1979.

Roucek, J. S., ed. *Juvenile Delinquency.* New York: Philosophical Library, 1958.

Rubel, R. J., and A. H. Goldsmith. "Reflections on the Rights of Students and the Rise of School Violence." In K. Baker and R. J. Rubel, eds., *Violence and Crimes in the Schools,* 73–77. Lexington, MA: Lexington Books, 1980.

Rubin, H. T. *The Courts: Fulcrum of the Justice System.* Santa Monica: Goodyear, 1976.

Rutherford, R. B. "Establishing Behavioral Contracts with Delinquent Adolescents." *Federal Probation* 39 (1975): 28–32.

Sanders, W. J. *Juvenile Delinquency.* New York: Holt, Rinehart and Winston, 1981.

Sanko, John. "Answers to Teen Crime at Hand." *Rocky Mountain News,* June 21, 1993, final ed.

———. "Kid Gun Law Generating Few Arrests." *Rocky Mountain News,* Nov. 11, 1993, final ed.

Sapon-Shevin, M. "Gifted Education and the Protection of Privilege: Breaking the Silence, Opening the Discourse." In L. Weis and M. Fine, eds., *Beyond Silenced Voices: Class, Race and Gender in United States Schools,* 25–44. Albany: SUNY Press, 1993.

Sarbin, T. R., and J. E. Miller. "Demonism Revisited: The XYY Chromosomal Anomaly." *Issues in Criminology* 5, no. 2 (summer 1970): 199.

Schafer, W. "Deviance in the Public School: An Interactional View." In K. Polk and W. Schafer, eds., *Schools and Delinquency* 145–163. Englewood Cliffs, NJ: Prentice-Hall, 1972.

Schafer, W., C. Olexa, and K. Polk. "Programmed for Social Class: Tracking in High School." In K. Polk and W. Schafer, eds., *Schools and Delinquency,* 34–54. Englewood Cliffs, NJ: Prentice-Hall, 1972.

Schafer, W., and K. Polk. "Delinquency and the Schools." In President's Commission on Law Enforcement and the Administration of Justice, *Task Force Report: Juvenile Delinquency and Youth Crime.* Washington, DC: Government Printing Office, 1967.

Schlapp, M. G., and E. H. Smith. *The New Criminology.* New York: Boni and Liveright, 1928.

Schmalleger, F. *Criminal Justice: A Brief Introduction.* Englewood Cliffs, NJ: Prentice-Hall, 1994.

Schmidt, A. "Electronic Monitors." *Federal Probation* 50 (1986): 56–60.

Schneider, A., ed. *Guide to Juvenile Restitution.* Washington, DC: Government Printing Office, 1985.

Schorsch, A. *Images of Childhood: An Illustrated Social History.* New York: Mayflower Books, 1979.

Schwartz, I. M. *(In)Justice for Juveniles: Rethinking the Best Interests of the Child.* Lexington, MA: D. C. Heath, 1989.

Seeley, Ken. "Breaking the Cycle of Teen Violence." *Denver Post,* Dec. 18, 1993, final ed.

Seligson, T. "Are They Too Young To Die?" *Parade Magazine,* October 19, 1986, 4–5.

Sellin, T. *Culture Conflict and Crime.* New York: Social Science Research Council, 1938.

Senna, J., and L. Siegel. *Juvenile Law: Cases and Comments.* 2d ed. St. Paul: West, 1992.

Sexton, P. *The American School.* Englewood Cliffs, NJ: Prentice-Hall, 1967.

Shah, S. A., and L. H. Roth. "Biological and Psychophysiological Factors in Criminality." In D. Glaser, ed., *Handbook of Criminology,* 101–73. Chicago: Rand McNally, 1974.

Shalloo, J. P. "The Emergence of Criminology." *Federal Probation* 6 (Oct.–Dec., 1942): 21–24.

Shaw, C. *The Jack-Roller: A Delinquent Boy's Own Story.* Chicago: University of Chicago Press, 1930.

Shaw, C., and H. McKay. "Are Broken Homes a Causative Factor in Delinquency?" *Social Forces* 10 (1932): 514–24.

Shaw, C., and M. Moore. *The Natural History of a Delinquent Career.* Chicago: University of Chicago Press, 1931.

Shaw, C., et al. *Delinquency Areas.* Chicago: University of Chicago Press, 1929.

Shaw, C., et al. *Brothers in Crime.* Chicago: University of Chicago Press, 1938.

Sheldon, W. H. *Varieties of Delinquent Youth.* New York: Harper, 1949.

Shepherd, R. E., Jr. "The Abused Child and the Law." In A. E. Wilkerson, ed., *The Rights of Children.* Philadelphia: Temple University Press, 1973.

Shibutani, T. *Social Processes: An Introduction to Society.* Berkeley and Los Angeles: University of California Press, 1986.

Short, J. "New Wine in Old Bottles: Changes and Continuity in American Gangs." In C. R. Huff, ed., *Gangs in America,* 223–39. Newbury Park, CA: Sage, 1990.

Siegel, L. J., and J. J. Senna. *Juvenile Delinquency.* 2d ed. St. Paul: West Publishing Co., 1981.

_____. *Juvenile Delinquency.* 5th ed. St. Paul: West Publishing Co., 1994.

Silberman, C. *Crisis in the Classroom.* New York: Random House, 1970.

Skinner, B. F. *The Behavior of Organisms.* New York: Appleton-Century-Crofts, 1938.

_____. *Verbal Behavior.* New York: Appleton-Century-Crofts, 1957.

Slawson, J. *The Delinquent Boy.* Boston: Badger, 1926.

Slocum, W. L., and C. L. Stone. "Family Culture Patterns and Delinquent-Type Behavior." *Marriage and Family Living* 25 (1963): 202–8.

Smith, C. P., and P. S. Alexander. *A National Assessment of Serious Juvenile Crime and the Juvenile Justice System.* Washington, DC: Government Printing Office, April, 1980.

Smith, C. P., D. J. Berkman, and W. M. Fraser. *A Preliminary National Assessment of Child Abuse and Neglect and the Juvenile Justice Sys-*

tem: The Shadows of Distress. Washington, DC: Government Printing Office, April, 1980.

Smith, C. P., D. J. Berkman, W. M. Fraser, and J. Sutton. *A Preliminary National Assessment of the Status Offender and the Juvenile Justice System*. Washington, DC: Government Printing Office, April, 1980.

Smith, C. P., T. E. Black, and F. R. Campbell. *A National Assessment of Case Disposition and Classification in the Juvenile Justice System: Inconsistent Labeling*. Washington, DC: Government Printing Office, January, 1979.

Smith, K. "A Profile of Juvenile Court Judges in the United States." *Juvenile Justice* 25 (1974): 27–38.

Snodgrass, J., G. Geis, J. F. Short, S. Korin, and the Jack-Roller. *The Jack-Roller at Seventy*. Lexington, MA: D. C. Heath, 1982.

Snyder, H., et al. *Juvenile Court Statistics, 1989*. Pittsburgh: National Center for Juvenile Justice, 1992.

Spergel, I. *Slumtown, Racketville, Haulburg*. Chicago: University of Chicago Press, 1964.

———. "Youth Gangs: Continuity and Change." In M. Tonry and N. Morris, eds., *Crime and Justice: A Review of Research* 12 (1990): 171–275.

Springer, C. *Justice for Juveniles*. Washington, DC: Government Printing Office, 1986.

"Springs Gets Tough, Creative in Combatting Violence in Schools." *Boulder Daily Camera*, Nov. 13, 1993, 10A.

Steele, B. F., and C. B. Pollock. "A Psychiatric Study of Parents Who Abuse Infants and Small Children." In R. Helfer and C. H. Kempe, eds., *The Battered Child*, 103–47. Chicago: University of Chicago Press, 1968.

Stetson, D. *Women's Rights in the U.S.A.* Pacific Grove, CA: Brooks/Cole, 1991.

Stevenson, R., and J. Ellsworth. "Dropouts and the Silencing of Critical Voices." In L. Weis and M. Fine, eds., *Beyond Silenced Voices: Class, Race and Gender in United States Schools*, 259–71. Albany: SUNY Press, 1993.

Stinchcombe, A. *Rebellion in a High School*. Chicago: Quadrangle Books, 1964.

Strachey, J., ed. *The Complete Psychological Works of Sigmund Freud*. Standard Edition. 1 London: Hogarth Press, 1966.

Straus, M., Gelles, R., and S. Steinmetz. *Behind Closed Doors: Violence in the American Family*. New York: Anchor, 1980.

"Street Gangs of Los Angeles." ZDF German Television production. Princeton: Films for the Humanities & Sciences. 1990.

"Study: New Laws Won't Keep Kids Away From Guns." *Longmont Daily Times-Call*, Dec. 13, 1993, 10B.

Sutherland, E. *Principles of Criminology.* New York: Lippincott, 1939.

Sutherland, E., and D. Cressey. *Criminology.* 9th ed. New York: Lippincott, 1974.

Swanger, H. "Hendrickson v. Griggs: A Review of the Legal and Policy Implications for Juvenile Justice Policymakers." *Crime and Delinquency* 34 (1988): 209–27.

Sykes, G. M., and D. Matza. "Techniques of Neutralization: A Theory of Delinquency." *American Sociological Review* 22 (1957): 664–70.

Symposium Planning Committee. *National Symposium on Children in Jail.* Washington, DC: Government Printing Office, 1980.

Szymanski, L. *Statutory Waiver Criteria.* Pittsburgh: National Center for Juvenile Justice, October, 1989.

Tannenbaum, F. *Crime and the Community.* Boston: Ginn and Company, 1938.

Tappan, P. W. *Juvenile Delinquency.* New York: McGraw-Hill, 1949.

Taylor, B. "When Cop Teaches, Teens Listen." *Boulder Daily Camera,* Dec. 29, 1991, 1E.

Taylor, C. "Gang Imperialism." In C. R. Huff, ed. *Gangs in America,* 103–15. Newbury Park, CA: Sage, 1990.

Taylor, I., P. Walton, and J. Young. *The New Criminology.* New York: Harper and Row, 1973.

———. *Critical Criminology.* London: Routledge and Kegan Paul, 1975.

"Teen Removes Monitor, Kills Boy." *Longmont Daily Times-Call,* Dec. 9, 1993, 6A.

Thomas, A. C. *An Elementary History of the United States.* Boston: D. C. Heath, 1908.

Thomas, W. I., and F. Znaniecki. *The Polish Peasant in Europe and America.* Vol. 4. Boston: Gorham Press, 1920.

Thornberry, T. "Toward An Interactional Theory of Delinquency." *Criminology* 25, no. 4 (1987): 863–91.

Thornberry, T., M. D. Krohn, A. J. Lizotte, and D. Chard-Wierschem. "The Role of Juvenile Gangs in Facilitating Delinquent Behavior." *Journal of Research in Crime and Delinquency* 30 (Feb. 1993): 55–87.

Thornton, W. E., Jr., J. A. James, and W. G. Doerner. *Delinquency and Justice.* Glenview, IL: Scott, Foresman, 1982.

Thornton, W. E., Jr., and L. Voigt. *Delinquency and Justice.* 3d ed. New York: McGraw-Hill, 1992.

Thrasher, F. *The Gang.* Chicago: University of Chicago Press, 1927.

Thurston, H. W. "Neglected Children." *Encyclopedia of the Social Sciences,* 398–403. New York: Macmillan, 1930.

Tiffin, S. *In Whose Best Interest? Child Welfare Reform in the Progressive Era.* Westport, CT: Greenwood Press, 1982.

Toby, J. "The Differential Impact of Family Disorganization." *American Sociological Review* 22 (1957a): 505–512.

———. "Orientation to Education as a Factor in the School Maladjustment of Lower-Class Children." *Social Forces* 35 (1957b): 259–66.

Traub, S. H., and C. B. Little. *Theories of Deviance.* 2d ed. Itasca, IL: F. E. Peacock, 1980.

Trexler, R. C. "Infanticide in Florence: New Sources and First Results." In L. DeMause, ed., *The History of Childhood,* 98–116. New York: Psychohistory Press, 1974.

Trojanowicz, R., and B. Bucqueroux. *Community Policing: A Contemporary Perspective.* Cincinnatti: Anderson Publishing Co., 1990.

Trojanowicz, R., and M. Morash. *Juvenile Delinquency: Concepts and Control.* 4th ed. Englewood Cliffs, NJ: Prentice-Hall, 1987.

———. *Juvenile Delinquency: Concepts and Control.* 5th ed. Englewood Cliffs, NJ: Prentice-Hall, 1992.

Tucker, M. J. "The Child as Beginning and End: 15th and 16th Century English Childhood." In L. DeMause, ed., *The History of Childhood,* 229–57. New York: Psychohistory Press, 1974.

Turk, A. T. "Conflict and Criminality." *American Sociological Review* 31 (June 1966): 338–52.

———. *Criminality and the Legal Order.* Chicago: Rand McNally, 1969.

Turner, J. H. *The Structure of Sociological Theory.* Homewood, IL: Dorsey, 1974.

———. *Sociology: The Science of Human Organization.* Chicago: Nelson-Hall, 1985.

Turner, J. H., and D. Musick. *American Dilemmas: A Sociological Interpretation of Enduring Social Issues,* New York: Columbia University Press, 1985.

Turner, J. H., R. Singleton, Jr., and D. Musick. *Oppression: A Socio-History of Black-White Relations in America.* Chicago: Nelson-Hall, 1984.

Turner, J. H., and C. Starnes. *Inequality: Privilege and Poverty in America.* Santa Monica: Goodyear, 1976.

"The 2.4 Million Children Who Aren't in School." *U.S. News and World Report,* Mar. 15, 1976, pp. 43–44.

Unger, K. V. "Learning Disabilities and Juvenile Delinquency." *Journal of Juvenile and Family Courts* 29 (1978): 25–30.

U.S. Bureau of the Census. *Statistical Abstract of the United States.* Washington, DC: Government Printing Office, 1964.

———. *Statistical Abstract of the United States.* Washington, DC: Government Printing Office, 1965.

_____. *Historical Statistics of the United States, Colonial Times to 1970.* Bicentennial ed. Pt. 2. Washington, DC: Government Printing Office, 1975a.

_____. *Statistical Abstract of the United States.* Washington, DC: Government Printing Office, 1975b.

_____. *Statistical Abstract of the United States.* Washington, DC: Government Printing Office, 1979.

_____. *Current Population Reports.* Ser. P-60, no. 137. Washington, DC: Government Printing Office, 1983a.

_____. *Statistical Abstract of the United States, 1982–1983.* Washington, DC: Government Printing Office, 1983b.

_____. *Statistical Abstract of the United States, 1984.* Washington, DC: Government Printing Office, 1984.

_____. *Statistical Abstract of the United States.* Washington, DC: Government Printing Office, 1986a.

_____. *Money Income and Poverty Status of Families and Persons in the United States—1985.* Washington, DC: Government Printing Office, 1986b.

U.S. Department of Health, Education and Welfare. National Institute of Education. *Violent Schools—Safe Schools: The Safe Schools Study Report to the Congress.* Vol. 1. Washington, DC: Government Printing Office, 1977.

U.S. Department of Health, Education and Welfare. Office of Education. "Delinquency and the Schools." In President's Commission on Law Enforcement and the Administration of Justice, *Task Force Report: Juvenile Delinquency and Youth Crime,* Washington, DC: Government Printing Office, 1967.

U.S. Department of Justice. *Federal Juvenile Delinquency Programs.* Washington, DC: Office of Juvenile Justice and Delinquency Prevention, 1980.

_____. *Dealing With Serious, Repeat Juvenile Offenders: Report of a National Conference.* Washington, DC: Government Printing Office, 1982.

_____. *Historical Corrections Statistics in the United States, 1850–1984.* Washington, DC: Government Printing Office, 1986a.

_____. *Jail Inmates—1984.* NCJ-101094. Washington, DC: Government Printing Office, 1986b.

_____. *Criminal Victimization—1985.* NCJ-102534. Washington, DC: Government Printing Office, 1986c.

_____. *Criminal Victimization—1986.* NCJ-106989. Washington, DC: Government Printing Office, 1987.

_____. *Report to the Nation on Crime and Justice,* Second Edition, Washington, DC: U.S. Bureau of Justice Statistics, 1988.

————. *Children in Custody—1989*. Washington, DC: Office of Juvenile Justice and Delinquency Prevention, 1991.

————. *Crime and the Nation's Households, 1991*. Washington, DC: Government Printing Office, 1992a.

————. *Criminal Victimization, 1991*. Washington, DC: Government Printing Office, 1992b.

U.S. Department of Justice. Bureau of Justice Statistics. *Report to the Nation on Crime and Justice: the Data*. Washington, DC: Government Printing Office, 1983.

————. *Sourcebook of Criminal Justice Statistics—1985*. Washington, DC: Government Printing Office, 1986.

————. *Sourcebook of Criminal Justice Statistics—1986*. Washington, DC: Government Printing Office, 1987.

————. *Sourcebook of Criminal Justice Statistics—1989*. Washington, DC: Government Printing Office, 1990.

————. *Sourcebook of Criminal Justice Statistics—1992*. Washington, DC: Government Printing Office, 1993a.

————. *Correctional Populations in the United States, 1991*. Washington, DC: Government Printing Office, 1993b.

U.S. Department of Labor. *Equal Employment Opportunity for Women: U.S. Policies*. Washington, DC: Government Printing Office, 1982.

U.S. Senate Committee on the Judiciary. Subcommittee on Juvenile Justice. *Hearings of August 12 and September 30, 1982*. Washtinton, DC: Government Printing Office, 1983.

U.S. Supreme Court. *Kent v. United States*, 383 U.S. 541 (1966).

————. *In re Gault*, 387 U.S. 1 (1967).

————. *Tinker v. Des Moines Independent School District*, 383 U.S. 503 (1969).

————. *In re Winship*, 397 U.S. 358 (1970).

————. *McKeiver v. Pennsylvania*, 403 U.S. 528, 535 (1971).

————. *Baker v. Owen*, 423 U.S. 907 (1975).

————. *Goss v. Lopez*, 419 U.S. 565 (1975).

————. *Ingraham v. Wright*, 430 U.S. 651 (1975).

————. *Wood v. Strickland*, 420 U.S. 308 (1975).

————. *West Virginia State Board of Education v. Barnette*, 319 U.S. 624 (1975).

————. *Breed v. Jones*, 421 U.S. 519 (1975).

————. *Ingraham v. Wright*, 430 U.S. 651 (1977).

————. *Swisher v. Brady*, 438 U.S. 204 (1978).

————. *Schall v. Martin*, 104 U.S. 2403 (1984).

————. *Stanford v. Kentucky*, 109 U.S. 2969 (1989).

Utah State Legislature. *Juvenile Court Act as Amended in 1969*. Salt Lake City: Utah State Legislature, 1969.

Vanek, J. "Keeping Busy: Time Spent in Housework, U.S., 1920–1970." In M. Richmond-Abbott, ed., *Masculine and Feminine: Sex Roles Over the Life Cycle*. Reading, MA: Addison-Wesley, 1983.

Van Waters, M. *Youth in Conflict*. New York: The New Republic, 1925.

Vardin, P. A., and I. N. Brody, eds. *Children's Rights: Contemporary Perspectives*. New York: Teachers College Press, Columbia University, 1979.

Vassar, R., ed. *Social History of American Education*. Vol. 1, *Colonial Times to 1860*. Chicago: Rand McNally, 1965.

Vaughn, J. B. "A Survey of Juvenile Electronic Monitoring and Home Confinement Programs." In *Juvenile and Family Court Journal* 40 (1989): 1–36.

Vedder, C. B., S. Koenig, and R. E. Clark. *Criminology: A Book of Readings*. New York: Dryden Press, 1953.

Vold, G. B. *Theoretical Criminology*. New York: Oxford University Press, 1958.

Vold, G. B., and T. J. Bernard. *Theoretical Criminology*. 2d ed. New York: Oxford University Press, 1979.

Wadlington, C. W., C. H. Whitebread, and S. E. Davis. *Cases and Materials on Children in the Legal System*. Mineola, NY: Foundation Press, 1983.

Walberg, H. "Urban Schooling and Delinquency: Toward an Integrative Theory." In *American Educational Research Journal* 9 (1972): 285–300.

Waldron, G., and J. Lynch. *Managing Juvenile Restitution Projects*. Washington, DC: Government Printing Office, 1978.

Walker, S. *Sense and Nonsense about Crime and Drugs: A Policy Guide*. 3d ed. Belmont, CA: Wadsworth, 1994.

Wall, J., J. D. Hawkins, D. Lishner, and M. Fraser. *Juvenile Delinquency Prevention: A Compendium of 36 Program Models*. Washington, DC: Government Printing Office, 1981.

Walt, Vivienne. "Gun Trade-Ins Pick Up Steam." *Longmont Daily Times-Call*, Jan. 9, 1994, final ed.

Wallace, E. W. "Physical Defects and Juvenile Delinquency." *New York State Journal of Medicine* 40, no. 21 (Nov. 1940): 1586–90.

Wallerstein, J., and S. Blakeslee. *Second Chances: Men, Women, and Children a Decade after Divorce*. New York: Ticknor and Fields, 1989.

Wallerstein, J., and J. Kelly. *Surviving the Breakup*. New York: Basic Books, 1980.

Walzer, J. F. "A Period of Ambivalence: 18th Century American Childhood." In L. DeMause, ed., *The History of Childhood*, 352–82. New York: Psychohistory Press, 1974.

Warren, M. "The Case for Differential Treatment of Delinquents." *An-*

nals of the American Association of Political Social Scientists 381 (Jan. 1969): 47–59.

_____. "Intervention With Juvenile Delinquents." In M. K. Rosenheim, ed., *Pursuing Justice for the Child,* 176–204. Chicago: University of Chicago Press, 1976.

Washington, Booker T. *Up From Slavery: An Autobiography.* New York: A. L. Burt Company, 1900.

Washington State Legislature. *Third Substitute House Bill No. 371: An Act Relating To Juveniles.* Olympia: House of Representatives, June 10, 1977.

Watson, J. B. "The Place of the Conditioned Reflex in Psychology." *Psychological Review* 23 (1916): 89–116.

_____. *Psychology from the Standpoint of a Behaviorist.* Philadelphia: Lippincott, 1919.

Weis, L. "White Male Working-Class Youth: An Exploration of Relative Privilege and Loss." In L. Weis, and M. Fine, eds., *Beyond Silenced Voices: Class, Race and Gender in United States Schools,* 237–58. Albany: SUNY Press, 1993.

Weis, L., and M. Fine. *Beyond Silenced Voices: Class, Race and Gender in United States Schools.* Albany: SUNY Press, 1993.

Weissman, I. "Guardianship: Every Child's Right." In A. E. Wilkerson, ed., *The Rights of Children: Emergent Concepts in Law and Society.* Philadelphia: Temple University Press, 1973.

Wells, H. G. *The Outline of History.* Garden City, NY: Garden City Publishing Co., 1921.

Werthman, C., and I. Piliavin. "Gang Members and the Police." In D. J. Bordua, ed., *The Police,* 56–98. New York: Wiley, 1967.

Wexler, D. "Token and Taboo: Behavior Modification, Token Economies and the Law." *California Law Review* 61 (1973).

Whitaker, C. J. *Teenage Victims: A National Crime Survey Report.* NCJ-103138. Washington, DC: Government Printing Office, 1986.

White, J. "The Waiver Decision: A Judicial, Prosecutorial or Legislative Responsibility." *Justice for Children* 2 (1987): 28–30.

Wilkerson, A. E., ed. *The Rights of Children: Emergent Concepts in Law and Society.* Philadelphia: Temple University Press, 1973.

Wilkinson, K., B. G. Stitt, and M. Erickson. "Siblings and Delinquent Behavior." *Criminology* 20 (1982): 223–40.

Williams, F. III. *Criminological Theory.* 2d ed. Englewood Cliffs, NJ: Prentice-Hall, 1994.

Williams, R. M., Jr. "The Sociological Theory of Talcott Parsons." In M. Black, ed., *The Social Theories of Talcott Parsons: A Critical Examination,* 64–99. Englewood Cliffs, NJ: Prentice-Hall, 1961.

Wilson, J. Q. *Varieties of Police Behavior.* Cambridge, MA: Harvard University Press, 1968.

Wilson, J. Q., and R. Herrnstein. *Crime and Human Nature*. New York: Simon and Schuster, 1985.

Wollons, R. *Children At Risk in America: History, Concepts and Public Policy*. Albany: SUNY Press, 1993.

Wright, J. "Student Attendance: What Relates Where?" in *NASSP Bulletin* 62 (Feb. 1978): 115–17.

Yinger, M. "Contraculture and Subculture." *American Sociological Review* 25 (1960): 625–35.

"Youth Violence Hits Record High." *Longmont Daily Times-Call*, Aug. 1, 1993, 8A.

Zelditch, M., Jr. "Some Methodological Problems of Field Studies." In W. J. Filstead, ed., *Qualitative Methodology*, 217–31. Chicago: Markham Publishing Co., 1970.

NAME INDEX

Note: Page numbers followed by n indicate footnotes.

SUBJECT INDEX

Parole, 269–271
Passion, criminals by, 99–100
Patrilocal norm, 140
Patrol work, 183
Peer subcultures, in schools, 170–173
Personality
  classification of, 236
  criminal, 82
  in structural-functionalist
    theories, 114–115
Physical disabilities, 102–103
Physically broken homes, 147
Physical type, 98–100
Police, 181–185
  approaches to juveniles, 192–
    194, 194–198
  capacity to respond to crime and
    misbehavior, 53
  disposition of juveniles arrested
    by, 67, 196–198
  gangs and, 188–192
  juvenile units and, 276–277
  officers' responsibilities and, 192
  prevention programs sponsored
    by, 198–200
  roles of, 200, 201–202
  screening of problem children by,
    193
  social class and, 131
  urban and suburban police
    departments and, 182–185
  willingness to arrest, 53
Police reports, 195
Possessing stolen property, definition
  of, 52
Poverty, 143–144
Pretrial hearings/conferences, 221–
  225
Prevention. *See* Community-based
  prevention/corrections programs;
  Delinquency prevention/correction
Preventive detention, 258–259
Primary cultural conflict, 128
Primary deviance, 106
Primary groups, 106
Prisons. *See* Adult prisons;
  Confinement; Incarceratories

Probation, 227–228, 242–247
  formal, 243, 246
  home arrest as, 245–246
  informal, 228, 242–243, 246–
    247
  restitution and, 248
Probation officers
  caseloads of, 244, 275
  cases handled by, 209, 211
  training of, 244
Problem children. *See* At risk children
Project DARE, 199
Proletarians, 116–117
Prosocial approach, by police, 192–
  193
Prostitution, definition of, 52
Psychologically broken homes, 147
Public education. *See also* Education;
  School(s)
  in England, 20
  socialization and, 146
Punishment
  rehabilitation versus, 234–237,
    257–258
  in residential programs, 252–253

Quarreling, in families, 149–150

Race. *See* Ethnic groups
Rape, definition of, 51
Rebels, 123
Receiving stolen property, definition
  of, 52
Recreational programs, police-
  sponsored, 199
Referees, pretrial hearings held by,
  223–224
Reform schools, in nineteenth
  century, 24
Rehabilitation, punishment versus,
  234–237, 257–258
Remedial education, 251
Residence, place of, 140
Residential prevention/corrections
  programs, 251–253

Please remember that this is a library book,
and that it belongs only temporarily to each
person who uses it. Be considerate. Do
not write in this, or any, library book.

364.36 M987i 1995

Musick, David.

An introduction to the
sociology of juvenile
c1995.